MW00986136

The Fugitive in Flight

The Fugitive

in Flight

Faith, Liberalism, and Law in a Classic TV Show

Stanley Fish

University of Pennsylvania Press

Philadelphia · Oxford

Published by
University of Pennsylvania Press
Philadelphia, Pennsylvania 19104-4112

Printed in the United States of America on acid-free paper
1 2 3 4 5 6 7 8 9 10

Library of Congress Cataloging-in-Publication Data
.
Fish, Stanley Eugene.
The fugitive in flight : faith, liberalism, and law
in a classic TV show
Stanley Fish.
p.   cm. — (Personal takes)
Includes bibliographical references.
ISBN 978-0-8122-4277-5 (hardcover : alk. paper)
1. Fugitive (Television program)   I. Title.
PN1992.77.F79F57   2010
791.45'72—dc22   2010017028

For Roy Huggins, the Only Begetter,
and David Janssen, the Heart and Soul

Contents

Part 1

Why *The Fugitive*?

IN THE SUMMER OF 1993, I was driving with my wife and her mother from some place to some other place. It was taking longer than we had anticipated, and everyone was getting hungry. We stopped at a restaurant simply because it was there and sat down for what turned out to be a not-so-bad-meal. The table next to us was close enough for me to hear the conversation. I was amazed to discover that our fellow diners were talking about *The Fugitive* (I had already been thinking about writing this book), and I began to have thoughts about providence and heavenly guidance when the conversation turned to an upcoming *Fugitive* conference in the late summer. When I heard that I couldn't help myself. I just went over, sat down, and gathered all the information they had. When I got home I made arrangements to attend the convention, and so it was that on August 24 I found myself in the Hollywood Roosevelt Hotel across the street from Grauman's Chinese Theatre (founded by Sid Grauman, a relative of Walter Grauman, who directed many of the key series episodes), where the movie version of *The Fugitive* was playing. I was ready to enter the world of diehard fans. I had thought I was one until I met the real thing.

My guide into that world was none other than Roy Huggins, *The Fugitive*'s creator. I had contacted him in June through his agent, Lee Rosenberg of the William Morris Agency. Huggins replied immediately and offered to help me in any way possible. True to his word, he met me at the airport, entertained me at his home, chauffeured me to various events, secured me a place at the speaker's table even though I was not a speaker, and, most important, arranged interviews with writers, directors, and actors who had worked on the series. Were it not for Huggins, I would not have been sitting down with Jacqueline Scott, George Eckstein, Stanford Whitmore, Alan Armer, Joseph Campanella, Walter Grauman, and Bob Rubin, or socializing at a party with Suzanne Pleshette and Earl Holliman. What I found in those conversations (some parts of which I will cite later) was a shared devotion to the series, both for the achievement it was and for the fellowship that attended its making.

That devotion was more than matched by the fans whose convention it was. They reminded me of the antiquarian scholars I had known (and been in awe of) in the academic world. They were learned in ways far beyond me. They knew episodes by heart. They could reel off lists of guest stars. They knew what the series' hero, Richard Kimble, wore, what names he had used, how many times he had been beat up, how many times he had fallen in love. When they walked onto a sound stage, they went immediately to the place where he had crouched behind a door or in a closet. They pointed out plot inconsistencies and mistakes, not in criticism, but with the affection one feels for the imperfections of a beloved. Some of them dressed like Kimble. They all had stories about the first time they saw an episode and the continuing role the series played in their

4

lives. They may not like this book. I imagine them thinking that it is too abstract, insufficiently in touch with the details and arcana of production, too prone to intellectualize the felt particulars they recall and caress. I want to say to them that I mean no harm.

The convention itself was a hoot: a medley of film clips, reminiscences, tributes, celebrations, performances of nostalgia, and at least one unstaged dramatic moment. A woman stood up and insisted she was the sister of David Janssen, the series' lead actor, a claim promptly and loudly denied by Janssen's mother, Berniece, who had a famously troubled (and disputed) relationship with her son.

In the middle of all this, something happened that I'm still trying to understand. As was my habit, I ran every morning. One morning I found myself thinking about a sequel to the Harrison Ford movie, already a huge success. (What I didn't know then was that many fans of the series engage in the same fantasy and write *Fugitive* scripts just for the fun of it.) By the time I returned to the hotel, I had sketched out an outline in my head, and I quickly scribbled it down on hotel stationery. That afternoon I read it to Roy Huggins.

In an instant our relationship changed. He became distant, even cold. He showed no interest in anything I said and seemed to want nothing more than to be quit of my company. What had I done?

That evening at dinner I put the question to Jacqueline Scott, the actress who played Kimble's sister Donna Taft, and her husband, writer Gene Lesser. They laughed and said that the moment I showed Huggins the outline, I was no longer the Duke professor who was going to honor his creation by making it the object of an academic analysis. I had become instead a competitor trying to horn in on the action that had belonged to him for thirty years (he was the executive producer of the movie). It was all over, they predicted, and it was. I never spoke to him or heard from him again.

I would like to think my intentions were honorable. I would like to think I was motivated only by enthusiasm for the project. I would like to think I wanted nothing for myself. I would like to think I was like the fugitive.

But again, why *The Fugitive*? In part because it has long been my habit to write while watching television. (I'm doing it now.) I don't use television as background noise. I pay a certain low level of attention all the time, and I pay undiluted attention some of the time. I find that allowing a storyline to occupy a part of my mind seems to free some other part to solve the problems that come up in the course of composing. In one instance, however, the strategy didn't work. In the 1990s when I was watching reruns of *The Fugitive* on the Arts and Entertainment Network twice a day, I couldn't take my eyes off it. In part it was the film noir style—black-and-white images of bleak, usually interior, scenes populated by men, women, and children with anxious and furtive looks on their faces. No one in *The Fugitive* ever relaxes, and as you watch you can't relax either, even though for long stretches absolutely nothing happens. It was the combination of nonstop tension with the (relative) absence of slam-bang action that attracted me, and as I now reflect on it, the same combination characterizes the literary works I have been reading and writing about for more than forty-five years.

These works, which appeared in the sixteenth and seventeenth centuries in England, are marked by an internalization of value and by a refusal to find meaning in external events as they emerge in time. In Milton's *Samson Agonistes*, for example, there is certainly a big event waiting for the hero and known in advance by the audience—Samson's pulling down of the Philistine temple, leading to his death and the deaths of the thousands he slays. The event, however, occurs off-stage and is reported by a horrified observer to Samson's father and friends, who begin immediately to speculate about its meaning. Rather than being a climax to the play's dramaturgy, this "great act" (Samson's phrase for a future he glimpses only in shadowy terms) is the occasion for introspection and interpretation, two actions that have been ongoing from the opening lines, when Samson complains loudly about his present situation and seeks to understand why the once-mighty champion of his people now labors in the mills of his enemies, "eyeless in Gaza." How could this have happened? What does it mean? Whose fault is it? Has God abandoned him? Has he brought about his own ruin? What can he do now? How can he live? How should he live?

These questions are asked and answered repeatedly by the succession of visitors to Samson's prison and by the hero himself, who is constantly reexamining his life in an effort to make sense of it. Although the plot moves in linear time and presents new scenes and characters, the structure of its concerns is static, and those concerns are relentlessly moral and psychological. Spectacular events do occur—the arrival, in full train and flower, of Dalila, the challenge to combat flung down by the Philistine giant Harapha, the summons to the temple—but they serve not to determine or clarify matters but to provoke further wrestlings (that's what "agonistes" means) with the existential questions rehearsed in the previous paragraph. The goal is not so much to reach a geographical place but to inhabit an internal one (what Milton in *Paradise Lost* calls a "paradise within") where the self has achieved a stability that persists no matter what slings and arrows of outrageous fortune it may suffer.

In short, *Samson Agonistes* is a drama of character, even though in many respects it has the trappings of melodrama. It is the same with *The Fugitive*, which presents its big event at the opening of every episode. Richard Kimble, a respected pediatrician in Stafford,

Indiana (a fictional town), has been wrongly convicted of killing his wife, Helen. The real killer is a one-armed man Kimble saw fleeing the scene as he drove up to his house. No one else saw the one-armed man, Kimble did not have an alibi, and his story was not believed. Now, the series' voiceover (William Conrad) intones, this innocent man is being transported by train to death row in the company of police detective Lt. Philip Gerard. The camera brings us inside the railway car where the two men sit joined by handcuffs. But then "Fate moves its huge hand," the train goes off the rails and topples over, allowing Kimble to escape and to begin running, away from the pursuit of the relentless Gerard (as he is always known) and in search of the one-armed man who alone can clear him and give him back his good name.

The (perhaps paradoxical) effect of re-presenting this very dramatic sequence every week (even before the credits are run) is to forfeit certain opportunities for drama. There is no question of "who-done-it" and thus no opportunity to lead the audience down the usual garden paths. (The concluding episode, "The Judgment," is, as we shall see, an exception to this general rule.) There is no real fear that Kimble will be captured, or if he is momentarily captured, we know he will once again escape, unless the producers wanted to bring the series to a premature end. There is no real hope that he will catch up with the one-armed man, or if he does momentarily, we know his quarry will slip away again so that the chase, and the series, can continue. We entertain no doubts as to the protagonist's innocence (the series is psychological in its emphasis but it is not a psychological thriller), and thus we neither expect nor desire any Hitchcock-like revelations about his character, which is established in the opening sequence—innocent, honest, law-abiding, and trustworthy—and never changes.

It is Kimble's steadfastness—his capacity for enduring the dangers and trials of a life on the run without undergoing any transformation, positive or negative—that anchors the series, and provides the still center around which various forces of disorder swirl. Kimble's refusal to allow circumstances to alter his character stands in marked contrast to another American fugitive, the hero or antihero of the 1932 film *I Am a Fugitive from a Chain Gang.* James Allen (played by the incomparable Paul Muni), like Kimble, is on the run

and hunted by a justice system that has convicted him of something he didn't do. In the last seconds of the movie, he encounters a woman who knew him before he was the victim of a legal process gone awry, and she asks, "How do you live?" As the shadows around his face turn to total darkness (it 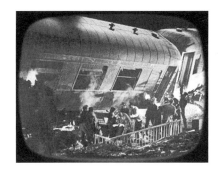 is the film's last moment), he replies, "I steal." Allen's innocence and integrity have not survived a world that does not believe in them; he has become what his pursuers mistakenly think him to be.

Richard Kimble never *becomes* anything. He is what he is from the first episode to the last, and what he is is severe, uncompromising, and, as we shall see, even more implacable in his way than the obsessed policeman who hunts him. The severity of the series' morality—its insistence on hewing to a narrow path in the service of narrowly defined values—is another source of its appeal, and, again, the same appeal draws me to the texts I have been thinking about for so many years.

Chief among them is *Paradise Lost*. After Milton's Adam and Eve have eaten the apple and engaged in sweaty post-fallen sex, they awake in shame and hide themselves in the thickets. A heavenly voice bids them come out and asks, did you eat of the tree after I told you not to? Adam replies in a lengthy speech in which he first considers taking the blame on himself, then decides that God would see through his subterfuge, then puts the blame on Eve for being so devilishly attractive that he could not say no to her ("her doing seemed to justify the deed"), an excuse that implicitly puts the blame on God for having made her that way. To this tangled web of self-extenuations the "Sovereign Presence" says only, "Was she thy God?" (X, 145). In other words, was she the appropriate object of your worship? In the moral life, according to Milton, the identification of one's primary loyalty comes first. Once that identification has been made, the choices and paths experience offers will arrange themselves around the obligation that, by definition, supersedes all others. Adam has made the mistake of thinking of Eve as a value in competition with the value of obeying God. He has forgotten that in a God-centered universe—a universe literally held together and given meaning by God—no creature, however beautiful and compelling, can be a candidate for one's primary allegiance, because as a creature, someone made by another, she lives only by virtue of the creator's sustaining spirit. Sever her from that spirit, and what remains is a lifeless husk as unworthy of affection and loyalty as the tree to which Eve bows down just after committing the original sin. Paradoxical though it may seem, Adam would have honored Eve and shown his love for her had he rejected her and refused to ratify and repeat her crime.

Milton's poetry is full of moments like this when a character or a speaker is tempted to substitute a lesser value for the primary one and must push the inferior value away, not in an act of ascetic renunciation, but in recognition of the fact that when all is said and done there is only one God, and you can have no other Gods before Him. There is nothing wrong about appreciating Eve or admiring the beauty of gems or the grandeur of trees as long as one does not prefer them to the deity who gives them both life and value. That is idolatry, being shackled, as Augustine puts it in *On Christian Doctrine*, to "an inferior love." "What or whom do you love?" is the great Augustinian question, and if, like Augustine, and Milton, you follow the injunction to love the Lord thy God with all thy soul and might, no other love can have precedence, although many other loves can have legitimate, if limited, claims on you.

The Fugitive is not a theological text, but its moral structure mimes theology's preoccupation with primary values and the awful consequences of falling away from them. The value the series embodies and promotes is not obedience to a deity (although there are several episodes about religion and faith) but the primacy of freedom; not freedom in the physical sense of the word (Kimble is running from the specter of confinement to be followed by death) but in the moral sense given to the concept by classical liberalism: freedom from attachments that own you and circumscribe your will. "True liberty," the great liberal thinker Isaiah Berlin tells us, "consists in self-direction: a man is free to the degree that the true explanation of his activity lies in the intentions and motives of which he is conscious."[1] The free man is the rational man, standing apart from the projects he may or may not take up and deciding between them by assessing them in relation to the principles of right action he has internalized. The unfree man, in contrast, is in thrall to his projects and feels compelled to pursue them; he cannot step back or break away. He is, says Berlin, "like someone who is drugged or hypnotized . . . we consider him to be in the grip of forces over which he has no control." It is control that is the mark of the free man who belongs only to himself and cedes that self to no one. He is, as the phrase goes, "his own man" and therefore owes nothing to anyone. If he happens to become indebted through circumstances or choice, he will labor mightily to discharge the debt so he can once again be free, which means that in some deep and almost tragic sense, he is alone even when he is surrounded by other people.

Berlin's account (and praise) of the man thus free fits Richard Kimble to a T. One might say that it is the exigencies of his situation that produce his reserve and preternatural caution: a man on the run and in constant fear of discovery cannot afford to let people get too close. But it is more than that. For Kimble, as we shall see, the danger in becoming too involved with others (a danger he repeatedly courts and then flees from) is not simply that he may be found out and betrayed, as he is many times, but that he may become so identified with those others that he would allow himself to be defined by them and their causes. As someone who doesn't want to be bound by anything and yet cannot say "no" to those who seek his assistance (because to do so would compromise his

---

[1] Isaiah Berlin, "From Hope and Fear Set Free" (1963), in *Liberty*, 2nd ed., ed. Henry Hardy (Oxford: Oxford University Press, 2002).

view of himself as a good person), Kimble is always putting himself in positions from which he must extricate himself, lest he leave a part of himself behind. He comes into town, bumps into someone with a problem or a crisis, feels obligated, by the oath he took as a doctor, to help, gives that help wholeheartedly and to an extent that leads those he aids to claim him as their own (he is now the most important person in their lives), and then must tear himself away or persuade his new best friends that they don't need him or anyone—persuade them, that is, that they can be just like him. Everyone Kimble encounters wants to possess him—women want him as a lover, men as a companion, children as a father; even villains want him as a partner in crime—and he wants merely to possess himself, something he can do only by standing aloof from everyone and everything. The longer he stays in one place, the more likely it is that he will be further drawn into the web of someone else's hopes and fears.

What rescues him is the appearance, just in the nick of time, of Gerard, who forces a rupture Kimble in fact desires. Kimble leaves every town promising to return and to think often of those he leaves behind. We know that he will never return (except in one special circumstance, to be described later), and that while he might remain in their thoughts forever, he will never think of them at all. His thoughts will be free of regret, nostalgia, longing, or anything else. He has removed these emotions as hostages before he exits, and he returns to the road and the running triumphantly secure, not in his physical person, which is always being threatened, but in the perfect equanimity of a being without inner anxiety. In fact Kimble has no inner life at all; he is the still, empty point in relation to which others, full of troubles and lost in the woods of their lives, orient themselves. Or don't; there are some the series

leaves behind because they are too far gone down the road of commitment and obsession.

These observations may seem to place too heavy a burden of
meaning on a piece of popular culture, but there are reasons to
think that the creators and producers of the series would recognize their intentions in my description of their achievement. I will
get to those reasons later, but I don't want to put them up front
because I don't want readers to think I am writing a book about
the production of a TV series and the personalities of the men and
women who brought it to the small screen (as television used to be
called). Other have told that story (see especially Mel Proctor's *The
Official Fan's Guide to "The Fugitive"* and Ed Robertson's *"The Fugitive" Recaptured*) and told it well. Nor am I writing a "tell-all" book
that promises to take you behind the scenes and reveal the tensions among the actors, writers, and directors. That would be an
interesting "take," but it's not mine.

What I *am* interested in is the moral structure of a series that
week after week at once celebrated and anatomized the ethic of
mid-twentieth-century liberalism, the ethic of self-reliance, with-
drawal from drama, personal responsibility, and a quiet, downplayed heroism that finds its expression in a commitment to family values and small-town life rather than in some grand epic action
designed to save or alter the world. It is the ethic, famously, of Sloan
Wilson's *Man in the Gray Flannel Suit* (1955), where the hero in the
end rejects a high-paying position in a pressure-filled industry and
decides instead to work at a less demanding job and spend more
time with his family (now a cliché uttered by disgraced politicians
who are forced to resign). Richard Kimble also wants to retire from
the danger and excitement of the road and spend more time with
his family. (Even though he meets and interacts with hundreds of

people, the relationship that means the most to him is with his sister; he calls her at every opportunity.)

The Man in the Gray Flannel Suit is a fifties novel—in fact *the* fifties novel, along with its opposite, *Peyton Place*, the TV version of which preceded *The Fugitive* in ABC's Tuesday lineup—and I invoke it because although *The Fugitive* ran from 1963 to 1967, it is a fifties program, focused not on issues or big political questions but on the struggles of ordinary men and women to find their place (and not someone else's) in an often hostile and indifferent world. Because that is *The Fugitive*'s focus, there is another book I am not writing: I am not going to explore the relationship between the series and the great events that were occurring at the time of its production—war, racism, riots, assassinations. I turn my eyes away from these events because the series does. It refuses to become a vehicle for the dramatization of the social and political issues that filled the nightly news and commanded the attention of editorial writers. Of course one could argue that by refusing political relevance, *The Fugitive* makes a political statement despite itself and without sufficient awareness of its own motives. This is a familiar kind of argument these days—it amounts to a form of intellectual "gotcha"—and it has, I admit, some force; but, again, I have no interest in making it.

In the end my analysis will be relentlessly abstract and internal, in keeping, I believe, with the abstractness and internality of the series, which insists on maintaining its own focus and not expanding it to take on the concerns of other shows. This does not mean that *The Fugitive* is sui generis. It has a documented novelistic source in Victor Hugo's *Les Misérables*, and it has antecedents and successors in the early history of television drama. It is an anthology show. The action occurs not in a fixed location with a re-

curring cast but in a different place each week as the main character or characters, for reasons tied to a basic plot structure, move
from town to town and encounter a whole new set of personalities,
along with the problems and demons they carry with them. Similar programs preceding or roughly contemporaneous with *The Fugitive* include *Wagon Train, Rawhide, Have Gun—Will Travel* (the title tells the story), *The Millionaire, Star Trek, Route 66,* and *Maverick*
(another Roy Huggins creation). Other shows inhabit a single locale, but the population is continually changing, again for reasons
tied to a basic plot structure: examples are *Ben Casey, Dr. Kildare,
The Rifleman, Gunsmoke, East Side/West Side, Bonanza, The Big Val-
ley,* and *Bus Stop* (also a Roy Huggins production). The difference in
formats is between who goes and who stays. In one, the hero goes
while the folks he leaves behind stay; in the other, the hero stays
and those he has befriended go away, usually with their problems
solved. Each format allows for a liberal use of guest stars and the
forming of relationships that die with the closing credits. Nor is the
fact that Richard Kimble is forced by circumstances to move from
place to place unique. Prior to *The Fugitive* was *The Rebel.* Contemporaneous were *Branded* and *A Man Called Shenandoah. The Incredible Hulk, The Invaders, The Immortal, Renegade,* and *Run for
Your Life* (also a Roy Huggins project) came later and were influenced by *The Fugitive.* No doubt there is an article or a book in all
those progenitors, analogues, and begats, but it isn't this one.

So why write this one? Why elevate *The Fugitive* above those
that came before it and those that followed in its wake? The simple
answer is because *The Fugitive* is better, and it is better because of
its insistence on remaining true to a narrow but powerful project
of charting the tensions between the vertiginous events of a world
ruled by Fortune (or in *The Fugitive*'s own vocabulary, by Fate) and

the centered self of a man who wants nothing but to be free—free not merely from the physical constraints of prison and the death chamber, but free from anything and everything.

Of course at this point my assertion of *The Fugitive*'s superiority is just that, an assertion. The task is to flesh it out and support it, and that is what I propose to do in the following pages. I will proceed by moving back and forth between discussions of individual episodes and the drawing of general conclusions about the series' themes and patterns. This method might seem to court the danger of allowing the argument to be overwhelmed by the succession of plot summaries; but the summaries *are* the argument. They are not limited to "this-happened-and-then-this happened" (although some of that will be necessary given that few readers will have committed entire episodes to memory); they track the appearance in particular episodes of the themes and patterns I see as informing and driving the series. Summary and argument will proceed in tandem and not as modes of analysis that are in tension. I want to give readers a sense of how the episodes unfold, and trace out the many ways in which episodes dissimilar in almost every respect are nonetheless deeply related by a small set of abiding concerns: (1) the nature of law; (2) the relationship between the law's formal judgments, as when it pronounces Richard Kimble guilty, and justice; (3) the relationship between evidence of the kind marshaled to convict Kimble and the evidence—intuitive, internal, unverifiable by visible measures—that leads so many to believe in his innocence minutes after meeting him; (4) the relationship between faith as a guarantor of knowledge and the knowledge provided by empirical inspection; (5) the relationship between the kind of integrity Kimble exemplifies—uncompromising, unshakeable, and curiously empty—and the obsessive attachments (to women, wealth, ambition, celebrity, and even good deeds) that disorder the lives of those he tries to help; and (6) the relationship of all these to the tenets of mid-twentieth-century liberalism and its dream of a world where rationality and freedom go hand in hand and everyone follows the advice of Polonius: "To thine own self be true . . . [and] / Thou canst not then be false to any man."

The shape of these concerns will emerge simultaneously with my readings of specific episodes, and I shall pause periodically to inventory, amplify, and consolidate my account of the series' master themes. The main body of the book will conclude with an analysis of "Runner in the Dark," an episode in which no one (except Kimble) can see, and the question of the relationship between inner and outer judgment is starkly posed. In the closing sections I shall return to the moment of *The Fugitive*'s creation by Roy Huggins, and the afterlife of the series, first in the form of the very popular 1993 Harrison Ford movie, and second in the form of CBS's attempt to revive the series in 2000. I shall make liberal and I hope illuminating use of the conversations I was privileged to have with those whose energy and talents made *The Fugitive* what it was—in a word, great. But let's begin at the beginning.

Part 2

The Fugitive
Stands Alone:
Morality
in Black
and White

The Fugitive Comes to Town
and Sets Everything Straight

THE PILOT EPISODE OF
The Fugitive is titled "Fear in a Desert City." The city is Tucson, Arizona, and the fear is equally distributed among the major characters. Monica Welles (played by Vera Miles) is afraid that her abusive husband will once again regain control over her life and the life of her young son. The husband, Edward Welles (played by Brian Keith as a man barely under control), is afraid of the mental and emotional instability that produces his aggressive behavior and drives his family away. The son, Mark (Donald Losby), is afraid that any man who gets close to his mother will turn out to be just like his father, someone who will abuse her and intimidate him.

And the fugitive, Richard Kimble, played in the role of his life by veteran TV actor David Janssen, is afraid of everything and everyone. Wrongly convicted of his wife's murder, Kimble escapes when the train taking him to the death house goes off the rails, and he begins to run. He runs from the police lieutenant who had him in custody (Philip Gerard, played by the great Barry Morse), and he runs after the one-armed man he saw in the vicinity of his house on the night of the murder. At every moment he is in danger of discovery (wanted posters bearing his image are everywhere). Every encounter, no matter how brief and seemingly casual, could be the one that returns him to prison and the prospect of execution.

The only characters who do not exude fear in this episode are the two policemen who produce it, not because they are overtly threatening, but because they are not. Edward Welles is a well-known and influential businessman, and he complains to the police that Kimble—who has befriended Monica Welles at the bar where they both work, she as a pianist, he as a bartender—is breaking up his marriage. Just as Kimble and Monica are getting into a cab, a police car glides up, and a police sergeant named Burden (is this an allegory?), played with quiet menace by the distinguished character actor Harry Townes, says to Kimble, "Mr. Lincoln" (the first of Kimble's many assumed names), "we'd be obliged if you'd get into the car."

Kimble does, and in the scene that follows no voices are raised, nothing remarkable is said, but the tension is wire-tight. The effect is Hitchcock-like; and indeed both the photography and the sense of threatening enclosure might well be an allusion to Janet Leigh's solitary automobile trip in *Psycho* as she makes her way to the Bates Motel. The world outside her car window is entirely ordinary, but everything she sees is a source of anxiety; no gesture seems innocent; no one stops her or speaks to her, yet the specter of surveillance hangs over every moment.

The surveillance is right up front in "Fear in a Desert City." The two policemen play a game of verbal tennis, with Kimble as the ball. They hit soft lobs. "Is this your first visit to Tucson? How do you like it?" one asks, and Kimble answers that he hasn't seen much of it but likes what he sees. "How do you like your job?" asks

the other, played by Dabbs Greer (his name is Fairfield, a bad joke if there ever was one), and before Kimble can reply, the first policeman does it for him. "Hasn't seen much of it, but he likes what he has, correct?" Discombobulated and nervous, Kimble rambles on about how even innocent men feel guilty in the presence of the law. After all, "there isn't a man in the world who doesn't have something he wants to hide, even you two." "That remark was not calculated to gain favor," is the quiet but chilling response from Burden. But he adds, "I wouldn't want you to think I was sadistic," and we suddenly see that the car has pulled up to Kimble's hotel.

Relieved, Kimble heads toward the hotel door only to hear Burden call out, "I don't know what's the matter with us; we insist on seeing you up to your room." Which they do, and finally Burden lets the shoe drop. "Edward Welles claims that you're breaking up his marriage." "Did you talk to his wife?" Kimble retorts with some spirit. "We are not in the marriage counseling business, nor are you" (a judgment that is literally true but, as it turns out in the next four years, substantively false). And then the words we have been expecting, all the more forceful because of the wait: "Leave Tucson tonight."

Quinn Martin, the series' executive producer, regarded this scene as one of the most important in the entire series. He felt, said critic David Thorburn, "that it established an assumption on which the rest of the series would be based."[1] That assumption, according to Thorburn, is that even innocent people may be misjudged and harmed by the forces of institutional authority.

But that is only half the story and not the important half. The important half concerns what innocent people do when this happens to them. Kimble's situation in the car is a miniature version of the situation that frames the series. He is as innocent of the charge that he is breaking up a marriage as he is innocent of the charge that he murdered his wife. (Edward Welles is the potential wife-killer in this story.) But in both cases the location of his innocence is entirely internal; it is something he knows, but the world denies, and denies for a very good reason: all the evidence is against him, and the only pieces of counter-evidence are the one-armed man, a specter only Kimble saw (or said he saw), and the testimony of Monica Welles, whom the police won't listen to because they don't recognize her as a party with standing. (She's a wife and she has her duties, doesn't she?)

Kimble's innocence, then, is a matter entirely hidden from view and empirical inspection; that is its weakness: there is nothing, apparently, that supports it. But that is also its strength. If Kimble's innocence exists without support from anything external to it,

---

1. Quoted in Ed Robertson, "*The Fugitive" Recaptured: The 30th Anniversary Companion to a Television Classic*, by Ed Robertson (Los Angeles: Pomegranate Press 1993), 38.

nothing external to it can undo it. Milton made the point long ago in his masque *Comus*, when his heroine says of her own innocence: thoughts of physical danger "may startle well, but not astound / The virtuous mind, that ever walks attended / By a strong siding champion Conscience" (lines 210–12). That is, virtue's internal location does not protect its bearer from the buffets of fortune, but no matter how violent fortune's ups and downs may be, virtue and its bearer remain always what they are. In this and 119 subsequent episodes, the plot currents swirl around Kimble—he is arrested, convicted, reviled; members of his own family believe he's guilty; Gerard hunts and haunts him; people he's just met assault and chase him; women alternately seduce and betray him; children accuse him of things he hasn't done—and through it all he remains essentially the same. The justice system has failed him; Burden and Fairfield push him around just to please someone who doesn't even live in their town (Edward Welles lives in Phoenix). None of this makes Kimble happy, but none of it makes him change.

But change is one of the two things plot usually produces. The other is surprise. In *The Fugitive* neither is central (except in a handful of episodes written by writers who apparently didn't know what the series was about). Surprise is largely absent because the plot is set and known in advance: Kimble's not guilty; Gerard is chasing Kimble; Kimble's chasing the one-armed man who, he is certain, really did it. The audience expects Kimble to be recognized by somebody at any minute; and it also expects him to get away again. Both expectations are regularly met, and as a result, the "device" that is thought to be the signature fact of the series—the device of the double pursuit—is not the source either of its energy or urgency.

What is? The interplay between characters, usually in the form of a one-on-one confrontation between Kimble and someone who needs his help, wants to help him, or wants to harm him. But even when this last is the case, the focus is not on the danger (which does hover in the background) but on what the interchange reveals about the psychological demons that drive people to acts of aggression and self-destruction. In the scenes between Kimble and Edward Welles, Kimble behaves more like the physician he is (and remains no matter what the situation) than as a man in fear of discovery. He tells Welles, "get yourself some help," and he asks the man if he knows what he is doing to his wife and child. Diagnosing Welles is as much a concern as avoiding his rage. What does he want? Kimble asks Monica. "To possess me," she answers; but he cannot possess her if he cannot possess himself, and it is clear in every scene that Edward Welles is a man out of control. (As I have already said, control of a certain kind is the chief virtue of the series.)

What Monica wants is what Kimble wants—to be free, not in anyone's thrall. When her husband is killed in the final act, Kimble says, "You can go home now; it's over." Minutes ago, she had been about to get on a bus with Kimble and run with him. But now she is free from the fear of being smothered by another, and while we don't doubt her affection for Kimble, she really doesn't need him any longer. Their parting is heartfelt, as partings often are in *The Fugitive*, but deep down both are more than a little pleased.

Although neither Monica nor Kimble get on the bus, this last scene returns us to the episode's opening moments, in which Kimble gets off a bus in the same station. Bus, bus station, bar, hotel room, the back seat of a car—the action, such as it is, unfolds in a succession of small, usually dark, spaces that shut out the larger world and its concerns so that the focus can be exclusively on the choices confronting the characters: the choice of whether to believe, to trust, to befriend, to betray. As Kimble parries the thrusts of Burden and Fairfield, the viewer sees the busy city scene *receding* as the car moves forward. Indeed, the forward motion, the sense of going somewhere, itself recedes. Kimble, Burden, and Fairfield might just as well be in a locked room or an abandoned building (both the locations of similar scenes in later episodes) as in a moving vehicle. Everything is narrowed to a point of stillness so that moral rather than social imperatives can be foregrounded.

The Fugitive as the Law's Chief Enforcer

The deemphasis of plot (which exists largely to get Kimble in and out of towns) goes hand in hand with the deemphasis of issues. Not that there aren't any issues hanging around in the period from 1963 to 1967: Vietnam, racial strife, student activism, assassinations, inner-city riots, the Civil Rights Act, presidential elections, the rebirth of conservatism, the Arab-Israeli conflict, the Cold War, the space race. These and other topics will occasionally be alluded to in *The Fugitive*, and even serve as the backdrop for an episode, but as a rule they do not take center stage. The characters never function merely as spokespersons for some position on the ideological spectrum. The stylized oppositions that structure political debate never structure an episode or become the focus of its attention. Like its hero, the show always stays on message, and the message—the primacy of self-possession in a world of distractions—relegates to the background the social and political messages that dominate other shows. *The Fugitive* almost always knows what it is about, and what it is about is moments of moral revelation and choice; moments the plot delivers, but does not—except as a momentary framing of an internal dilemma—produce.

I am not saying that Kimble's plight plays no role in the drama, just that it does not drive the drama. That is why the most extended account of the "back-story" events occurs in a flashback that is disconnected from the episode in which it appears. The episode is called "The Girl from Little Egypt." Kimble has been accidentally hit by a car driven by Ruth Norton, a stewardess (played by Pamela Tiffin), and while he is unconscious, he dreams of the night his wife was murdered. Richard and Helen (Diane Brewster) quarrel about adoption; he's for, she's against. Richard storms out of the house

and drives aimlessly, stopping at a point above a lake. He sees a boy in a boat, fishing. The stillness and isolation of the image—bathed in light even though it seems to be dusk—are almost portraitlike. The strong impression is of a self-contained world, safe from external demands and intrusions. It's just the boy, the boat, and the fishing pole. No significance attaches to the activity (if sitting silently in a boat is an activity); it does not invite interpretation; it does not invite anything, its self-completeness not so much repelling the observer's gaze (that would be too active) as remaining oblivious to it. In this case the observer is Kimble, who smiles, perhaps because the boy represents the child he now may never have (after a stillborn birth, Helen Kimble cannot have children) or because he recognizes in the still tableau the self-sufficiency and integrity he prizes above everything.

There is a plot consequence to this plot-less moment: The boy never sees Kimble (of course he doesn't; he's not looking outward), and the one piece of evidence that might have placed Kimble elsewhere than in his house is lost to him. At the trial (which Kimble revisits in another flashback), the prosecutor points out that, "As a matter of fact, you've heard him sitting right there testify that he didn't see you." "As a matter of fact." Here as elsewhere, all the facts point in one direction; the truth is, quite literally, out of sight.

As powerful as the flashback scenes in "The Girl from Little Egypt" are, they play no role in the story, and, in fact, are discounted early on when Ruth Norton overhears Kimble's hallucinatory ravings. When he awakes, she calls him "Dr. Kimble." "I was innocent," he says. But she has already come to that conclusion: "People usually don't lie when they are delirious." (End of that question.) There are policemen all over the episode, questioning Kimble (now going by the name George Browning), standing next to him at a party during a discussion of capital punishment. The villain of the piece—Paul Clements (Ed Nelson), the cad who seduced Ruth Norton and hid from her the fact that he is married and has two children—finds out that George Browning is not Kimble's real name. But all of this goes nowhere. The viewer is being told, Look, we know that in other dramatic presentations of men on the run the danger of discovery supplies much of the suspense; but in this one, you don't have to worry; you are free to attend elsewhere.

Elsewhere in this case is the drama of Ruth Norton's coming to terms with the betrayal she has suffered and letting go of the obsession that still ties her emotionally to Paul Clements. In the final act Kimble forces the issue by contriving a confrontation between Ruth and her illusions. As usual, the place of confrontation is an enclosed place, in this case Clements's living room, where a nice suburban gathering is in full swing. Kimble has told Ruth that they're going to a party (hardly something he would arrange if he were concerned about discovery), but is vague about its host, who is appropriately shocked when he opens the door and has to introduce his occasional fling to his very permanent wife. In the course of the next few moments, Ruth is brought to her senses, and as she leaves she says to Clements, "You have a lovely home, Paul. Next week I'm going to move somewhere, and I won't be in the phone book."

Later she and Kimble have a farewell drink in the same restaurant Clements used to take her to. Kimble predicts that she will one day have her own comfortable suburban life. She is free of the entanglement that possessed her and prevented her from being herself. Now that she is possessed by no one—always the desired state in *The Fugitive*—Kimble can leave, not as the pursued fugitive, but as the restorer of order to a world gone momentarily astray.

That is Kimble's real role in the series and its great irony: Kimble is the chief enforcer of the values of the establishment that has condemned him. Indeed, he takes its values more seriously than do the law officers who pursue him, for he does not limit himself, as they do, to legal infractions of good order. He is alert to *any* infraction of good order, and he moves immediately (and instinctively) to correct it. Edward Welles isn't breaking any laws when he sits at a bar and stares fixedly at his estranged wife. Paul Clements isn't breaking any laws when he sweet-talks and deceives a vulnerable young girl. Yet they draw Kimble's disapproving attention as much as if they had robbed a bank, and he won't leave town until their disruptive and deviant behavior has been stopped, one way or another.

Kimble is vigilant even when the situation is purely domestic. In "Fun and Games and Party Favors," he is the chauffeur and general factotum for a wealthy family that includes a weak father (always a figure of danger because he fails in his responsibility to keep things in their proper place), a domineering mother (emblematic of the forces that must be kept in check if civilized society is to be protected), and a pampered daughter (who threatens to carry the seeds of disorder into a second generation). Before he exits the scene, Kimble straightens them all out.

One night the parents (played by Joan Tompkins and Tom Palmer) return from a social evening to find a teen-age party out of control (fast and loud music is always a sign of danger in *The Fugitive*). Indignant, the parents ask Kimble, "Where were you?" and he replies with stinging scorn: "Where were *you*?" Earlier in the evening he had confronted the daughter (played by Roy Huggins's daughter, Katherine Crawford) and her pool-boy beau (actor Mark Goddard) as they were about to elope. "People wait, animals don't," he barks. *Self*-restraint, not the restraint imposed from the outside by legal or governmental structures, is what Kimble preaches; it is what distinguishes us from the lower orders and from those human beings who are without self-control. When the girl expresses her frustration by flirting with one of the louts who crashed her party, her boyfriend rescues her from his clumsy advances and tells her, "Go take a cold shower"; that is, extinguish those runaway emotions and come to your senses by refusing to give in to your senses.

In the end, tutored by the moralizing chauffeur, the father takes command; the mother bridles her will; and the daughter agrees to wait until her boyfriend (who turns out to be middle class despite his blue-collar job) finishes medical school, after which he will be just like Kimble was before "fate" (named as the villain in the famous voiceover introduction to each episode) misidentified him as a lawbreaker, when in fact he is the very embodiment of the law and of good, middle-class values.

Kimble's moralizing influence on those who encounter him can work even after he is no longer around. In "The 2130," he is running after the first scene. He is again a chauffeur, this time to

Dr. Mark Ryder, a prominent medical researcher (played by Melvyn Douglas), and his spoiled, troubled daughter, Laurie (Susan Albert). Laurie comes home with a dented fender and asks Kimble to take the blame. He says the right thing: "If I take the blame for you, I'm not helping you." But then he relents and tells her father (of whom she is afraid) that he was the driver. What Kimble doesn't know is that she hit somebody, and when the police come calling (someone saw the incident and took down the license plate number), he knows he can't stay.

Chagrined at having been taken in by Kimble, Dr. Ryder decides to feed the fugitive's history into a large computer in the hope that it will be able to predict his movements. The cat-and-mouse game between Kimble and his mechanical adversary takes up much of the rest of the episode, but in the background is the unresolved story of the girl who told a lie. It is resolved when her father tells her that his research reveals a man who, except for the moment of supposed violence against his wife and his running away from an accident, has always been exemplary. "I think I'd be sick if I thought I was hounding an innocent man." Conscience-stricken by her father's words, Laurie confesses, but claims that the man she hit stumbled into her car. We could have told that to the police, Ryder says. His daughter replies, "I wasn't afraid of the police; I was afraid of you." At that moment, far from Kimble physically, but feeling the pressure of his moral presence, father and daughter undergo a change, one facing up to her responsibilities, the other realizing that raw data don't tell even half the story.

In another episode, "Coralee," Kimble carries out his law-and-order mission underwater. He has been working for a salvage-boat captain (played by Murray Hamilton) whom he suspects of being responsible for a diving "accident." Suspecting that he is being suspected, the captain orders Kimble to dive into deep waters so he can cut off his oxygen supply. Realizing what is about to happen, Kimble unhooks himself from his suit and swims to safety. When the police arrive in pursuit of Kimble, they are told he has just descended into the water, but when they pull up his line, they find he has escaped. They also find he has attached to the line evidence of the captain's crime, the damaged helmet worn by his victim. At the moment Kimble evades authority, he is in the act of enforcing it.

The Fugitive Provides Evidence the Law Cannot See

In "Coralee," as in every other episode, Kimble's normative rules are those he carries inside him, not those encoded in a statute or proclaimed by a fallible justice system. No matter what the outward world thinks of him or does to him, he is sustained by an inner probity that cannot be shaken. In the episode "Flight from the Final Demon," he meets his mirror image, a man whom the world has judged innocent but who is, in fact, guilty.

The story gets going when Sheriff Bray, played by Carroll O'Connor, suspects that the man giving him a massage and calling himself Al Dexter is really Richard Kimble. Bray is about to take Kimble/Dexter down to the station for questioning when one of Dexter's coworkers, Steve Edson (played by Ed Nelson), decks him, and he and Kimble run out of the health club and drive away in Edson's car.

"Why?" asks Kimble. Edson acknowledges that what he did wasn't that smart. "I could have got killed back there." A seemingly

conventional sentiment, which is, we later find out, an expression of a death wish.

As the two flee the scene, Edson discovers that Bray, who shot at the car, has wounded him. Immediately, Kimble feels obligated to stay with Edson until he is well. ("We'll stay together until we

get this patched.") Edson, however, is more interested in Kimble than in his wound. "Must really be something—running away all the time. Did you kill her?" "For what it's worth," Kimble responds, "I didn't." "For what it's worth, I believe you," is the reply. Edson continues to obsess on Kimble's situation, but it becomes clear that he is talking about himself. "You know you're innocent and everyone thinks you're guilty. Sometimes it works down to where it's just a fine line, so fine that a jury would have to be more than human to even give you a fair verdict." In other words, the world can be wrong, but the heart cannot; the heart knows.

What Kimble's heart knows is that he is innocent. What Edson's heart knows is that he isn't. He tells Kimble, "I was in front of a jury five months ago, for murder." A fight with the brother of his girl-friend, he explains. It could have gone the other way, he acknowledges, but he was acquitted. The fine line has been crossed in the wrong direction, just as it was in Kimble's case, and for both the true verdict lies elsewhere than in the public, visible record. Kimble carries his innocence within him, and it repels the judgment of an accusing world as if it were an invisible shield. Edson carries his guilt within him, and it pursues him more relentlessly than does the brother of the man he killed. The final demon of the episode's title, the demon (or angel) that always counts in *The Fugitive*, is the inner self, and, by definition, one's self cannot be escaped; one can't run from it. Kimble needn't run from it—it is his refuge; he runs *with* it, and therefore he is always standing in the same place even when he is crouched in the back of a truck or hiding in the woods. Edson, too, is always in the same place, pursued by an enemy he can't outrun, spiritually dead even when the machinery of the law has allowed him to live (the mind is its own place). He wants to be punished so that he can stop punishing himself. Sheriff Bray, still on the scent, intuits this: "Kimble," he says to his deputy, "is running with a man who deep down wants to get caught."

Kimble figures it out, too. In a later scene Edson proposes that he and Kimble and the girlfriend (who has now turned up) should run away together, but Kimble isn't having any: "No, I'm sorry, Steve, I can't help you anymore.... No one can help you. Why don't you tell her why you've been running?" That is, you can only be helped by yourself, by acknowledging the guilt that is already kill-

ing you. Edson does tell her, and Kimble comments like a Greek chorus: "A man with a conscience who has committed a crime can't live with it; so he finds his own punishment."

Soon the pursuers close in, and Kimble and Edson run. It is not clear whether Edson intentional-

ly puts himself in harm's way so that Kimble can escape, but that's what happens, and he is shot by the deputy. The story has two epigraphs. The first is given by the girl as she kneels over Edson's body. "He found a way to stop running." (He sentenced himself to death.) The second is intoned by William Conrad, who is heard as the portentous moralizer at the beginning and end of each episode. Kimble has often thought "he would gladly trade places with any man on earth." Now he knows "any man but one." Better to be pursued by the slings and arrows of outrageous fortune than by the horror of a diseased self.

"Flight from the Final Demon" is notable (yet typical) because the double conceit at its center—one man falsely accused, the other falsely freed—is not a device of plot but of character. The point is not to see Kimble endangered and then escape (what else is new?), but to contrast the moral situations of Kimble and his flawed companion. As always, the real dramatic focus is less on Kimble's plight (although that hovers in the background and propels events forward) than on the opportunity for change afforded those he encounters. It is an open question as to whether Steve Edson changes, because in the end we're not sure whether he has sacrificed himself for Kimble, committed "suicide by cop," or is just running away again.

There is no doubt about the matter in another early episode, "Nightmare at Northoak." This fan favorite opens with Kimble dreaming that he has been cornered in an alley by Gerard who, it seems, is about to shoot him. A loud sound ensues; however it is the sound not of a gun but of a tire blowout, and it wakes Kimble up. (He had been sleeping in a meadow.) What he sees is a school bus that has run off the road and is partly in flames. The schoolchildren are disoriented, the bus driver is unconscious, and the situation looks desperate, but of course Kimble rescues them all. He does not, however, get off the bus in time—he had gone back twice to carry out the wounded—and an explosion knocks him unconscious. When he next wakes his vision is blurred (the play of sight and blindness is very important in *The Fugitive* and we shall return to it), and he is lying in a bed surrounded by anxious and grateful people. It turns out he has been taken to the house of Sheriff Al Springer (Frank Overton), the father of one of the children he has saved. Because Kimble can't see, he's not yet aware that he's in a lawman's house.

While Kimble is still barely conscious, the sheriff's son, egged on by a newspaper photographer, takes a picture of the town's new hero, and, although half of the man's face is covered by a compress, Gerard, scanning the newspaper in a city far away, recognizes Kimble. The plot question then becomes will Kimble be able to get away before Gerard arrives and verifies his identity?

The real question, however, is what the sheriff's wife, Wilma (Nancy Wickwire), will do, for this is her story. She bosses the ladies of the town around and insists that everything be according to rule. Her husband, Al, jokes, "I call the little woman the real sheriff of Oak County," meaning that she is the one in the family with an extra-firm sense of right and wrong. She responds, "I stick to the letter of the law; my father was a judge." In saying this, Wilma echoes (unintentionally, of course) Gerard's response in the pilot episode, when he is asked by his boss whether he ever thinks that there may be a one-armed man after all: "I enforce the law, the law pronounced him guilty; I enforce the law." Let others, he adds, "debate and conclude. I obey." At least at this point in the episode, Wilma Springer is Gerard's double.

The distinction between the letter of the law (what has been established as a matter of legal fact) and the spirit of the law (what is really true, despite the weight of evidence) structures the dilemmas the series' characters repeatedly face. On which side will you stand is the question always being asked, and the answer given determines the moral status and subsequent moral life of the person who gives it. Wilma Springer undergoes her test when she comes upon her husband in the act of fingerprinting Kimble. Al explains to her that a policeman named Gerard believes the man they know as George Porter is really an escaped murderer. Her first instinct, indicated by a facial expression, is to dismiss this idea as absurd, just as her husband has done. But then she picks up the newspaper with Kimble/Porter's picture in it, and as her husband leaves the room, she muses aloud, connecting the dots between Gerard's call and the fact that, earlier in the day, Kimble had been found wandering in the woods. She had assumed, with everyone else, that he was still suffering the aftereffects of a concussion and didn't know what he was doing. But now she sees that he was trying to run away, and as she turns around to face Kimble, the conclusion she has come to is plain on her face.

"I am Richard Kimble," the fugitive acknowledges immediately, "but I'm innocent." Unlike so many characters in other episodes,

Wilma doesn't say, "I believe you; someone like you just couldn't be a murderer." Instead she asks a question about process. "Was it a fair trial?" The word "fair" tells us where she stands: a fair trial is a trial that is *procedurally* correct; the question of the truth of the verdict it has delivered is not to the point. He replies, "Well legally, yes," but legally is all she's interested in, and when Kimble asks her to help him escape, she says, "You want me to be an accomplice?" "You know any other human being I can ask?" he retorts. The appeal is from one human being to another, notwithstanding what the law, backed up by all the evidence, had concluded.

Wilma leaves the room, obviously torn, and turns to her husband. "Al?" "Yes?" "Nothing." It looks as if she is going to follow her original instinct and let Kimble slip away. Her husband meanwhile is declaring, "He's my kind of man; he knows I'm just doing my job." Wilma says fiercely to herself, "It is right. It is right." And then blurts it out: "He is Richard Kimble."

The sheriff enters Kimble/Porter's room just as the fugitive is trying to get out the window. Kimble resigns himself to capture and holds out his hands for the handcuffs. "That won't be necessary," his captor says. Kimble is still the sheriff's kind of man; although procedure requires the handcuffs, Al Springer trusts him. Kimble's status as a convicted murderer is one thing. What the sheriff knows about him as a man is another, and that knowledge trumps.

Gerard arrives to find a town hostile to him. He must wait for extradition papers and is persuaded to have dinner at the sheriff's house. At dinner, the Springers' son cries because he is the one who took the picture that got Kimble caught. Gerard says to Wilma Springer, "He did the right thing, just as you know that you did." Wilma is no longer so sure. She asks, "Did he kill his wife?" Gerard replies, "The Law says he did," an answer she herself would have given a short time ago. But now she's after something different. "That's not what I mean. Did he really kill her?" "Really" means not in relation to evidence and procedure, not according to probabilities or circumstances, but as things really are. The way things really are will often not be supported by appearances and indeed will affirm against them. Merely by uttering "really," Wilma Springer signals that she has crossed a line.

Later, when everyone is back at the jail, the townspeople line up to shake Kimble's hand. Wilma is last in line, and she passes him a key. When Gerard goes back to check on his prisoner, he is overpowered, and Kimble escapes. When Gerard accuses the sheriff of having passed the key, Wilma says, "You're wrong. I gave it to Mr. Kimble." Then "you'll be arrested," Gerard responds, but before he can act, there is a Spartacus moment: everyone present declares, No, I did it. Gerard is angry, stymied, and frustrated, but can do nothing. Sheriff Springer and his wife smile at each other in the knowledge that they are on the same side.

And what side is that? It is the side of belief in the face of contrary evidence. In almost every episode of *The Fugitive*, people are given the choice of believing what the world tells them or believ-

ing in Kimble. It is, quite literally, a trial of faith, and those who come through it are often rewarded with a changed life. When Kimble says to Wilma, "You know any other human being I can ask?" she is incapable of responding; the right response is given by her husband when he declines to handcuff the convicted murderer. The sheriff is the human being who responds without being asked. An officer of the law, he knows instinctively that the law has made a mistake. His wife knows that in the end and becomes the human being Kimble doesn't have to ask. We know as the episode ends that she will never again be the rigid, judgmental sheriff of Oak County. She has been saved.

The Fugitive Is Tempted to Forget Who He Is

What makes "Nightmare at Northoak" so good is that it doesn't allow Kimble's story to overwhelm the story of the protagonist whose moral life (as opposed to physical life) hangs in the balance. Kimble's situation impels the plot forward and precipitates crises, but the crises are not his: they belong to Wilma Springer; it is she who must find her way. Kimble's actual escape is downplayed so that the focus in the epilogue can be entirely on her transformation. But in another early episode, "Never Wave Goodbye," the proportions are out of whack, and the real story of the episode can easily be missed by the viewer who is attending to some uncharacteristic bursts of cinematic action. (This episode, as some fans have noted, has some affinities with the immensely popular Harrison Ford film, which, good as it is in many respects, is most un-*Fugitive*-like.)

One of the things that makes "Never Wave Goodbye" an untypical *Fugitive* episode is that most of it takes place in the light and out of doors. The town is Santa Barbara; there is sunlight everywhere. Kimble, here called Jeff Cooper, works as an apprentice to a sailmaker and is often on a boat out at sea, a vast expanse entirely unlike the confined enclosures in which the "action" of *The Fugitive* usually occurs. There are other differences. Kimble is in love. In almost every episode, he enters into some kind of relationship with a woman. Most of the time, he is the object of her pursuit, but he usually manages to keep his distance, avoiding romantic entanglements as he avoids all entanglements, in part because he fears that closeness will lead to discovery, in part for the deeper reasons I have already introduced. In "Never Wave Goodbye," however, he is head-over-heels, and the feeling is reciprocated. The woman, Karen (the sailmaker's niece), is played by the beautiful Susan Oliver, and they make a handsome couple. In one extended scene they enjoy an idyllic afternoon on a small yacht. Kimble does two things that are entirely uncharacteristic: he does a Cary Grant imitation, and he sings a song (very badly). He also smiles all the time—not the tentative, quickly withdrawn, half-smile we see in other epi-

sodes, but a full, unselfconscious smile, carefree and without reservation. Obviously, this isn't going to last. It's no accident that the boat is named *Tranquilizer*. This is a narcotic moment, an interlude of forgetting.

The spell is broken when Kimble reads in the *Los Angeles Times* that a one-armed man has been arrested for assaulting a woman. He tells Karen, who has declared her love for him and begged him to stay, that he has to see a man in the county jail, and if "he's the right man, I'll be back." Of course Gerard has also seen the news story, and we know the two are headed to the same location.

They arrive at the building at the same time, and suspense builds as they just miss each other, getting on and off of elevators, coming in and out of the same door minutes apart. Kimble ascends to the jail floor, where he does get to see the one-armed man. He is not the one Kimble has been searching for, and he prepares to leave. But in the course of their brief conversation, Kimble lights the man's cigarette and leaves the match, a mistake he will soon rue. Just as he is about to exit, Gerard spots him, but there is a locked door between them, and before Gerard can get it opened, Kimble is running. As Kimble comes out of the building, Karen, who has followed him in her car (he of course has taken a bus) to Los Angeles, rushes to him, and they run together with Gerard and police officers in pursuit. They hop a bus, get off, hop another, and in a scene that could have been plucked from a hundred action films (that's what's wrong with it), they finally get away. Meanwhile, Gerard finds the match, which has the word "sails" on it; he begins to think about what it means.

Back in Santa Barbara, Kimble resolves to stop running. He has told Karen who he is, and she of course believes his story. He reasons that Gerard will assume he has fled to another part of the country as he has so many times before. Perhaps if he stays put he will be safe.

That's the end of Part 1. Yes, it's a two-parter—not the only one in the series, but the only one aside from the famous finale that keeps you watching because you want to know what *happens* next, as opposed to what complexities of character and moral choice will be revealed next.

In Part 2, the sequence of events unfolds in predictable melodramatic fashion. With burnt match in hand, Gerard tracks Kimble down, and he arrives in Santa Barbara just before a dinghy race Karen and Kimble intended to enter. Karen has received a phone call from a friend warning her that a policeman is looking for an escaped murderer who may be working at a sail shop. She alerts Kimble, who then concocts a plan that is as improbable as it is conventional. Kimble and Karen will capsize the dinghy in an area frequented by sharks just as the fog rolls in. They will smear blood on their life jackets and escape in a rubber raft. Gerard will believe they are dead and give up the hunt; they will then hitch a ride somewhere and start a new life.

What? Is this *The Fugitive* we're watching? Is Kimble going to

give up the search for the one-armed man? Will he forget about
clearing his name and reuniting with his family?

Never mind. It doesn't work, of course. When Kimble and Kar-
en don't come back, Gerard commandeers a coast guard boat and
looks for evidence. The blood-stained life jackets are found, and
the coast guard captain decides to turn back. Gerard, however, will
have none of it. He steals a raft—there is a wonderful shot of him
rowing into the fog wearing a suit and a tie—and the current brings
him to the shore where Karen and Kimble have landed.

There's more, but it will have to wait while I back up and retrieve
a plot line I have deliberately omitted. It's easy to miss, but it is in
fact the true plot line, the one that tells us this is really an episode of
The Fugitive, although disguised as something else. This plot line belongs to Eric, another sailmaker who has disliked Kimble from the
start and warned Karen away from him. He is played, with a Scan-
dinavian accent, by an incredibly young-looking Robert Duvall. Eric's story is revealed in stages. Lars Christian (played by Will Kulu-
va), the owner of the sailmaking shop, and Eric's uncle, reminds him:
"Once you were a fugitive, too, a twelve-year-old fugitive from the Gestapo." The implication is that Eric should be sympathetic to Kimble because they share a similar past. But it turns out they don't. Eric
was smuggled out of Norway not only because he was fleeing the
Nazis but because he was in trouble with the underground. He had
betrayed his cousin to the Gestapo—something, of course, Kimble
would never do, something a person of integrity would never do.

He now seems bent on doing it again. He says to Kimble, "I think
you are running from someone. I think I can find out. I *know* I can
find out. You'd better start running again." Kimble doesn't run, but
Eric gets another chance to get rid of him when Gerard arrives. Eric
identifies Kimble, leads Gerard to his room, tells him that he is

probably sailing, and, later, accompanies the detective on the coast guard cutter. He asks another passenger, a doctor also enamored of Karen, "Why did she go with him? He was a criminal; he was no good. Why did she go with him?" The doctor begins to answer, but stops himself and says, "I don't think you'd understand." What Eric wouldn't understand is a judgment that did not proceed from an official source. He's like Gerard, but worse. Gerard doesn't care whether Kimble is actually guilty; he just enforces the law. Eric thinks that Kimble is guilty *because* the law says he is. He has no conception of a truth, either of fact or character, that exists apart from the determinations of authority.

And then the moment, the true *Fugitive* moment. It is Eric who remembers an old rubber raft, and remembers, too, a repair kit he saw open on a bench. He concludes that Karen and Kimble took the raft and plan to escape in it; he tells Gerard, who says, "If she's found abetting an escaped fugitive, she'll have ten years to think

about it." When Eric hears that, he suddenly gains a measure of self-awareness. "What have I done?" he cries, in what is perhaps an allusion to the last-minute realization of Alec Guinness's character in the 1957 film *Bridge on the River Kwai*, that by cooperating with the Japanese he has betrayed everything he loves. Gerard goes to the captain and tells him what Eric has said. But when Gerard commands Eric, "Tell the captain about the raft," for the first time in his life Eric defies authority: "I don't know what you're talking about," and maintains that denial even when Gerard grabs him by the shirt.

That's the last we see of Eric as the plot moves on to storms, sharks, rocks, and near-drownings. It is Kimble who gets the moral spotlight in the final scene when, after Gerard has washed up on the shore half-dead, the fugitive decides to save him rather than escape to another life where he would be sure his nemesis no longer hunted him. Although Karen is horrified, this is exactly what we expect of Kimble. It's not news to any regular viewer. What is news, or what should have been news if the episode had been true to the series' spirit, is what Eric finally does—shake himself free of the shackles of authority and confront for the first time the obligation of deciding for himself what is right and what is wrong.

I have lingered so long over what I consider a flawed episode because its flaws allow us to see what a genuine episode of *The Fugitive* is like. First of all, "Never Wave Goodbye" is exciting, not intermittently, but all the time. That's good if what you want is drama that grabs the viewer's attention and never lets up, filling every moment with car chases or, in this case, with boat chases. But *The Fugitive* depends on slow moments, and one of its favorite devices is some natural disaster (flood, hurricane, mine cave-in, bus crash) that stops the action and forces a small number of characters to confront their inner demons. (In one episode, "Landscape with Running Figures," Kimble and Mrs. Gerard are trapped in a deserted ghost town and pour out their hearts, each in ignorance of who the other is.) After the talking has done its work, some plot device (the winds die down, the rescue party arrives) starts the action again, and everyone exits to take up their lives, but significantly changed. (Except, of course, Kimble.)

Karen doesn't change. The title "Never Wave Goodbye" refers to the fact that she has twice before lost a beloved figure and fears having to wave goodbye again. But that is a slender reed on which to hang a psychological drama, and it fails to be compelling. When an episode of *The Fugitive* really works, the woman with whom Kimble is involved (the involvement needn't be romantic) is either conflicted or haunted or twisted. Karen is just pretty, and she is still pretty when she waves goodbye to Kimble.

I have already remarked on the abundance of sunlight. True, fog and poor visibility set in halfway through Part 2, but too much of this episode reminds you of what a nice place Santa Barbara is. The fact that Kimble wants to stay there is another tipoff that this is a *Fugitive* episode only by name. What makes Kimble Kimble is the steadfastness both of his purpose and his character. Indeed they are the same thing. It is because he is innocent and refuses to be defeated by the contrary judgment made by the world that Kimble persists in his quest for the one-armed man. Those who believe in him moments after meeting him do so because they recognize he is simply not the kind of person who could have done what the legal system said he did. It follows then that he should not be portrayed as someone who could be tempted by something so trivial as Southern California (what doth it profit a man to gain a beach and lose his soul?). By portraying him as such a person in this episode, the writers lose hold of their own creation.

They are in firmer control in a later episode, "The Brass Ring," which is a film noir version of "Never Wave Goodbye." The link between the two is Robert Duvall, who plays a man confined to a wheelchair as the result of an automobile accident. The setting is another Southern California town, more honky-tonk than Santa Barbara (the episode was filmed at the Santa Monica Pier), where Duvall (Leslie Sessions) and his sister Norma (Angie Dickenson) run a gift and bauble shop. Norma is involved with Lars Morgan (John Ericson) in a plot to kill Leslie, who has been awarded

$100,000 in damages after the accident. What they need is a drift-
er who can be seduced by Norma into performing the deed. This is
where Kimble ("Ben Horton") comes in. He is looking for a job, and
Lars tells him there is a job at the Sessions' shop. When he walks
into the shop, Kimble sees Norma, and the moment is electric
with sexual tension in a manner reminiscent of the scene in *The
Postman Always Rings Twice* (1946) when John Garfield first sees
Lana Turner. The job is to be Leslie's caretaker, and Kimble takes
it even though his patient is incredibly hostile, especially to his sister. "You've got the job," he says, but "I'll be watching you and her."
In another story this might indicate that Leslie is obsessed with his
sister's honor, but what Leslie is worried about, rightly, as it turns
out, is his sister's malign intentions.

Norma and Kimble become involved, but they remain in different movies. She is still playing the Lana Turner or the Barbara Stanwyck (*Double Indemnity*) role, using her wiles in an effort
to draw Kimble into her web. It doesn't work. Kimble tells her up
front that there is no long-term future to their relationship. "No
speeches, no promises." (This is Kimble warding off attachments
in advance.) It is obvious that Norma is falling in love with Kimble, and she is enough changed by her new feelings that she tries
to warn him off. "You better get as far away . . . as you can; I'm no
good for you, I'm no good for anyone." At the same time she keeps
trying to lure him in, telling him about a dream in which "a man
carries me off and sets me free." She interprets the dream as a comment on her situation: "I'm in prison, and Leslie's keeping me there.
It's either my life or his." Kimble replies, "Sounds like a nightmare,"
and leaves.

He returns to his duties and to Leslie's rehabilitation, which
is progressing in a way that exceeds everyone's expectations. The

once-immobile man is now able to get up on his own and be taken to the bank, where he withdraws all his money and puts it in a suitcase. Lars and Norma see their future slipping away and resolve to act. When Kimble returns from an errand, he finds Leslie dead (Lars has done the deed) and is immediately blamed. The police are called, and Kimble runs, ending up in Norma's apartment, where he confronts her. She embraces him and apologizes, saying, "Lars made me do it." She also has a plan. She will tell the police the truth (or part of it) and then meet him somewhere, and they can then be together. "I'm wanted on a murder charge," Kimble tells her. She responds in a way that puts her on the side, if not of the angels, at least of those who know integrity when they see it: "That's crazy. I know you, and you couldn't kill anybody."

Norma has not, however, crossed completely over to the bright side, and when the police come knocking on the door, she turns Kimble in, reasoning (selfishly) that if she can't have him, she might as well have Lars and the money. But then, as Kimble is being led away and Norma stands watching at the top of the stairs, she undergoes a change of mind, a conversion, calling out, "Lieutenant, he's not the one who killed my brother. Lars and I planned it together." The lieutenant relaxes his grip, and Norma descends the staircase in a way that reminds us of another Norma—Norma Desmond, who also had her spotlight moment on the way to incarceration. She turns to Kimble: "What I said upstairs, I guess I meant it." That is, I guess I really do love you and found out too late what it means to be true to your best self. She gets into the waiting police car and gazes out with resignation, regret, and longing at Kimble, who says and does nothing.

This is *The Fugitive*'s version of a "happy" ending—no one is happy. Lars is caught, Leslie is free from his confinement, but at the price of his life. Norma is free of her prison, not the one she complained of (life with Leslie), but the prison of her self-obsessed thoughts, and she is rewarded with the prospect of a physical prison. Kimble is alone—no Lars, no Leslie (who wanted to go away with him and possess him), no Norma—and that's just the way he likes it. Kimble not only escapes capture; he escapes Norma, or more precisely, he escapes the feelings he has for Norma, feelings that led him for a time to misjudge the situation he had stumbled into.

Surrendering to his feelings is a danger in another episode, "The Walls of Night." This is a late episode (#117), and it is in color, as was the entire fourth season. It's easy to understand why the network went to color—everyone was doing it, and it was what the advertisers and the viewers wanted—but color is all wrong for *The Fugitive,* which is a black-and-white show both cinematically and morally. The starkness of the moral choices the characters typically face is not enhanced but overwhelmed and blurred by pastels. Sunlight may, in Justice Louis Brandeis's phrase, be the best disinfectant; but it is not the best frame or foil for what is important in this series. Color is a liability for a certain kind of drama (which may be why color remakes of great black-and-white films are often disasters), and it must be muted, as it is in this episode, by having the crucial scenes occur at night.

Working as a trucker in Portland, Oregon, under the name Stan Dyson, Kimble has fallen in love with dispatcher Barbara Wells (played by Janice Rule), and she with him. To date, most of their meetings have been at lunch. What Kimble doesn't know is that Barbara is on "day parole" and must return to prison every night as she waits for full parole. When Kimble asks her to join him at a small resort for a weekend during a break in his run, she cannot accept, but doesn't tell him why. Disconsolate, he goes alone, and is overjoyed when she unexpectedly turns up. Although she doesn't tell him, she is now a fugitive, too.

This is the first moment of choice in the episode. The second occurs when Kimble and Barbara leave the resort and get into the truck, ostensibly to return to Portland. By this time, Barbara's parole officer and her boss (both of whom care for her) are trying to track her down. They guess that she has gone to meet Kimble, and call his truck to tell him what's going on. Immediately, Kimble says to Barbara, "Why didn't you tell me? You've got to go back." But she wants to just keep going. Don't worry, she tells him, nothing will happen to you. It is then he lets her know that he is a fugitive, too, but with a difference. "We're running for different reasons. My only hope is to keep running; yours is to stop." She can square herself with the law by surrendering to it; he can square himself from the law only by evading it. The priority, Kimble implies, is to be right with oneself, as he is when he insists on taking her back.

But then he wavers, and begins talk about fleeing to Canada with her. When he gets out of the truck for a few minutes, Barbara receives a radio call from her boss and the police, who have now learned who Kimble is. They ask her to give them her location, but she tells them he is coming back to the truck and signs off. This is the third moment of choice. She chooses not to believe that he is a murderer.

The final and decisive choice occurs as they drive through the night. The police cannot track them because the radio is turned off, but they know what Kimble's options are, and one of them predicts he will turn north and go to Canada. In short order the truck comes to a crossroads (sometimes *The Fugitive* isn't subtle), with signs pointing one way to Canada and the other to Portland. (Barbara is contentedly asleep.) Kimble turns toward Portland.

When Barbara awakes she sees a sign indicating they are only six miles from Portland. "But you're running into a trap," she exclaims. Yes, I know, he replies; all those calls were because "they're not after you, they're after me." He tells her to take credit for turning him in, and gets out of the truck just as they pull into the truck yard. But before Kimble leaves he says, "I would have liked Canada, but I wouldn't have liked myself very much."

This is a complicated statement. He wouldn't have liked himself, first, because he would have given up the quest for exoneration and the return of his good name, as he was all too willing to do in "Never Wave Goodbye." And he wouldn't have liked himself because he would have been the vehicle and abettor of someone else's swerve from the straight and narrow way. He could never like himself if he had been the cause of her being unable to like herself. He must take her back not only for her sake but for his. Kimble's bottom-line concern is with his own integrity, and nothing—including helping a friend evade the law that has wronged him—can be allowed to stain it. When push comes to shove, he would no more sell his soul for California or Canada than he would kill his wife.

The Fugitive as Liberalism's Best Exemplar

In the short-lived revival of *The Fugitive* (CBS, 2000), a hunted and hungry Richard Kimble (portrayed by Tim Daly) sits at a lunch counter. When the person next to him gets up and leaves half a sandwich, Kimble reaches for it. The "real" Kimble would never have done that. Instead he would have offered to work for food or just walked away, not simply because he prizes his moral dignity (although that's certainly part of it), but because he abhors having to depend on anyone, even on someone who leaves a sandwich he couldn't finish. It is not only that Kimble doesn't want to be captured by Gerard; he doesn't want to be captured by *anything*. Clearing his name is his immediate goal, but his long-term, life-project goal is to be independent, to be without obligations burdening him, to be without entanglements he cannot step away from, to be without attachments—persons, things, vocations—he can't leave behind.

In "The Other Side of the Mountain," he encounters one of the many men and women (here one played by Sandy Dennis) who want to possess him because they are not in possession of themselves and believe that only in someone else can they find security. Kimble tells her, "You can get down from this mountain. You don't need me; you don't need anybody. It's all in yourself." Or it isn't, and if it isn't, no amount of money, number of friends, record of achievements will be enough. If it is, no amount of deprivation or loss will diminish the treasure that lives within. This is the lesson *The Fugitive* repeatedly teaches, and it is the lesson its hero always embodies, except in those moments when the writers and producers forget who he is. He is the fugitive who never moves, even when he is hopping a freight or hitching a ride. Like Ben Jonson's Sir John Roe, he may often experience a "change of clime," but "not of mind," and that mind, that self, remains unaffected by everything by which it is buffeted and assaulted.

In "Landscape with Running Figures," a policeman says to Gerard, "When a man is on the run, he's stripped of everything, and all that's left is an animal." Kimble is stripped of nothing at the same time he is apparently stripped of everything—name, reputation, family, honor, profession, possessions. In the course of 120 episodes, he is beaten, lied to, imprisoned, kidnapped, robbed, hunted and betrayed, but whatever happens to him, his conviction of his innocence and his unwillingness to compromise his integrity sustain him. But while words like "innocence," "integrity," and "independence" accurately describe Kimble, they also point to a darker side of his character, which is the darker side of the mid-twentieth-century liberalism he represents and repeatedly affirms.

The precise definition of liberalism is a matter of controversy, but few would disagree that at its heart is a freestanding individual who bends the knee to no one, nominates his or her own values, and avoids obsessive, enslaving attachments either to persons or causes. What is important about the self in this picture is its capacity to choose rather than any of the choices made in the course of its independent way. In liberal thought, John Rawls observes, "The self is prior to the ends which are affirmed by it" and remains what it is when one end is replaced by another. Michael Sandel glosses (without approving) Rawls's statement:

> The priority of the self over its ends means I am never defined by my aims and attachments but always capable of standing back to survey and assess and possibly to revise them.[2]

The freedom of such a self, then, is negative, in the terms made famous by Isaiah Berlin's essay "Two Concepts of Liberty": "I am normally said to be free to the degree to which no man or body of men interferes with my activity. . . . The wider the area of non-interference the wider my freedom" (15). Liberty in this sense, Berlin

---

2. Michael Sandel, ed., *Liberalism and Its Critics* (New York: New York University Press, 1984), 5).

continues, "means liberty *from*"; and it is his view that "the desire not to be impinged upon, to be left to oneself, has been a mark of high civilization" (19, 21).

The list of things that might impinge on the self is very long and includes anything that impedes the self's mobility and holds it hostage. That would include, as Berlin notes, unpaid debts, which, because they exert a continuing claim on the self, a lien against its estate, prevent it from getting up and moving on freely. That is why Kimble can never leave a town until the obligations he has incurred—sometimes by choice, more often by accident—have been discharged; not primarily because of his concern with those whose lives he has touched (although that is certainly part of it), but because he cannot bear to be encumbered.

The best example of this compulsion to be free of encumbrances is an episode titled "Scapegoat." It often happens that Kimble is recognized and called by his own name rather than by the name he has assumed. The serial change in names is not only a strategy dictated by his status as a fugitive; it is an emblem of Kimble's independence of anything external to him. William Conrad, the series' omniscient chorus, makes the point as the story begins: "The name on the time card is Hayes. The name is easily changed, or dropped, or forgotten. Every identity Richard Kimble has borrowed has vanished for good when he moves on."

Except this one time.

Act I opens with Kimble, using the name Bill Hayes, in line for his paycheck. Suddenly, a fellow worker calls out, "Eddie Fry, aren't you Eddie Fry?" Kimble denies it, and the man concedes the guy he was thinking of was murdered back in Black River, South Dakota. Kimble knows immediately that a loose thread has been left hanging from a former life. He says, "All right, I'm Eddie Fry," by which he means, that's the name I went by, and whatever events were set in motion when I wore that name are my responsibility, because "I" am the same no matter what I call myself. He then is told that Justin Briggs (John Anderson), a man who had employed and later turned on Fry, was convicted of his murder, largely on the testimony of Briggs's housekeeper, Janice Cummings (Dianne Foster), who had seen a drunken Briggs attack Kimble with a chair and a knife for having stolen the affection of both Cummings and Roy (David Macklin), the younger of his two sons. When Janice went to get the police, Kimble, who had been hurt but not fatally, ran into the woods. The last thing he wanted, of course, was to have a conversation with the police.

And yet Kimble decides he must go back to Black River and set things right, despite the danger he courts in returning to a scene where trouble surely awaits him, and despite the fact that in doing so he both makes himself more vulnerable to discovery and interrupts the search for the one-armed man, the key to the restoration of his good name. He feels compelled to go not only because of the injustice being done to Justin Briggs—an injustice that mirrors the one done to him—but because he cannot bear being even indirectly responsible (he did nothing wrong; he just left town) for a harm he must now redress. As he travels back (on the bus, of course) to Black River, he remembers Justin Briggs's words: "I taught my boys to do an honest day's work and mind their own affairs." This might as well be Kimble's motto; for while he spends a great deal of time minding other people's affairs, it is only because their problems have been thrust upon him. He did not seek them out, but once implicated in them, he cannot disengage until they are resolved. Doing an honest day's work and leaving others free to do the same according to their lights is the life Kimble wants to get back to. His involvement in the lives of others is an unintended and unwanted consequence of the situations that befall him because he is a fugitive. You can bet that when he is once again Richard Kimble and in secure possession of his life, that life will be, by choice, incredibly boring.

When he arrives in town and walks into the one restaurant-bar, everyone is shocked, not only at the sight of someone believed to be dead, but because a live Eddie Fry is a rebuke to the town's collective action, an action now revealed to have been hasty and disastrously so. For it turns out that Briggs escaped from jail and was hunted down and killed. The townspeople, as Briggs's lawyer, Bertram Ballinger (Harry Townes

again), observes, are now awash in guilt, and they must purge themselves either by acknowledging a wrong or by finding a scapegoat.

The town takes the scapegoat route and nominates Janice Cummings for the position. It was her testimony that convicted Briggs; she, the townspeople decide instantly, is the cause of their present distress (along with Eddie Fry). Janice's landlady evicts her. Her boss at the restaurant fires her. The elder of Briggs's two sons, Vin (Don Quine), vows to make her pay. At Briggs's trial, Ballinger had accused the town of seizing on an excuse to get rid of a man it didn't like, a man who held himself aloof. Now it doesn't like Janice Cummings and is set to do the same thing all over again.

Meanwhile, Kimble has a problem. The man he had come to save (so that he can absolve himself of blame and return, undetected, to the chase) is dead. How can he now wipe the slate clean? The answer is that he transfers his sense of an obligation that must be discharged to Briggs's sons, even though the elder has always despised him and the younger feels betrayed by him. ("Why did you run away, Eddie?") He knows that Vin has a gun and is looking for Janice. Kimble goes to her rooming house and urges her to leave town with him so that Vin will have a chance to cool down: "Let's give Vin Briggs a chance to get his senses back." But as they emerge into the street, Vin is waiting for them and begins to shoot. They get away, and the town constable hides them in the courtroom, the scene of Justin Briggs's conviction. By now the townspeople are entirely on Vin's side—they begin to say that Justin Briggs wasn't really a bad fellow, always minded his business—and he quickly finds out where Janice and Kimble are.

The final confrontation takes place in the courtroom where Kimble and Janice have been joined by Roy. There is no help to be expected from those outside. The constable has conveniently discovered that he must leave for a nearby town. Vin bursts in, gun in hand, and forces Janice to sit in the witness box and relive

her testimony. She refuses to recant. After a scuffle, Roy, too, has a gun, and the drama shifts to the tension between the two brothers. Roy says he believes that Janice believed their father was trying to kill Eddie Fry. Then why did Fry run away? Vin counters. Now Kimble reveals himself: "My name isn't Eddie Fry. I was convicted of murder just like your father. I ran for the same reason your father ran." Roy triumphantly says,

"He came back; he tried to help us; you can't blame him." But Vin can, and he raises his gun. Roy, facing *his* moment of moral choice, shoots, wounding his brother and thereby saving him from an irrevocable act. (He is becoming like Kimble.) Kimble sends Roy for a doctor, and when Ballinger (who has heard the shot) arrives on the scene to ask what happened, Kimble replies, "I shot him." This is his final payment to Justin Briggs; he has saved both his sons.

But the town will not let it rest. The restaurant owner, Janice's former employer, says to Ballinger, "Why would both Roy and Fry confess to shooting Vin? I say we'd better find out before Fry gets away again." "Too late," Ballinger tells him. "Fry left town two hours ago." And then he adds, "You pack of hyenas go home." But Fry/Kimble has not left town. Ballinger, now protecting Kimble, tells him how to get away. Once again, Kimble has worked his therapeutic magic. Ballinger, the Thersites-like cynic, believes. Janice is vindicated. Vin hasn't shot anyone. Neither has Roy. Only the town itself has not responded; it remains the moral cesspool it has always been, which just shows that Kimble can't save everyone. But then again he doesn't owe the town anything. Kimble's ministry is limited to those with whose lives he has become entangled. When they have received what he can give them, he can move on, and never think of them again. Except when it turns out, as it does in this episode, that something he did, inadvertently, has had consequences of which he was unaware. Then he is compelled to return to a place he was done with, in part to make some wounded people whole, but in larger part so that he can clean things up and leave nothing of himself (in the way of an obligation) behind. In "Scapegoat" he finally gets away free from Black River, even though it took him two tries.

The freedom Kimble achieves, to borrow Berlin's vocabulary

again, is a negative one. It is a freedom *from* that involves holding yourself aloof from anything that would own and possess you, even if that thing is one of your own "aims and attachments." The danger to a truly free self can come from within as well as from without. A cause to which you are too attached can erode your liberty even if you think of it as freely chosen. This is what Berlin means by positive liberty: the liberty to choose what one will be mastered by, as opposed to the state of negative liberty in which you are mastered by nothing and can therefore walk away from anything.

In "Ballad for a Ghost," Kimble encounters someone even more determined to be free of attachments and obligations than he is. Hallie Martin (played by Janis Paige) is a well-known singer who

has come to make a record at the small nightclub of her ex-husband, Johnny (Mark Richman), who is still carrying a torch for her. She arrives accompanied by her father (Paul Fix) and her sister Nora (Anne Helm), who resents the attention everyone pays to her celebrity sibling. Kimble is working as an assistant to Johnny. His primary responsibility is to man the lights and coordinate the lighting sequence with the performers. Hallie and Kimble (calling himself Pete Glenn) meet and quickly tumble to each other's secrets: Hallie's resemblance to Helen Kimble has often been pointed out to her, and she recognizes Kimble immediately. Kimble in turn observes that Hallie is injecting herself with morphine, and putting this together with a few other things, concludes, correctly, that she is suffering from an inoperable and fatal brain tumor. Because all this is revealed fairly early, certain possibilities of suspense are forfeited (there is a minor sub-plot involving a sheriff, but it doesn't amount to much), and the focus can be squarely on Hallie and her way of dealing with the hand fate has dealt her.

What she does, at least on the surface, is make life miserable for everyone, especially Nora and Johnny. When Kimble asks, "Why do you want such hate from everybody?" she replies, "Only from the people I mean the most to." Kimble immediately understands (they share an ethic): "You're going to cushion the blow for Nora and Johnny." That's the nice way of putting it. She wants to leave the world owing no debts, and were her death to generate grief and longing, those emotions would constitute a claim on her that she could not discharge from the grave. Hence the plan to alienate those she loves so they will feel no loss and perhaps even feel relief at her passing. There would be no loose emotional ends that had not already been tied up. As Kimble observes in a later scene, everyone dies, but "at least you can do it the way you want—everything paid." That's the way Kimble wants it—everything paid and he completely free—and before the episode ends, he is able to impart the lesson to another. Johnny has found out about Hallie's condition and has figured out what she's trying to do. He wants to go to her, to say he understands and still loves her. But Kimble stops him: "You're always saying, don't do me any favors. Maybe she feels the same way, too." Johnny then does Hallie the favor of letting her think he no longer has any feelings for her, and they part coldly. So we have another *Fugitive*-style happy ending: not everyone reconciled in loving harmony, but everyone left alone to savor an integrity that demands the destruction of entangling relationships. It is brilliant and, at a deep level, chilling.

The Fugitive Refuses Attachments and Causes

But if negative liberty can be chilling because it refuses the appeal of fellowship and fellow feeling, positive liberty—the liberty that involves the freedom to choose the master or principle one will serve—can be equally chilling, as we see in "Not with a Whimper." Kimble hitches a ride to a small town in West Virginia because he has seen a newspaper item reporting that his medical school mentor—someone to whom he owes everything—is gravely ill with a heart condition. He stops at a coffee shop and orders coffee and a piece of pie. What kind of pie? he is asked. "Apple" is the predictable answer. This guy is nothing if not American. The counterman sees Kimble looking at the story about his teacher, Dr. Andrew Emmett "Mack" McAllister, and offers this opinion: "He's crazy." Why? Because he's an anti-smog crusader at war with the plant that sustains the economy of the town.

Kimble leaves the coffee shop after having aroused the counterman's suspicions (he is a true-crime magazine reader), and proceeds to the hospital, where he is immediately recognized by McAllister's longtime nurse. She feels that a visit with his former student, now a fugitive, will upset him, but Kimble insists on seeing his old friend (played by Laurence Naismith), who, although he is obviously ill, is also full of zealous energy. He has moved to Hempstead Mills because of the high incidence of smog. "I'd hoped to die from a lung disease," he tells Kimble. "So it could prove your theory," Kimble replies, in a tone that implies disapproval. If your life is driven by a theory you have, the theory has you. You can't detach yourself from it or put it on the shelf for a while. It leads you to do things you wouldn't otherwise do and "you" become an extension of its narrow and exacting vision.

In McAllister's case what his obsession leads to is making a bomb he will use to blow up the polluting factory in the hope that his cause will then receive the attention it deserves. Confined to a wheelchair, he can't do it him-self, and so he sends Kimble and a young lady admirer (the factory owner's daughter, played by Lee Merriweather) to deliver a package (he tells them it's a smog-measur-ing device) to the lab of one of the factory's scientists. It is to go off Saturday at high noon, when no

one is supposed to be at the plant. But, unbeknownst to McAllister, a group of schoolchildren is scheduled to tour the factory at that very time. What follows has a bit of the action melodrama about it as Kimble, once again, must come to the rescue, get the children out, and defuse the bomb, all while the police are hot on his trail. (The counterman in the opening scene has figured out who he is.)

He does it, of course, but the true focus of the episode is the rela-tionship between the doctor and the cause that deranges him. Vari-ous explanations are offered—he is old, his physical condition has affected his mental capacities; but the heart of the matter is that McAllister has allowed himself to be completely subordinated to a cause—an end—and that cause has become his master. When that happens, Berlin explains, the individual begins to think of himself as the representative of a larger whole, "a tribe, a race, a church, a state," and as such entitled to impose his will on "recalcitrant 'mem-bers'" who are being disciplined or even harmed "for their own sake." McAllister's nurse, who knows what he is planning to do, asks if his concern with pollution warrants doing something that might get people killed. He replies, "Millions of people have died from bad air, and if something isn't done about it, millions more will die in the future." In short, the end justifies the means, the logic often embraced by the apostles of positive liberty. After it is all over, Kimble delivers the judgment: "Mac was a brilliant man; what he did was wrong . . . what he did was fight for something he believed in—a cause. He was just too old and sick to know how to do it." That is, it's okay to believe in something so long as you can step away from it when it asks too much, so long as the attachment to it does not efface your identity and erode your independence.

In "Running Scared," the attachment someone cannot step away from is ambition. Michael Ballinger (James Daly) was the prosecuting attorney at Kimble's trial. That case jump-started his career, and he is now a candidate for governor, much to the distress of his wife (Joanne Linville), who sees the man she married disappearing before her eyes. ("Here's to the man I married, wherever he may be.") He pops pills; his hands tremble; he can think of only one thing.

At this moment of crisis in a marriage, Kimble reappears and becomes, as always, a catalyst. He has returned to Indiana because he has seen a newspaper story about the death of his father. He very much wants to see his sister, Donna (Jacqueline Scott), both to comfort her and draw comfort from her. A complicated set of arrangements (put into motion by Donna's husband) brings him together with the Ballingers and also with Gerard, who has gotten wind of Kimble's reemergence. The plot takes many turns, but at its center is the effort of Mrs. Ballinger to help Kimble avoid the authorities. She fears that her husband, who has spotted Donna in a Fort Wayne hotel (where she is registered under another name) and figured out what is going on, will get credit for Kimble's recapture, and once again be propelled forward in his political ambitions. "If you get caught," she tells Kimble, "no one but Michael Ballinger wins, and I lose a husband."

It doesn't work. Ballinger finds Kimble in his own hotel room (where his wife has stashed him) and is determined to turn him in. His wife comes back and intercedes, crying, "If he gets captured, you'll be captured too—you'll be a prisoner." As they quarrel, Kimble slips away. He leaves the stage to the episode's true protagonists, who trade recriminations. Ballinger tells his wife that every

man has his own dream, and the governorship is his. "That nomination means more to me than anything." "What are you going to do?" she asks. "About us?" he counters. "I'm not sure that there is any more us." He stalks out.

This is Harriet Ballinger's moment of truth, and she fails it. She runs after her husband and tells him where Kimble has gone (to an athletic event where he will meet up with his sister). Initially desperate to save her husband from his addiction to power, she ends up enabling it by providing him with the information that puts him back in the chase. Once more in pursuit of his political dream (which is her nightmare, although she has now chosen it), Ballinger rushes off to find Gerard. He's running again, not as Kimble runs—in order finally to stop running—but as one runs after an obsession to which he has long since surrendered. (It is Ballinger who is "running scared.")

In "A Taste of Tomorrow," the form obsession takes is hate. Like Kimble, Joe Tucker (Fritz Weaver) was wrongly convicted (of embezzlement) and had been on the run for four years. But unlike Kimble, Tucker has not maintained his inner equilibrium and lives only for revenge. A policeman accurately describes him when he

says, "Take a little hate, feed it for a long time," and you end up "with a half-crazed animal." The irony is that Tucker's innocence has now been established, and those pursuing him only want to apologize and bring him the good news.

He won't accept it. Another fractured mirror image of Kimble, Tucker is the innocent judged guilty, pronounced innocent again, but too much in love with his misery to let go of it. When Kimble, who has become involved in the usual accidental way, tells him that the truth is now known and that even his accusers and doubters (including his own daughter) want to make things right, Tucker just won't believe it. Kimble exclaims, "You want to hate; you don't want to be free; you just want to hate."

The central character of "Decision in the Ring" doesn't want to hate; he wants to be a victim. I remarked earlier that while "issues" sometimes inhabit the edges of a *Fugitive* episode, they never take center stage, and this is true even in an episode where the quintessential American issue—race—can hardly be avoided. Joe Smith (James Edwards) is a promising black boxer managed by Lou Bragan (Academy Award–winner James Dunn). At the end of a hard fight, he has cuts that must be attended to, and the cut-man (also black) fumbles the job and is fired. Kimble, here known as Ray Miller, who works in the building as a maintenance man, wanders by and stops to help. Naturally he gets the job.

It turns out that Smith is a former medical student who has left school to make his fortune in the ring. He is also suffering the effects of having been hit in the head too many times. Kimble suspects brain damage and, with the help of Smith's wife (Ruby Dee), tries to talk him into quitting the ring. He resists, even though as a former medical student he knows Kimble is right. It is not that he is drawn by the money (although he doesn't disdain it); rather what attracts him to the boxing life is his feeling that his peers accept him as a man: his racial identity is irrelevant. That would not be the case, he fears, if he were to leave the safety of the sporting world for the white world of medicine. "People pay me to see me fight; would they pay me if I were a doctor?"

In the ethos of liberalism, escaping the confines of racial identity and racial thinking is a good thing. But Smith has not escaped race; quite the reverse, for he allows the specter of race to dictate his choices. He may be free of the unpleasantness of prejudice, but he is not free in the sense of being indifferent to prejudice. Prejudice owns him insofar as a hyper-awareness of it determines his actions. When he says to Kimble, "Here I'm not black or white, I'm Joe Smith the fighter," he takes his identity from a profession rather than from something inside him. Being a fighter is fine as long as it is something you can walk away from; but if it is a refuge from the world, fighting becomes your prison, and freedom requires that you relinquish it. Kimble urges Smith to the better fight, the fight that vindicates his individuality and demonstrates his independence of external judgments of any kind: "Why don't you fight to make them accept you as a doctor? Or maybe you're too afraid to try."

Smith does not reply, but when the police come looking for Kimble (he has been found out in the usual accidental way), and he is told that his cut-man is a murderer, he replies, "I don't believe it."

After the police leave, Smith asks Kimble directly, Did you kill your wife? Kimble responds, "Arrested, tried, convicted, and innocent," and Smith reaffirms his status as a man of integrity who is able to recognize his fellow: "I believe you." As Kimble escapes with the help of a disguise Smith has provided, the boxer says, "I hope you get away." Kimble returns the good wish: "I hope you do, too." That is, I hope you break free of the prison you have made out of the boxing ring and make your own choices. Seconds later Smith tells Lou, who has come to escort him to the big fight, "Get me a doctor, I'm hurt. I've been hurt for a long time." We learn in the epilogue that Smith has acted in time and will heal; but he is already healed in the most important respect: he no longer clings to the false security of a protective cocoon. He has made his decision in the ring to leave it and be a free man.

The Fugitive as Doctor to Obsession

That is a decision Gerard can never bring himself to make. He is the most dramatic example in the series of someone who cannot let go of an obsession. Described in the prologue to every episode as "obsessed," Gerard's inability to detach himself even for a moment from his pursuit of Kimble is regularly a topic of discussion (he and his boss are talking about it the first time we see him in "Fear in a Desert City"), but in "Landscape with Running Figures," considered by many to be one of the series' best, his crippling obsessiveness gets a two-part episode of its own. If Kimble is the third and corrosive partner in the marriage of the Ballingers, he is even more so in the marriage of Marie (Barbara Rush) and Philip Gerard.

As Part 1 opens, the Gerards have interrupted a long-promised vacation because of a report that Kimble has been spotted in a small town in Missouri. As the police and Kimble play a cat-and-mouse game in back streets and alleys, the tension between the Gerards grows. Marie says, "Life without Kimble; what a pretty dream." Gerard says, "I wouldn't have come here if I didn't think there was a chance of getting him." He leaves, and Marie waits for her husband to call. When he doesn't, she decides to go back to Stafford. But a storm has closed the roads, and, determined to get away from a husband who is busy not being her husband, she gets on a bus heading in the opposite direction. When asked for her name by the ticket seller, she replies Lindsay (her maiden name). She is in effect divorcing Gerard on grounds of desertion.

But then by a twist of fate (always forcing things in *The Fugitive*), Marie is thrown together with the alienating party. Kimble has hitched a ride out of town, but he doesn't get along with the driver, who puts him off just at the point where the bus carrying Marie has stopped. Kimble mingles with the passengers and gets on without Marie spotting him. Soon after, the bus goes off the road. Kimble gets out and is about to leave when he hears Marie cry out, "I can't see." He turns back (as he always does), examines her, and finds that she has a concussion. He determines 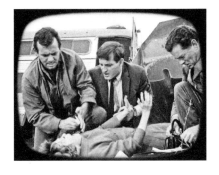 that she must be taken to a medical facility, and they go off together in a truck. She says to him, "Whoever you are, you're very kind." She doesn't even have to see him to know what kind of person he is. (But later she will go against her knowledge.)

Meanwhile Gerard is coordinating the search for Kimble. He becomes aware that his wife has left their hotel and cannot be found. But one anxiety overwhelms the other, and when pressed about his wife, he snaps, "Kimble, Richard Kimble, that's all I want to hear about."

That's also what his wife wants to hear nothing about. While her husband runs toward Kimble, she runs away from him—or so she thinks—but in fact she clings to him as her only protection in a dark world. The truck they share stalls, and together the fugitive and the blind woman walk into a town, only to find that it has been abandoned in advance of approaching floods. No one is there, and the electricity is off. Even though it's an entire town, it is just like the small rooms and dark alleys where the true action of *The Fugitive* typically occurs.

Kimble and Marie go into the inoperative telephone exchange— an image of blocked communications—and settle down for a conversation, unencumbered, at least for a while, by the ties and pressures of the world outside their confined but privileged space. What do you do? she asks. Jobs, odd jobs, he says. She almost tells him her real name, but he's stepped out to deal with three teenage louts who have taken over a bar. In his absence, Marie gets through to an operator—Kimble had told her to keep pressing a certain key—and manages to make contact with her husband. "I want you to come get me," she says, at first telling him nothing about her physical condition. He replies, "Is this a test, a choice between you and Kimble?" "No, there's been an accident." Alarmed Gerard asks, "Are you all right?" "A little too late to ask," she responds, and adds, "If you have to think about it Philip, don't come." She rings off.

Gerard thinks about it, looking all the while at a wanted poster of Kimble, and finally decides: "I want to go to my wife." He has pulled back from his obsession long enough to regain some sense of priority and balance. There may be hope for him.

Back in Tilden (the name of the abandoned town), Marie hears someone come in; she thinks it's Kimble (whom she knows as Carver), but it is one of the louts, who proceeds to terrorize her until Kimble returns and drives him and his friends away. "Those people, who were they?" she asks him. "They're people who are gone. You don't have to think about them anymore." The landscape has been cleared again; the world has receded; the space they occupy is once more wholly private, and as time seems to stop, they tell each other the story of their lives. She guesses that he's been married and asks, "Were you happy?" "It's been a long time. I don't remember." For once the tables are turned on Kimble. He is usually the one who forces others to engage in painful introspection, which they resist. Now it is he who resists, at least initially; but soon he recollects the early years of his marriage, first in San Diego and then in Stafford. He describes the simple pleasure of a small town (he doesn't name it). She responds by telling him about the small town she lives in, and they laugh as they recognize the similarities which, they think, characterize all small towns. (When you've seen one, you've seen them all.)

Brooding on her own situation and ignorant of Kimble's, Marie observes, "Where I come from nobody runs. It's a perfect circle—nothing to run to and nothing to run from. The only thing to do is wait around until the movie theater changes its bill." This evocation of a world where little happens and nothing ever changes is a representation of the ideal toward which Kimble, in all his frantic exertions, is moving. He runs and lives an extraordinary life so that he can stop running and live a life of extraordinary ordinariness. It sounds dull (though both he and Marie reminisce about it with affection), but then Kimble is basically a dull person; it is only the accident of a fate he didn't choose that has made him seem interesting.

It is that dull but reliable person Marie responds to, and she holds nothing back. "I lost my husband to a will-o'-the-wisp who twists in and out of my life. He's the little man who is never there, and he was never there again today." The irony hardly needs comment: the will-o'-the-wisp whose capture would set her free is sitting right there, although she can't see him. And yet she does see him for what he really is—"nice and kind." But then her eyes are opened when Kimble lets slip a detail that alerts her to his identity. At that moment the lights actually go back on and (ironically) the light of understanding recedes. The restored world blinds her to what she has come to know about the person she has been traveling with. Now she can only think of holding Kimble there until her husband reaches them. (Whereas Harriet Ballinger wants Kimble to escape, Marie Gerard longs for him to be captured; but their motives—to detach their husbands from Kimble—are the same.) "Promise, you'll stay with me until someone comes," she implores. She even comes on to Kimble, clumsily; she tells him that she will reward him and that he won't have to "worry about publicity." But when Gerard calls back, Kimble answers and hears, "This is Lieutenant Gerard; I want to speak to my wife." Kimble hangs up and says, "You'd do anything to keep me here, anything." When she replies, "Yes, anything," she has become just like her husband: obsessed. When he turns to leave, she cries, "Kimble, you can't run away from me," exactly the kind of thing her husband has said a hundred times. Marie runs after him and falls in the street, pleading for help; once again, Kimble comes back. He is what he is, even if she is changing by the minute.

In the end, an ambulance arrives, and Marie is saved. Gerard gets there just seconds after Kimble escapes. Business as usual. In the epilogue, Gerard is at his wife's bedside and acknowledges what he has become. "There'll be another time, and when the call comes, I'll go; he's stuck in my throat. Sometimes I feel that Kimble is all around us." Of course it is he who brings Kimble with him wherever he goes; he has allowed his obsession to infect everything, even the one relationship he thinks of as an oasis. "You're the only part of my life he can't ever get to, the only thing he can't touch. If I lost that there would be nothing left, nothing but the thought of Kimble to be choking me." Marie decides to let her husband believe that she has not been touched; as the episode ends her fingers close over his. Does it mean they are now allied by a shared obsession, or does it mean that because of the strength of their relationship, there is the possibility they may someday be free? It's hard to tell.

There is no ambiguity about the status of another obsessive, the central character in "With Strings Attached." He is a young concert violinist, Geoffrey Martin (Rex Thompson), who plays a rigorous concert schedule under the hard-driving direction of his coach and guardian, Max, played to an Erich von Stroheim turn by Donald Pleasence. Kimble is the newly hired chauffeur, Frank Carter, and from the moment he enters the house, things begin to happen: Geoffrey's pet canary is killed; his Stradivarius is broken; he reports that Max injured his hand with a paperweight. On its face (there's the play between what is visible and what is true again), the evidence says that Max is abusing Geoffrey, but soon Kimble, who is, after all, a pediatrician, begins to suspect that Geoffrey himself is the orchestrator of these events and is planning to do something terrible.

What he is planning to do, it turns out, is kill Max, who he believes is responsible for his feeling of being trapped and confined. But Max, once a concert violinist himself until drinking ruined his

career, knows better. In an exchange just before a big concert, Geoffrey says, "You took something from me, Max. I'm taking it back. My
freedom." Max replies, "You haven't any freedom. You lost it when
you were given the great gift of genius. Don't you understand that?"
Earlier Max had called genius not a gift but a burden, a "terrible"
burden. It is a burden from which Geoffrey cannot be free: it is not
external to him, but lives within him. (He is attached to the strings
in the strongest sense; apart from them he has no self.) Max can
free himself of drink by an act of the will. Kimble can free himself

of the taint of guilt by evading capture long enough to find the one-
armed man. But short of a lobot-
omy (and even that might not do
the job), Geoffrey cannot be free
of his genius. He thinks he can escape it by destroying its outward
vehicles—the violin, his concert
schedule, Max—but even if the ex-
ternal scaffolding that supports his compulsion to perform is dis-
mantled, the compulsion will survive and still rule his life.

Needless to say, Kimble arrives in the nick of time, even though
he is now dodging the police, who get a glimpse of him when they
come to the house. Kimble confronts Geoffrey, who has Max at gun-
point. After a back and forth in which Kimble makes it clear Geoffrey will never get away with it even if he kills him too, the young
man snaps and starts shooting. But when the police, looking for
Kimble, rush in, they find that instead of shooting Max or Kimble,
Geoffrey has shot his violin. He cries, "I only wanted to be free; it's
all I ever wanted; just that, only that; just to be free, free, free." But
he was born with strings attached, and wherever he is and whatev-

er he does, they will not relax their hold. In case we missed it, William Conrad intones the moral: "Some men can never be free from birth. They are their own jailors, their own prisons."

Even the desire to be free can also be a prison, if by "freedom" is meant not freedom from external constraints—the classically liberal freedom of formulating one's own life plan—but freedom from any constraints whatsoever, even the constraints of an internalized morality. Freedom embraced for its own sake—without reference to some inner compass that keeps one on the right path in the midst of temptations and distractions—is a freedom that undermines the self by depriving it of an anchor and a center. It is really not freedom at all, but bondage to whim, chance, and opportunity. It is directionless movement impelled by nothing more substantive than the way the wind blows. It is the freedom Milton excoriates when he declares in a sonnet, "License they mean when they cry liberty."

This is the freedom—the dark side of Berlin's "negative freedom"—that is embraced and celebrated by the motorcycle gang that gives the episode "The Devil's Disciples" its title. The leader of the gang is Hutch, played to slimy perfection by Bruce Dern. Hutch has taken the leadership away from Don (Lou Antonio) and in the process taken his girl, Penny (Diana Hyland). Although most of the gang members have day jobs, on weekends they act out the fantasy of a life without responsibility, riding where they like, doing what they like, taking what they like. (One is reminded of Matthew Arnold's devastating characterization in *Culture and Anarchy* of the freedom-mongering Englishman who insists on his right to "enter where he likes, hoot as he likes, threaten as he likes, smash as he likes.")

The plot revolves around the death of Disciple-member Tommy Joe, who was killed in Vietnam. Tommy Joe had gone there in the wake of an aborted robbery attempt. His own father had turned him in, and he was given the choice of jail or military service. Hutch is telling everyone that Tommy Joe's death must be avenged, which means that his father, who set the fatal events in motion, must be killed.

Kimble enters the scene when the gang rescues him just as he was about to be captured by the police. They assume he is like them, an enemy of authority, a lawbreaker. Hutch asks him, "What makes you special?" Kimble responds, "I'm nothing special," which is in fact true. The status that leads him to be the quarry of so many law enforcement officers has been forced on him. He is, as I observed before, relentlessly ordinary, although Hutch and the others have a stake in thinking otherwise. They look up to him as a "higher" version of what they aspire to, someone who flouts society's conventional prohibitions. (Boy, do they get their man wrong.)

Even though he is a captive of the gang, Kimble immediately involves himself in the moral dynamics of the situation. When the police arrive, looking for him, Kimble and Don hide in a bathroom. Don boasts that Hutch "does okay for us, man; we're loose, we're free." Kimble points out that they are cowering in a toilet. "You call that free?" He adds, "Penny's Hutch's chick, and no one can say anything different; you call that free?" Later Penny asks what Kimble's trying to do with Don. "I'm no high-school dropout. I know that Caesar stuff—divide and conquer." Kimble corrects her, "Divide and rule, and it's Machiavelli." This exchange does two things: (1) Penny shows herself to be someone worth caring about; she is literate, and potential material for the middle class; and (2) Kimble steps into his tutelary role; there's work for him here.

Penny doesn't think so. "You've seen Hutch walk all over Don; you think that's going to change?" "It will have to," Kimble answers, "for himself, for some kind of life for you." Penny then gets off one of the best lines in the series: "You must have talked your wife to death." She identifies the true arena of Kimble's action: he talks to people; he tries to appeal to their better natures; he helps their better natures emerge.

It pays off. Penny aids in Kimble's escape. Don sees what's happening and doesn't let on. Hutch figures out what she has done and slaps her around, injuring her. Don insists on taking Penny to a doctor, and when they get there, she tells him the real story. It was Hutch who was responsible for the robbery. Tommy Joe took the rap for him, and he has projected his guilt on to Benson, Tommy Joe's father. "Why are you telling me this?" he asks. "Because I don't want to get mixed up in any killing." The two have now pulled away from the false freedom of the motorcycle gang and are moving toward the real freedom of being true to themselves and to a standard of behavior they themselves nominate. No longer the devil's disciples, they are now Kimble's disciples, which means they are on their way to being no one's disciples.

Before he left with the injured Penny, Don had promised Hutch that he would meet him at Benson's place. He now goes there, but with a new intention. He finds Hutch and the others terrifying Benson. Don tells them the real story. "If you want to square things for Tommy Joe, the guy you want to kill is Hutch or me." The gang turns on Hutch, who cries, "I never needed you anyway; I don't need anybody." The claim is one of total independence, freedom from everything and everyone. But there is a difference between being free to follow your own understanding of what is right and being free from any conception of right. The first freedom—the freedom of the man who knows who he is and what he values—is what Kimble enacts even when his physical being is the most constrained. The other freedom is the freedom of being without value and therefore without being. That is Hutch's condition: he is the plaything of his freedom; he doesn't have it, it has him; it is his obsession.

The Fugitive as Rational Man

Obsession is, quite literally, the condition of being out of your mind, of having surrendered the free play of mind to a fixed and confining point. As Geoffrey, the mad violinist of "With Strings Attached," is taken away by the authorities, someone asks, "What will happen to him?" A policeman answers, "It's up to the doctors." That is, it is up to medical science to determine whether or not he can be returned to sanity by undergoing treatment that will wean him away from his genius and render him normal, someone who will live a "balanced life," moving freely from context to context and not being confined to only one. This faith in medical science belongs to the liberalism that informs the series; for liberalism privileges the realms of fact and rational choice and looks askance at forms of thought (like religion) which bind men to conclusions arrived at in advance of free and unfettered investigation. A liberal walks into a situation with a diagnostic eye and refuses to accept prepackaged answers to questions and problems.

Richard Kimble is such a person; he is, after all, a physician, a man of science, and in "An Apple a Day" he champions science against the idée fixe of a homeopathic practitioner. As the episode opens, Kimble is being pursued by the police. He runs, trips, and falls unconscious at the bottom of a hill, where he is found by a middle-aged couple, Mr. and Mrs. Crandall, who take him to the house of their doctor, Josephus Adams (Arthur O'Connell). But Adams is not a real doctor. He has a certificate from something called the American Natural Medical Institute. He dispenses herbs, honey, and potions and inveighs against "allopaths," conventional physicians who charge large fees and like to cut people open. He is assisted by his niece, Sharon (Kim Darby), and by his wife, Marianne (Sheree North), who is the manager of the clinic and the driving force behind its ever-growing mail order business. Marianne is a brassy blonde of a kind that always signals danger and disorder in *The Fugitive*. She is addicted both to money and sex (she comes on to Kimble), and she abets the efforts of her husband to make his patients addicted to him and to the suspiciously habit-forming "cough syrup" he sells as a substitute for X-rays.

It is that syrup—made in part from the honey Adams harvests from his own bees—that is given to Mrs. Crandall (Amzie Strickland), who suffers from a persistent cough. When Kimble hears the cough, he is alarmed—he feels indebted to her, and by the laws of his universe it is a debt he must repay. He asks what the X-rays showed. This immediately brands him as someone sympathetic to allopaths. Sharon triumphantly tells him of a patient with a

very high fever who was treated by her uncle, and the fever broke after four days "without any of those fancy antibiotics." "Kind of a miracle, isn't it?" she comments. But Kimble has no truck with miracles and prefers the explanations made available by science and empirical observation. "With mod-

ern medicine," he explains, "the fever could have been broken overnight. These days pneumonia is no more dangerous than a bad cold." "These days." The criticism is muted but unmistakable. Sharon and her uncle live in a medieval animist world where nature provides remedies to those in tune with Her. Kimble lives in the modern world where nature is not worshiped but mastered by the efforts of independent Cartesian investigators. When Sharon tells him that Josephus calls his remedies "God's own elixir," Kimble replies drily, "He ought to know; he's part of the family." That is, Josephus lives in some dream world where he consorts with folk deities and ignores the proven results of laboratory procedures.

All of this talk is interrupted and mooted when Mr. Crandall carries Mrs. Crandall into the house. Kimble examines her and says to Adams, "Your patient's dead." Kimble decides it's time to leave, but as he is waiting for the bus, he learns that Sharon broke down at Mrs. Crandall's funeral, sobbing, "She didn't have to die," before passing out. The bus arrives, but, concerned for Sharon, Kimble rushes back to the house, where he finds that she has been attacked by the bees (after a quarrel with Marianne she accidentally knocked over a beehive) and has passed out again. Josephus is about to administer an ointment and some natural spirits, but Kimble stops him. "She's in a diabetic coma. She needs help, and she needs it now. She could be dead in a few hours. We'd better get her to the car." "We don't agree with your diagnosis, Doctor," Marianne retorts, letting him know that she knows who he is. Kimble leaves with the girl anyway, and when Josephus indicates that he's beginning to think Kimble's diagnosis may be correct, Marianne tells him that his "friend" is a convicted murderer. He responds, "If you knew he was a murderer all the time, didn't it bother you having him in the house?" "I thought it would be exciting," she admits, drawing Josephus's disgusted reply: "I think he was too decent a man to have anything to do with you." His eyes are open not only to his wife's true nature, but to the folly of allowing an unexamined belief to blind him to the reality of medical facts. His recognition that Kimble is a good man coincides with his recognition that he has surrendered himself to an obsession. An apple a day should not keep the doctor away. What you want in Richard Kimble's world is a doctor (like him) who is always on call and puts his faith in up-to-date medical knowledge not in faith.

Josephus's conversion to the world of empirical cause and effect is complete when, at the end of the episode, after his niece has been saved, he tells Kimble (who is of course about to get on a bus), "You were right about all of it." "All of it" includes not only Sharon's medical condition, but the superiority of experimental science to folk remedies, and the danger of giving oneself over to nature. In *The Fugitive*, nature is not man's friend but an anarchic force that must be kept at bay and controlled by man-made devices and structures. That force can take the form of a disease that disorders the body; of bees that attack once they escape an enclosure; of women like Marianne who are engines of hunger (the human equivalent of sharks) and always want more—more money, more sex, more material possessions, more possession of your being. "Marianne will be gone," Josephus tells Kimble. She is expelled along with the false allure of natural medicine.

Josephus frees himself from the forces to which he has been bound just in time. Others Kimble encounters are not so fortunate. In "This'll Kill You," Charlie Paris (played brilliantly by Mickey Rooney) is a washed-up comedian who has been reduced to running a Laundromat in a one-horse town. Like Josephus, he has two obsessions that prevent him from owning himself: One is gambling, and the second is his Marianne, Paula (Nita Talbot), another of the predatory blondes who lure weak men to their destruction in the series. (Kimble is never tempted by them; just as he is immediately known for what he is by those who believe in him, so does he immediately know those who walk the wrong side of the street.) His obsessions combine in a deadly fashion when a desperate Charlie (he is broke and on the run from organized crime figures who want to kill him) tries to lure Paula; he writes to her claiming that he owns a string of laundries. Charlie knows that only a lie would bring her to him, and therefore he must also know, in some part of his being, that when the lie is discovered she will discard him. In fact Paula is already paving the way to disaster, because Pete Ragan (Phillip Pine), a mob messenger-boy, has followed her, figuring, correctly, that she will lead him to Charlie.

Kimble (as Nick Phillips) is Charlie's assistant, and he is literally in the middle of all this. But he is unable to work his usual magic, because the forces he must defeat live within the man he would save from them. Charlie has invited his demons—externalized in the forms of Ragan and Paula—to converge on him, and for the most

part Kimble can only watch as they close in. Early on in the episode, Kimble could see what's coming. A woman had come on to him in a bar, and later, when Charlie sends him to intercept Paula, he realizes the woman is Paula. It is only a matter of time before she hooks up with Ragan, who immediately offers her five thousand dollars to lead him to Charlie. She declines, but only because she believes she will get more from Charlie. When Charlie finally admits to her that he has nothing ("I haven't got a quarter"), she goes to Ragan immediately.

Kimble sees Paula and Ragan together and draws the obvious conclusion; he tries to warn Charlie. Charlie refuses to believe him, and declares, "If you're going to marry someone, you've got to have faith in them." Kimble implores him: "She sold you out, Charlie." But Charlie tells him to leave. On his way out, Kimble sees Paula and says to her, "He didn't believe a thing I said; I hope you got a good price." (It was $7500, not the proverbial 30 pieces of silver.)

The rest unfolds with the inevitability of a Greek tragedy. Charlie confronts Paula with Kimble's accusation, and she claims Kimble forced himself on her. Charlie protests that Nick is not that kind of guy, but she shows him fresh bruises (stigmata) she received from a sexual encounter with Ragan. It's faith in Kimble against visible evidence, and physical evidence wins, as it did in his trial. Kimble had already acknowledged that he was on the run, and Charlie, incensed at what he thinks to be his friend's perfidy, informs the police that Nick can be found at the Laundromat.

But then, almost immediately, Charlie spots the wad of money in Paula's purse and stumbles onto the truth. In the world of *The Fugitive*, however, this is not good enough. All Charlie has done is assent to physical evidence more powerful than the physical evidence he had assented to moments ago. What is required is a faith that persists independently of *any* physical evidence. Charlie doesn't have it, and by the inexorable logic the series embodies and exacts, he must be punished.

Charlie tries to do the right thing and warn Nick. He drives to the Laundromat, but as a consequence of Paula's betrayal, he is followed by Ragan and an imported hit man. Everyone arrives at the same time—the police, Charlie, the killers, and Paula. The police go into the building looking for Kimble. Charlie is shot as he gets to the front door. Paula gets to Charlie just as he is dying. His last words are, "I can't think of anything funny." Kimble slips away, having been able to do nothing but watch helplessly.

The Fugitive Spreads a Secular Faith

Both "An Apple a Day" and "This'll Kill You" turn on the issue of faith, but in ways that may at first seem contradictory. In one, faith is derided in favor of a reliance on hard, physical fact. In the other, faith is required, and the man who relies on what he takes to be hard physical fact is undone. How can these two episodes be reconciled? I am aware that one might say this is a TV series and not a philosophical tract, but there is ample evidence—to be presented later—that the writers and producers of the program had a coherent understanding of what the series was about and adhered to it. The series is a continual meditation on a set of limited themes, and faith is one of them. It would not be too much to say that the proof text of *The Fugitive* is Hebrews 11:1 "Faith is the substance of things hoped for, the evidence of things not seen." The evidence of things seen is what has gotten Kimble into his predicament. The evidence of things not seen—the evidence that resides within and is affirmed only by faith—is what keeps him going and connects him with others who look into his heart and see what is written on its fleshly tables (2 Cor. 3:3).

Those who are unable to look inside and remain confined to the limits of what is empirically verifiable see in Kimble only the marks of a fugitive, and draw their conclusions accordingly. They stand on the other side of the series' great divide, and sometimes Kimble just leaves them there. After all, he can't save everybody. But when that somebody is his own brother, he cannot walk away; he must fight for his soul and bring him over to the faithful side. That is what happens in "Home Is the Hunted," an episode in which the dynamics and demands of faith are foregrounded. Fittingly enough, very little happens, even though Kimble has returned to Stafford where, as the narrator reminds us, a thousand people know him and Gerard is, quite literally, just around every corner.

Kimble is in Stafford because he has read that his father, also a physician, has given his treasured medical library to a local university. His sense of foreboding is deepened when he goes to the family home and finds a "for sale" sign in front of it. He phones his sister, Donna, and is told that his father has had a heart attack, and that he and his daughter's family have moved to a house in the suburbs. Donna agrees to bring their father to the old family home to meet Kimble. She finds Richard's

younger brother, Ray (Andrew Prine), tinkering with his racing car (a Porsche with the name "the Kimble special" inscribed on it) to tell him that his brother has returned. Ray is unresponsive and says that he has to prepare for a race. At this moment we begin to suspect this episode will be Ray's story.

Kimble and his father, John Kimble (Robert Keith), meet. The ailing doctor, a pediatrician like his hunted son, has been worrying about his own parenting skills. "I loved you first, and I'm afraid I loved you more," he tells Richard. Donna comes into the room and adds her account of the trouble Ray keeps getting himself into. Sometimes, she says, "I think Ray doesn't care whether he lives or dies."

When Ray finally comes to the house, the meeting between the two brothers is tentative and awkward. It doesn't get any better when Richard rehearses Ray's bad behavior—drinking, driving too fast, losing jobs, spending money he doesn't have, casting off old friends, in short the very forms of behavior that in *The Fugitive* always signal a life out of control and a soul in danger. Ray responds to the rehearsal of his failings by blaming them on his brother. After the trial and conviction, Ray's fiancée left him ("Her father could only see me as Richard Kimble's brother"), and employers let him go as soon as they found out who he was. Everyone believed Kimble to be guilty.

"Do you?" Richard asks his brother, who answers, "The jury believed it; the appeals court believed it." Ray adds, as his father walks into the room, "What difference does it make? Dad never cared about me." For one of the few times in the series, the fugitive loses his control and slaps his brother, recoiling against himself even as he does it. When some stranger cites the world's evidence against him, Kimble can receive the judgment without flinching, but when his own brother will not take him on faith, it is more than he can bear.

This is a moment of great psychological complexity. When people who barely know Kimble affirm their belief in him, it is because, like him, they are centered, secure in their identities and able to recognize and respond to someone similarly secure. (Again, it takes one to know one.) But those whose inner gyroscopes spin wildly are unable (it is an incapacity that goes to the core of their troubled being) to connect with him; only if they are somehow made whole can they acquire the equanimity and self-confidence (a phrase that should be taken literally) that allow them to see what is truly there, to see what is inside. Ray has nothing to center him because he has never felt supported or loved. The irony is that the means of his recovery to wholeness is also, in his mind, the obstacle to it. He has always wanted to be like his brother, but at the same time he has always felt that his brother stood between him and what he desires—the love of his father, the prize for which his fiancée, his friends, and his racing trophies are inadequate substitutes. His brother, both as a role model and as the recipient of the father's love, is what he wants, and also what he resents. He must be healed (if he is to be healed) by the one who wounded him.

It happens in a single scene that takes place in the old family home against the backdrop of the danger posed by Gerard who, having sensed that something is afoot, is closely monitoring the activities of the Kimbles. Richard's father and sister urge him to leave town; they fear (correctly) that Gerard is closing in. But he is adamant: "Before I go I've got to make [Ray] believe I didn't do it."

But how can he accomplish that? At first he turns to the method that has always been used against him, the marshalling of external evidence. He reminds Ray of the years they spent living under the same roof and of the relationship they shared. "Did you see any killer in me then? Can't you believe me?" The response is anguished: "I want to, I've tried to. Make me believe you." Now the fugitive realizes that piling up evidence is not going to do it because evidence doesn't produce belief. "I'm supposed to relive the million pieces of our lives again so that they all add up to you believing me?" "Million pieces" is telling; it signals Richard's realization that a hundred million pieces wouldn't do it; nothing "adds up" to belief. How then is it produced? He finds the answer when he walks outside the house, thereby exposing himself to the possibility that Gerard (who is already in the neighborhood) will see him. Alarmed, Ray asks, "What are you doing?" "Some things require a lot of proof," the fugitive replies. "I'm going to prove to you that I'm not afraid to die." Ray is amazed. "You mean . . . you'd let him take you just to prove to me that you aren't . . . ?" Richard's answer says it all. "If I were drowning, wouldn't you jump in for me?" He is telling his brother that he, not the fugitive, is the one in real trouble, and that he, the fugitive, would do anything to help him; and he is also telling Ray, you are just like me. When Ray understands this, and understands that he would in fact do the same thing were their positions reversed, he joins his brother in a fellowship of unconditional love and becomes the whole person he had never been before.

When the two exit the room, John Kimble asks his elder son, "Is it all right?" and the response is, "It's all right." No explanations, no chain of reasons, no elaborate Q.E.D., just a quietly shared conviction that the circle of the faithful has been enlarged by one.

In the epilogue, John Kimble talks to Gerard, who asks about Ray. "Ray's been thinking about giving up fast cars," he tells the policeman. The younger Kimble no longer needs to run from a self with which he is profoundly uncomfortable. The Porsche that he drove in races originally belonged to his brother; courting death by driving it too fast was his way of trying to be one with his brother and to destroy him at the same time. Now that he really is one with his brother, he doesn't need the car; he doesn't need to go anywhere; he is home. (In the epilogue Conrad quotes the refrain from Robert Louis Stevenson's "Requiem": "Home is the sailor, home from the sea.") For Ray, this is the day the running stopped.

Fans and commentators have remarked on Ray's absence from the rest of the series. "Why was he not used in future episodes?"[3] The answer is that there would be nothing for him to do. The role of the loyal and helpful sibling already belongs to Donna. Ray's role

---

3. Kenneth Ardizzone, comp., "*The Fugitive*": *Views and Reviews* (Shelbyville, Ky.: Wasteland Press, 2006), 93.

has been to highlight in a particularly focused way the series-long opposition between visible evidence and belief, and once he has done that, he quite properly vanishes from the stage.

Of course belief or faith can find an object not worthy of it; it can be blind. This would appear to be the case in "Nobody Loses All the Time." This is a late episode and displays the weakness that characterizes the beginning of the fourth season. Too much time is taken up by a chase sequence that has Kimble hopping freights, stealing ambulances, and assuming unconvincing disguises. But there is a fugitive heart to the story, and it involves, of all people, the one-armed man. Kimble sees the man (played by Bill Raisch) on a newscast about a local fire, and he leaves his job as a bartender to find him. The one-armed man, accompanied by a woman, is still on the scene when he sees Kimble approaching, and as he runs away, the woman he has left behind is struck by a car. What will Kimble do? As William Conrad intones the Hippocratic Oath, which enjoins physicians to minister to the ill even when they are under threat, Kimble has to choose between pursuing the man he's been chasing for years and helping the injured woman.

It is of course no choice at all, for Kimble is always faithful to his sworn oath. He accompanies the woman, Maggie (played by Barbara Baxley), to the hospital and treats her, saving her life. He also questions her in an effort to locate her friend. But Maggie resists him, even when he tells her, "He killed my wife." She responds, "I'll never believe that." Why? Because "he talks to me, he even listens to me; and he cares about my troubles." This evidence of what her heart knows overrules any evidence the world may offer, even when its bearer is the man who has saved her life. Structurally she is in the same position as Nurse Ruthie (Joanna Moore), who (predictably) falls for Kimble. When the nurse is told that the handsome doctor is a fugitive and a murderer, she says, "I'll never believe he did it."

Only Gerard refuses to enter the circle of faith. He had come to town alerted by the police, who have been alerted by Maggie. Going through her belongings, Gerard discovers a picture of her with the one-armed man, and understands why Kimble has risked everything. So you believe his story? a local policeman asks. Gerard replies, "It's not my job to believe him; it's my job to catch him."

He of course doesn't. When Gerard tracks Kimble down, he is with Maggie, and she is still refusing to betray her man ("I can't tell you"). But neither will she betray Kimble. When Gerard bursts into the room, Kimble goes out a back way and she blocks the entrance with her wheelchair. So everyone ends up being faithful in his or her fashion. Maggie is faithful both to Kimble and to the one-armed man (a hard feat in this series). Ruthie is faithful to Kimble. Gerard is faithful to his obsession. And all three persist in their faith in the face of contrary evidence. Maggie believes in the one-armed man despite everything she's been told about him. Ruthie believes in Kimble despite what the police tell her. Gerard believes in his mission despite the evidence that he may be pursuing an innocent man. And what do their beliefs get them? Not much, for as the episode ends, they are all alone: Ruthie and Gerard without Kimble (in different ways), Maggie without the one-armed man. The reward of belief is more often than not wholly internal; all it gives you is the feeling that to your own self you have been true.

That tension between belief and evidence as it plays out in the law is the explicit subject of "Man in a Chariot." The man in the chariot is G. Stanley Lazer (Ed Begley), trapped in a wheelchair as the result of an accident whose significance becomes clear only at the end of the episode. Before the accident, Lazer was a high-profile defense lawyer. Now he is reduced to teaching law, a task he describes contemptuously as being a nurse to a bunch of kids. Kimble has seen Lazer boasting on a TV show that had he been Richard Kimble's lawyer, he would have obtained an acquittal. Kimble contacts Lazer and says, "I want your help." Lazer replies, "I've never lost a capital case," and resolves to be-

gin examining the transcript immediately. Kimble interjects, "Isn't there something you should ask me? . . . Whether I'm guilty?" Lazer dismisses the question: "What's the difference? I'm not a judge, I'm a lawyer."

This early exchange hints at what will soon become apparent: Lazer is interested only in the forensic arena in which he can display and exercise the skill of outmaneuvering the prosecution. Kimble is interested only in being believed. When Lazer announces triumphantly, "I've pinpointed enough technical errors to put you back in the dock," Kimble looks disappointed. He doesn't want to get off on a technicality. He wants exoneration; he wants the record wiped clean. When Lazer proposes to mount a mock trial in his class—literally a trial run—Kimble objects; but Lazer explains that since his students hate him (he bullies and berates them mercilessly), the test of his case will be helpfully severe. "If I can get an acquittal before that jury, I could defend you in front of the Spanish Inquisition."

In Lazer's mind, his relationship with his students is a mere strategic convenience; it provides him with the perfect stage setting for his experiment. But very soon it becomes the heart of the story—not Kimble's story, but his own. The mock trial has barely started when he takes over the role of defense attorney.

As the "trial" continues Lazer begins to spar with Lee Gould (Robert Drivas), a star student who is acting as the prosecuting attorney. Gould is skillful, and as the evidence against Kimble piles up (just as it did in the original trial), Lazer becomes more and more shrill and even abusive. After a particularly heated exchange, in the course of which Lazer taunts Gould, calling him "cheap, infantile, and gutless," the young student leaves the classroom in great distress. Kimble, who has been watching on a remote hookup, catches up with him, and they go for a beer.

Gould is ready to quit, but Kimble says, "He picked you because he thought you'd give him a good fight, but when he took the gloves off you ran." Gould decides to stay with it, and Kimble

goes back to confront Lazer. (This is his role: the healer, the reconciler, the enabler.) "That boy worships you, although I don't know why." And yes, "he's good, making the great Stanley Lazer look bad, and if it weren't for your vanity, you would be proud of him." Of course, Lazer could feel pride in Gould's performance only if he thought it was his job to produce it. In his mind, however, his real job is one he can no longer practice: "I'm not a teacher; I didn't choose the work, and now I rot in a classroom." (He cannot see that the classroom podium can be as powerful a chariot as the lawyer's summation.) As he rambles on, he reveals the back-story behind his present situation. He was injured when the car being driven by his drunken wife crashed. She was killed, and he was disabled. The real damage, however, was done to his spirit; Kimble is trying to tell him that he must heal himself by coming to terms with his condition and learning to recognize and value what he has.

Lazer begins to do that in his summation when his plea for Kimble is transparently a plea for himself: "Consider the defendant. What he asks from you is only compassion. . . . He was exiled to a world he hated . . . and he built a wall around it. This is the man you are asked to judge, and I commend him to your mercy." The verdict the jury (of students) delivers is "Not guilty," but it has nothing to do with Kimble. Lazer's students have forgiven him and redeemed him.

Lazer knows it. He tells Kimble, "That verdict was mine, not yours. You won the case for me and brought me back to humanity." He adds, "I couldn't win for you. You'll have to find your one-armed man." "Then you do believe I'm innocent?" asks Kimble, and Lazer replies, "Of course." Lazer, the man who put his faith and energies into the legal system, reveals himself to be a believer independently of any evidence. At the beginning of the episode, Kimble was just someone he could get off; he was a means to Lazer's professional rehabilitation. Now the fugitive is the man who has saved him. He joins the long list of those who just know that Kimble is innocent, and he knows it at the moment he knows—and learns to live with—himself. "Get going," Lazer says. "I have a few young minds that need twisting." Taught by Kimble, he now accepts his role as teacher. He no longer needs Kimble and, apart from the lawyerly skills whose inadequacy he has acknowledged, he has nothing Kimble needs. Kimble says, "Thanks, Professor," and Lazer says the right thing. "Thank *you*."

The Fugitive Encounters Religious Faith

The faith Lazer achieves in Kimble and in himself is entirely secular, but faith is of course a theological concept. Its theological meaning is explored in a two-part episode starring Eileen Heckart as Sister Veronica, a nun who is trying to get to Sacramento—that is, to a state of grace. It is only near the end of Part 1 that we find out she is undertaking the journey in order to renounce her vows. Sister Veronica considers herself a failure because when a troubled young Indian boy reached out to her, she did not respond, and he was later executed for committing a murder. She no longer has faith in her vocation. The irony—unavailable to us as viewers until the end of the episode—is that she exhibits the faith she thinks she's lost at every moment she persists in an entirely baseless confidence that she will reach Sacramento, despite the fact that she has no money and is driving an ancient jalopy that wheezes along with smoke blowing out of its radiator cap. What she needs is a miracle—at the beginning William Conrad defines miracle as "an effect in the physical world which surpasses all known human power"—and the miracle Providence provides is Richard Kimble. When he first appears and diagnoses a plugged fuel line (fuel is a metaphor throughout for grace), she says, "I was just marveling at how Providence can work." The title of the two-part episode is "Angels Travel on Lonely Roads," and contrary to the striking appearance of Sister Veronica, who is resplendent and authoritative in a full habit, the angel, the vehicle of grace, is Kimble.

He doesn't think so. Indeed, at every turn Kimble resists understanding the succession of near-escapes and fortunate coincidences that befall them—work turns up just as they are broke; he draws to an inside straight in a poker game—as anything but the workings of natural, if unpredictable, causes. It's just the hydraulics and the mechanics of fuel lines and fuel pumps, nothing else. After one of Sister Veronica's invocations of the "higher authority" ("What possible set of natural circumstances could have brought us together?"), he says, "Faith is a wonderful thing, Sister, but there is also reality." The reality, as he see it, is that he is going to ride with her only until they reach Ravenna (a town in California, but also a city in Italy famous for its mosaics depicting events in the life of Christ); but when he tries to hop a freight, the car he chooses is detached from the train and shunted off to another track, where it just stops. Defeated, Kimble goes back to the car, where Sister Veronica smiles knowingly and says, "Mr. Walker [Kimble's current alias], perhaps you had better drive."

The opposition between a fact-based realism and a faith that looks beyond the calculation of merely physical effects is not as stark as Kimble takes it to be. Indeed he has already exhibited his own style of faith before he encounters Sister Veronica. Running from the police yet again, he spots two young thugs mugging a man who had fallen to the ground. He scares them off, checks to see that the man is not badly hurt, and lifts his wallet; not, however, for the money—he shoves that back into the man's pocket— but for the papers of identification. (The morality of these matters has changed; today we would regard identity theft as the more serious offense.) Kimble can continue in his quest for justice only if he does not reveal himself; in his eyes the means that allow him to remain undetected are legitimately seized, but he thinks it illegitimate to rob people of what he can still earn honestly. (He takes evident pride in doing every job, however menial, to the best of his ability.) One can quarrel with the principle, but principle is what it is, and adherence to principle is itself a form of faith because it declines the temptation to take the shortest way between point A and point B. It subordinates empirical reasoning (the more money I have, the better equipped will I be to avoid capture) to the demands of timeless imperatives—imperatives that tell you what you must do rather than what it would be strategic to do. The difference between Kimble's faith and Sister Veronica's faith is that hers includes the structure of an ecclesiasti-

cal institution while his rests only (as far as we ever know) on an internalized ethics. In short it is the difference between religious faith and liberal faith.

That difference narrows to almost nothing in the course of their adventures. At several points they change places. Just when they need it, an unoccupied, fully furnished, unlocked cabin turns up. In the respite from the road this "miracle" provides, Sister Veronica begins to hone in on Kimble, saying to him, "A man who drifts from job to job . . . Doesn't fit." And a little bit later, "I know you're running." Kimble reacts and scoffs at the very mode of perception on which he depends: "You look at a man's face and right away you can tell what he is? It just doesn't work that way . . . ." Yet in every episode of the series, someone looks at Kimble's face (one female character exclaims upon meeting him, "Boy, do you have a face!") and right away is certain of what he is—a good, innocent man. It's what he counts on when, over and over again, he asks people he barely knows to trust him. That is, he counts on people who will discount the evidence cited robotically by Gerard—he was charged, convicted, and sentenced—and respond to something they see inside him. That's the point of his saying to Sister Veronica that the Devil doesn't walk around with horns. Don't look to the public record about me, he pleads; look to the inner truth of my character. In this compressed and complicated statement, Kimble conflates several assertions: (1) evil does not always announce itself by visible signs, and (2) visible signs are not a true index of reality, (3) in my case, the signs or labels that have been placed on me do not tell the real story, and yet (4) when it comes to me, what you see is what you get. What sounds superficially like a rejection of faith-based thinking is an affirmation of faith-based thinking that does not rely for confirmation on the presence either of horns or halos or on the occurrence of miraculous effects. If he has any quarrel with Sister Veronica, it is that her faith waxes and wanes (mostly waxes) with what she takes to be the small and large miracles that allow them to go forward. His faith is a steadier thing, and it subsists even when—especially when—everything goes wrong; it subsists too without the support of the machinery of organized religion.

As Part 1 ends Kimble is tutoring Sister Veronica in the true nature of *her* faith. When she tells him that she is renouncing her vows because of a single failure, he says, "Even in religion, there is a practical side. What you're looking for is the parting of the waters, a few loaves and fishes that feed the multitudes." He reminds her of all the small successes she has had and of the cumulative effects of her service, but she can't get past the fact of her despair and declares, "I'm the worst kind of fugitive of all—a fugitive from God." Kimble says, "I hope you'll change your mind when we get to Sacramento," and she replies, "*If* we get to Sacramento." They have changed places. Kimble queries, "If?" She answers, "It's your word,

Mr. Walker." And he comes back: "But it's a switch hearing it from you. What happened to all that faith of yours?"

They do get to Sacramento at the end of Part 2, after further adventures including an interlude in which a young pretty wom-an (Ruta Lee) falls for Kimble and tries to get him to stay with her, and a car chase that ends in a fortuitous crash which fatally harms no one but permits Kimble and the sister to escape and keep on going. As they part, they acknowledge the distance they have traveled in each other's direction. Kimble thanks her for putting him in touch with his deepest self. "Because of you another side of me came up for air. Drawing to an inside straight—quite impressive for a realist. A gambler would take that to mean that he was to go on playing the game." She decides to continue playing, too. After visiting with Father Kerrigan, she will return to her convent. They part secure in their different but mirroring faiths.

"Angels Travel on Lonely Roads" is anomalous in *The Fugitive* because it foregrounds the ceremonies and vestments of Christianity. Aside from the ever-present habit and a few theatrical prayers, however, there is nothing particularly Christian about the story. Another episode, "Ill Wind," is the reverse. Overt references to Christianity are absent, but the story is drenched in Christian significance. The plot is simple. Kimble is a migrant worker in California. Just as he is about to move on, a storm threatens, and everyone seeks shelter in a stable. (Yes, a stable.) Meanwhile Gerard has seen a newspaper photo of Kimble in a group photo of laborers, and he heads for the farm named in the article. He arrives just as the storm begins, and he and Kimble are thrown together in a succession of crises, including a crisis that threatens the detective's life. Acting as a chorus to the action, one of the workers—in love with the girl who has fallen for Kimble (known to them as Mike Johnson)—improvises a running ballad about a girl and a fugitive outlaw, "a man destined for hell." Kimble's fellow workers are obviously lower-class and uneducated, but they love and trust him. The leader of the crew, Lester Kelly (John McIntire), is one of nature's noblemen who, although he knows that Mike is on the run, declares early on, "What a man was ain't nearly as important as what he *is*."

But when Gerard asks him where Kimble has gone and threatens him with a year's imprisonment, which would have been a disaster for his family, Kelly gives up the man he likes and admires. When he does, his daughter Kate (Bonnie Beecher) accusingly cries "Pa!" branding him as a Judas-like betrayer of a leader everyone looks to for guidance. Gerard and the local sheriff trap Kimble in a building—there is a great moment when Kimble turns and sees Gerard blocking his way, looking larger than life and utterly implacable—and they hustle him into a car. But the storm whips up, and they are forced to join the Kellys and the other workers—all of them hostile to Gerard—in the stable.

There is of course a baby in the stable; not the Christ child, but a child who has been refused entry to a better inn because she is sick, perhaps with typhoid. The foreman of the ranch shrinks from the fevered child, but Kimble ministers to her much as Christ does when he ministers to lepers, although he does so under Gerard's watchful supervision. They all wait to see if the fever will break (if it does, then the illness is not typhoid.)

In the remainder of the episode, two plot strands unfold in counterpoint: Kimble takes on the role of Gerard's defender, both as an officer of the law whose authority must be acknowledged and as a human being whose physical person must be protected. In the other plot, the migrant workers labor to understand what Kimble is doing; all they can see is the foolishness of coming to the aid of someone who wants to capture and, with the state's help, kill you. Kimble's serial and massive turning of the other cheek begins when Kate throws a pitchfork at Gerard and Kimble pulls the detective away from its line of flight at the last second. Kimble asks the girl to promise she won't do anything like that again. She assents but reminds him that the others feel as she does. At this point Gerard says, "What you did didn't surprise me." At some level he knows what kind of man Kimble is, but it does not alter his resolution to bring him in. Kimble too declares that he has not swerved from his purpose: "You know I'll try to get away if I can." "That doesn't surprise me either," is the reply. The two men know and have taken the measure of one another. They form a kind of unit—educated, mid-

dle-class, professional men who adhere to the codes they have sworn to uphold.

The workers, however, know only the codes of survival and tribal loyalty. Kimble is one of theirs, Gerard isn't. It's as simple as that. They cannot abstract away to a realm of principle that intervenes between their immediate desires and what might be thought to be *generally* right. They can't, that is, abandon their tribalism in favor of liberalism. Their perplexity grows when shortly after the baby's fever breaks—an outcome they attribute to Kimble as savior—a part of the stable falls in, pinning Gerard down and severing an artery in his arm. Kimble asks for help: "Get me a stick and a piece of cloth." Lester's wife, Naomi (Jeanette Nolan), exclaims, "We can't think all complicated like you do; we just help our own." Helping one's own is the essence of identity politics; actions follow from local affiliations. "Thinking complicated" means moving away from the imperatives of the present situation—he's my enemy, my pursuer; here's a chance to get rid of him by letting him bleed to death—and allowing the present situation to be configured by an obligation it neither declares nor contains, the obligation to do what is right rather than what is self-serving and expedient.

For Kimble that kind of thinking is effortless; he doesn't have to reach for it because it defines him and constitutes the core of his (liberal) being. His friends, who have never read Plato or Kant or Isaiah Berlin, can't follow him even when they try. Kimble says Gerard will die if he doesn't receive a blood transfusion and asks for volunteers whose blood type (B) matches the injured man's. No one volunteers, and Kelly says, "He's lucky he's got us to keep him from digging himself a grave." But his wife senses that something is eluding them. "He's saying what we're doin' ain't right." She doesn't quite know what "right" means, but she at least has begun the journey from a perspective that locates obligation in kinship to something larger. Her daughter struggles to follow. She says to Kimble, "If that man lives, he sees you killed. Why are you trying to save his life?" Kimble replies, "For a doctor, all life is worth saving." That is a doctor, like Christ, doesn't save only those he thinks worthy; he saves those who are his brothers and sisters in humanity. Kate just can't comprehend it: "All I get out of it is that you want me to help him kill you."

And then a remarkable moment that is at the heart of the episode and the series. Without any intervening deliberation or reflection, Kate turns on a dime and reverses herself: "But all right. If you want it [my type B blood], he can have it; he can have all of it." No better illustration of a leap of faith (with the exception perhaps of Abraham's willingness to sacrifice Isaac when God tells him to) could be found. Kate will do something that goes against everything she believes and desires because she believes even more in the person who asks it of her. I will do what I think wrong, even to the extent of risking my own life ("he can have all of it"), if that is what you require. This selfless (in the strictest sense) gesture aligns her with Kimble as a healer and makes her literally a redeemer. She spills her blood so that another—and another whom she despises—might live. She is the third type of Christ (after the baby and Kimble) in the episode, and the most effective. The tube going from her vein into Gerard's is an image of unification as well as redemption: her blood brings together the educated and the untutored, the professional and the hourly worker, the establishment and the fringe. Nature seems to signify Her pleasure by stilling the storm. Gerard is revived by the transfusion. Kimble moves toward the door. Gerard threatens to shoot. The migrant workers place themselves between him and his target. Gerard attempts to pursue Kimble, but, weakened, falls down, crying out in anguish, "Kimble, Kimble." Or, in other words, "Kimble, Kimble, why has thou forsaken me?"

The synopses of this episode in *The Fugitive* series guides emphasize the relationship between Kimble and Gerard, but the characters know that the real story is the story of what is happening to them. In the epilogue, the Kelly family continues to ponder the significance of Mike's actions. Mrs. Kelly says, "I don't un-

derstand why Mike went to the trouble to save all that meanness."
Her daughter responds immediately, "Even a life like that is worth
saving," drawing from her father
a wry observation, "Sounds like
some of the stuff Mike was talking." Not only is Kate a redeemer,
but she has been redeemed. And
what she has been redeemed for
is the middle class and its "complicated thinking." She may still
inhabit her old life on the surface,

but on the inside she has been transformed. Kimble the civilizer,
the bringer of liberal values, has been here.

In "Joshua's Kingdom" Kimble arrives in another town to perform the same service, this time in opposition to a religiosity gone
bad. Suitably tempered and moderately practiced, religion—like
violin-playing, political engagement, environmental concern, professional dedication, connubial affection, motorcycle-riding—is
a perfectly healthy part of liberal/rational life. But when the demands of religion are such that no aspect of one's daily existence
is exempt from them, when religion is obsessively followed to the
point of leaving no room for good old-fashioned empirical common sense, then it joins the long list of things from which one must
free oneself.

This is the lesson Joshua Simmons (Harry Townes yet again)
must learn so that he can wear the faith of his biblical namesake
without turning it into a crabbed and negative thing. Kimble's in-
teraction with Simmons begins when he sees the man's daughter,
Ruth (Kim Darby), being harassed by Pete (Tom Skerritt), a former
deputy sheriff with too much time on his hands. Kimble half in-

tervenes, and the ex-deputy throws off a remark about Ruth's fallen virtue. There is no direct confrontation, and when Pete leaves, Kimble asks about a job. He's told to go see the town veterinarian, who is more than happy to take him on. The first thing the vet and his new assistant do (after Kimble, ever the apostle of order, cleans up the hospital) is go out to Simmons's place to look at an ailing horse. There Kimble encounters Ruth again and finds that she has a child who is sick. He says that a doctor should look at the boy, but Joshua thunders, "We don't believe in medicine; we don't impose our beliefs on others, and we do don't want others to impose their beliefs on us. God is the healer." As he says this he looks askance at Kimble and his daughter, suspecting there's something between them. The child's father was a young man who left for the army the day after he and Ruth made love for the first and only time. The young man died, the baby was born, and Joshua now darkly quotes scriptures about fallen women. His biblical literalism blinds him to everything.

Kimble tries rationality, reminding Joshua that he is perfectly willing to give medicine to his horses: "What kind of religion have you got—one kind of God for animals, another for a child?" But Joshua has an answer. In Genesis, he points out, God assigned to man the care of animals, but God himself takes care of us. And as for his grandson, "The Lord wills life and death," he says to Ruth. "Ask him, not a stranger." Kimble is the stranger in two senses; he is an outsider, and he is a stranger to the belief system that dictates Joshua's every thought and action, the belief system that informs him so completely that he has no agency of his own.

Things come to a head when the baby can't be wakened. Ruth takes the boy to the veterinarian's house, hoping to find Kimble, who sees immediately that the child is anemic and needs blood.

Ruth doesn't even know his blood type, but Kimble determines that it is the same as his own, and with the veterinarian's help he gives the child a transfusion. This is not a magical moment, as it is in "Ill Wind." It is much more prosaic, the victory of science and empiricism over religious faith of the wrong, illiberal kind. The Lord may take care of us, but in the mainstream Protestant theology of which Kimble is a wholly secular representative, he helps those who help themselves.

He also works in mysterious ways, as Kimble reminds Joshua when they have a final confrontation. Enraged to find that Ruth has taken his grandson to Kimble, he shouts, "I told you to go to the Lord. . . . No man can do the work of the Lord." But this time Kimble is ready for him, and rather than denigrating his faith he interrogates it with the benign skepticism his liberal rationalism teaches. "How do you know I wasn't sent here? Why did I come to this house? Why this town? Do you know?" These questions are designed neither to affirm Joshua's faith nor to dismiss it, but to put it in its proper place, which is in a realm inaccessible to us except through mediations, of which Kimble may or may not be one. This is liberalism's most generous response to religion. It says to Joshua, yes, it may be that it is from your perspective that things are ultimately disposed, yet we live not in the ultimate, but in the here and now, where we must make decisions and take actions with the help of the resources the world affords us. So let's get on with it and do what we can in the knowledge that whatever we do is overseen by a power greater than ours. In short, don't abandon your faith in the Lord; just don't allow your faith in Him to undermine your perfectly reasonable faith in the power of rationality and science to aid us in coping with the problems this mortal life presents to us. It is the same lesson administered to Josephus in

"An Apple a Day," where the dethroned deity is Nature and the vehicle of a secular grace is Kim Darby (as she is here); the writers liked this story enough to tell it twice.

Joshua does not respond directly to the lesson, but we see its effects when the police (whom he has called) close in on Kimble. As the policemen arrive, they see a man they believe to be Kimble running; they take off after him, led by dogs that have been given the scent. But when the dogs corner their quarry, the man turns out to be Joshua, who is wearing Kimble's jacket. Kimble of course has escaped, and the stage is left to Joshua, whose story this really is. The sheriff (John Milford) asks, "Why did you help him escape?" Joshua replies, "Me, Sheriff ? It was the Lord. The Lord giveth and the Lord taketh away. Blessed be the name of the Lord." Simmons delivers these lines not in the sanctimonious tone he had employed earlier, but in a tone that is detached, even ironic. (Irony, as Richard Rorty has taught us, is the paradigmatic liberal stance: it stands to the side of commitments and does not give itself to any of them.) It is almost as if he were saying, "I'm not going to give you the real reason; I'm going to give you the reasons I would have given an hour ago when I was a different person." The real reason is that he now believes in Kimble, and because he believes in Kimble, he now sees his daughter's true worth and is able to love his grandson without reservation. In short, he is a graduate of the Richard Kimble school of civilizing liberalism, and he passes his final exam with flying colors.

The Fugitive as Professor

In "The Chinese Sunset," Kimble's pupil is less intense, almost comic, but equally in need of instruction. The Chinese Sunset is a residential motel on Los Angeles's Sunset Strip where Kimble, calling himself Jack Fickett, has a job as bellboy, pool boy, concierge, janitor, or, as he puts it, general factotum. He uses that phrase to describe himself when speaking to Penelope Dufour (Laura Devon), a beautiful young woman who is the "companion" of shady bookmaker Eddie Slade (Paul Richards), just out of prison and desperate to get financing for a new scam. Penelope doesn't understand the phrase, and Kimble/Fickett explains it to her. She says where she come from "girls with looks don't need books." "It's a question of values," Kimble replies. Offended—"Something wrong with my values?"—Penelope stalks off.

The next day she's back. She is determined to marry Slade and knows that his ex-wife was college educated. She is afraid Eddie will ask himself one day, "What am I doing with this dummy?" and so she has a proposal for Kimble. "I've got to get me some kind of quick education. I was wondering if you could teach me some things." At this state she conceives of knowledge as just another kind of material possession. She has a  few jewels (including a nice pair of diamond earrings) and now imagines having a few new facts and a couple of pieces of grammatical knowledge. Kimble compliments her for wanting to improve herself. She demurs: "I don't want to change. I want to look like I've changed." In short, she doesn't want any of that "complicated thinking."

But of course Penelope has no control over where she will end up once she begins. Kimble soon has her reading Aesop's *Fables*, and when he asks her what she thinks is going on in one of the stories, she replies with some reflections, admittedly inchoate, on the moral status of the characters. She's on her way whether she wants to be or not. What we have here is a version of a very old story told in *Pygmalion, Born Yesterday,* and *My Fair Lady*: a young lady of low birth and upbringing who is tutored by an educated establishment male to the point where she has internalized values and forms of behavior that were at best opaque to her when she first encountered them.

There is tension between the teacher and his pupil, and it is centered on the word "shortcut." Kimble talks about the difference between people who walk the straight and narrow path and those who take shortcuts. Penelope says, "You say shortcuts as if it were a dirty word." To Kimble it is, for it names the practice of preferring your ends to the extent that you will employ any means to achieve them. This end-justifies-the-means morality is liberalism's chief target. Liberalism argues for the deferring of desire and for the adherence to impersonal procedures that may produce outcomes you don't like.

Penelope takes the lesson she is learning to Slade, who tells her that no one is straight, everyone hustles, everyone takes shortcuts. Upset, Slade seeks Kimble out and tells him, "That girl has a beautiful independence of mind, and I don't want her thinking and educated." You're wrong, Kimble replies, "She has an energy inside her, a drive to grow." It seems that he is right, for one night Penelope forgets to put on her cherished diamond earrings, previously the visible sign for her of her value. She wonders aloud "if that means I'm starting to shine inside like Jack says."

Slade decides the best way to get the old Penelope back and break the spell of Kimble's influence is to demonstrate that the ordinary Joe will always go for a deal, even one that seems a bit shady. He dangles the bait of a scheme that pays off twenty to one, and sure enough he has a bunch of the motel residents on the hook. Penelope tells Kimble, "I should have known Eddie was right. Human nature. I guess you're the only person I ever thought could beat that rap." That is, you may be the one person in the world who never bends his principles in order to go for the main chance. She adds that the suckers Slade is conning will soon learn even if Kimble won't: "[I guess] you better go and save those decent people of yours." No, he responds, "You've got to do it." She refuses, and Kimble says, "I thought you were learning something."

But she was. When Kimble tells the marks they are buying into a scam, they don't believe him—one of the few times in the series that his natural credibility fails. But then Penelope walks in and tells them the truth, as she says, "straight from the horse's mouth." They ask her why she did it. She replies, pointing to Kimble, "Ask the Professor here." She doesn't do what she does because she has broken with Slade. She still loves him, and that is why her act is impressive and significant. She affirms and professes the truth *despite* her mar-

ital hopes, and as a reward she receives the professor's benediction. ("By George she's got it!") "What you did in there proves that not everyone hustles; you're growing and changing." She nods wryly: "I'm not sure I'll like it." "You will when you get there," Kimble assures her. When she gets there she may not

have diamond earrings, but she will be in possession of herself, and that, in liberalism's economy, is a treasure greater than any other.

In the epilogue Penelope passes her final exam. A policeman tells her that Jack is a fugitive wanted for the murder of his wife. She retorts, "I bet my diamond earrings that he never done—" and here she stops to correct herself—"did it." This is a marvelously compressed moment. She displays the formal effects of her education by recalling and applying the rules of grammar. And she testifies to the inner transformation that education has wrought by being willing to wager everything on an integrity she now shares. She predicts that Kimble will "come back and clear himself." "That will be a long road," the policeman offers, and she responds with a proverb she first heard from Jack: "You know what they say—a journey of a thousand miles begins with a single step." And she adds, "Just something an old professor of mine used to say." She is now the professor, in the sense both of having mastered and professed the requisite formal and moral skills and of being able now to tutor others. Conrad's voiceover says of Kimble: "A man who would lose himself in order that he may some day find himself." But it is she who has lost her earlier self (the good-looking girl who didn't need books) in order to find a new and better self (a woman of integrity who doesn't need anything).

The Fugitive Leads the Blind to See

Like others Kimble brings to true self-knowledge, Penelope must shed the handicaps—in her case a lack of education and an over-reliance on a physical beauty that cannot be sustained—to which she is attached because they provide her with "reasons" for her destructive behavior. She must trade outside glitter for the true shining that lights her inside. I remarked earlier that the play of sight and blindness in relation to the priority of faith—of interior over external evidence—is a constant in the series. Kimble is blinded for a time in "Nightmare at Northoak." Marie Gerard is blind for much of "Landscape with Running Figures"; she sees Kimble most accurately when she doesn't see him at all. When she regains her sight, she re-imagines him as her enemy and nemesis. Kimble is himself blinded in "Second Sight," and even in that condition, he is able to bring moral insight to a photographer who uses his skills to blackmail people. (The man looks through a lens, but is unable to see truly.) In "Dark Corner," Mattie Braydon (a luminous but deadly Tuesday Weld) wills a blind-

ness that protects her from seeing herself and from having others see her as she really is: a manipulative, possessive seductress who craves power over everything and everyone. (As her sight comes back, Kimble says, "Poor Mattie may have to see again.")

All these relationships to blindness (physical and moral) are on display in "Runner in the Dark," an episode that brings together in one sustained meditation many of the series' themes. The story be-gins in a small, dark basement room where Kimble plies his pres-ent trade of maintenance man in an apartment building. A wom-an who has asked him to fix a leaky faucet is watching television; she is horrified when the program identifies the man she is wait-ing for as a murderer and a fugitive. When Kimble arrives, she pan-ics, and, realizing he has been recognized, he runs. Kimble spots a police car coming down the street and climbs over a wall; he drops down onto what looks like a small estate with extensive grounds. It turns out he has stumbled into the Beacon Manor Home for the

Blind. No one there is capable of recognizing him (at least by sight; the recognition of his inner value will occur as usual), and Kimble quickly ascertains there are no TV sets in the manor. Nevertheless, he is not safe: The most alert inhabitant of the home is Dan Brady (Ed Begley), an embittered former police chief who spends his days and nights keeping tabs on everything and everyone; he seems glued to the headphones connecting him to the radio. It is obvious that it is only a matter of time before Brady figures out who Kimble is, and a portion of the plot turns on Brady's investigative skills and the conclusions he's likely to draw. But the dramatic denouement is delayed, in part by Brady's desire to stage Kimble's capture in a way that will return him to his former glory.

Meanwhile Kimble, who has passed himself off as a representative from the Good Neighbor Society, has a larger than usual cast of

characters in need of his brand of tough-love therapy. First there is Brady, who cannot come to terms with a life in which he can no longer issue commands, bring criminals to justice, and enjoy the plaudits of a grateful public. Brady can't bear to be without duties and powers. He has a desperate (obsessive) need to be needed. That is why he is always trying to get his fellow inmates (in more than one way, the manor is a prison) to come to terms with their limitations—precisely what he is unable to do. (He says, "I take it upon myself to keep folks busy.")

The person Brady most wants to help is Claire Whitaker (Diana Van der Vlis), who was in the garden when Kimble climbed over the wall. The first thing she said upon sensing his presence was, "I need a little help." That, it turns out, was a very difficult sentence for her to utter. She doesn't want to rely on others—"I'll never ask anyone for anything"—yet she pushes away all offers of further medical consultation and refuses to learn how to manage her environment. Instead she stays in her room, more or less immobile, unable even to put a record on the phonograph and unwilling to come down the stairs for meals. Brady has tried unsuccessfully to encourage her to do even the smallest things; but Kimble is immediately able to make some headway, more or less tricking her into turning on the record-player by herself. She is emboldened enough to try the stairs at dinnertime, but she trips and is caught by another resident, Bob Sterne (Peter Haskell).

Sterne's quick action tells Kimble (now going by the name Phil Meade) that he is not blind at all. Sterne had been driving a bus full of schoolchildren when it overturned and caught fire. He went back into the fire four times and saved 22 of the 24 children on board. When he awoke in the hospital, he was blind, but then, after a while, his sight began to come back. He chose to hide his sightedness—he is hiding in manufactured darkness—because he doesn't want the awful truth to come to light. (The light the others are deprived of is the light he fears; the blindness they lament is his cocoon.) On the day of the accident, he had been drinking (a fact that did not come out during the investigation), and he is convinced that he is responsible for what happened and for the deaths of the two children. Sterne is punishing himself by assuming an affliction that is not really his and immuring himself in the prison cell of his room.

Kimble will not let him off the hook. Sterne confides that the only thing he ever sees in his mind's eye is "those two kids trapped in the bus," and as a result, "I never wanted to see again. I just wanted to be left alone." The solitude he seeks is not the solitude of a man at peace with himself, as Kimble is, but the solitude of a man who is wearing his guilt as a hair shirt and refusing to do anything that might relieve its burden. "Let go of your guilt," Kimble admonishes, although he knows what the cost will be. "It's nice to be a hero, but you may have to give that up to ease your conscience." Sterne's guilt is both his penance and his protection from seeing things as they are and from being seen for what he is. His guilt is his treasure—later Brady says to him, "If you didn't enjoy your punishment, you would put an end to it"—and only if he lets it go can he find a measure of peace.

Meanwhile, Claire had gone out for a walk—she promised Kimble, with whom she has fallen in love, "I will try again"—and become lost. Kimble finds her and gets her to walk back on her own. When she arrives, she says to everyone, "Phil Meade is a pernicious man; he makes people do their best despite themselves." Just so! That is what Kimble does. He is the traveling prophet of Emerson's message in *Self-Reliance*: "Nothing is at last sacred but the integrity of your own mind." "Nothing can bring you peace but yourself."

Brady mistakenly thinks he can find peace by bringing in Kimble on the very day the town council is voting on his successor. He alerts Sterne to Meade's true identity as a murderer—to his credit Sterne immediately says, "I don't believe that"—and persuades him to hold a gun on the fugitive while the three go downtown to police headquarters. Sterne asks, "Why don't you call the real police?" Brady replies, "I am the real police, and all I need to prove it is your eyes." In the car Sterne says to Kimble, "You were convicted but say you're innocent; I wasn't even tried, and you know, you're the lucky one." (Sterne is like Steve Edson in "Flight from the Final Demon"; he wants the law to punish him.) Kimble is lucky because his inner weather is calm even when the storms rage around him.

When they arrive at police headquarters, Brady tells Sterne to handcuff him to the prisoner. But when Brady enters his triumph turns to chagrin as the council members and the new police chief see that he is attached to Sterne, not Kimble, who has slipped away. Brady finally has his moment of self-knowledge. "Gentlemen, I have been a fool." That is, I have been blind in even more ways than I saw.

He is a fool not only because he has been fooled by Sterne and Kimble, but because he has allowed his desire for personal glory and his bitterness at being blind to blind him to the duty he owes to the law and to the profession he has served for thirty-eight years. If Sterne's and Claire's selves are impoverished and small, Brady's is too large and too ambitious for precedence and command. The balance Kimble exemplifies, the balance of someone who can live within himself without either shunning the world or needing to command it, has escaped Brady, but he achieves it when he says to the man who will replace him (an apostle of modern methods who rejects the "lone gunman" model of an earlier time), "I used to be good at giving orders . . . I can also follow orders if you ever need my help."

So everyone is finally on the right path. Brady has learned to be content with what he can do and not pine after lost glories. Claire has learned that she can in fact do something, and if one thing, why not many things? Sterne has learned to accept responsibility for his actions. (As the episode ends, he has been charged with aiding and abetting the escape of a fugitive; he gets the punishment he wants.) They have all been runners in the dark, even though they did their running without physically moving; and they have all come into the light even though (with the exception of Sterne, who was in the dark when he could see) they remain physically blind.

And Kimble? He hasn't learned anything; he has just been himself and, by the simple force of example, brought others to the place where they are able to do the same.

The Fugitive Stops Running

The Fugitive was the first series to be graced with a planned—and announced—ending in which everything was tied up: Kimble vindicated and back in Stafford, Gerard proven wrong, no more reason to run. The two-part conclusion, entitled "The Judgment," was an event that drew international attention. Everyone in the world, it seemed, tuned in, and the final installment remained the most-watched single television program episode in history until it was eclipsed by the "Who Shot JR?" episode of *Dallas* in 1980. There were questions about the wisdom of writing a conclusion to the story; some felt the syndication value of the series would be diminished if viewers knew how things would turn out. Such concerns, however, assumed that the interest of the series lay in its plot and in the answer to a question—who, after all, did kill Helen Kimble? But, as I have argued repeatedly, the plot exists largely as a device for bringing Kimble in and out of towns where he could serve as a catalyst for the life-changing decisions of others. It is what those others—men and women whose lives intersect with Kimble's in ways that produce moral/psychological crises—do that is at the heart of every episode, at least of every episode that knows what the series is about.

This means that the writers and director of "The Judgment" faced a dilemma and had something of a formal problem. How could they satisfy the expectations of a huge audience, expectations all bound up with plot, and yet be true to the series as it had unfolded in 118 previous episodes? The solution they came up with was to give Part 1 over to plot intricacies, which meant introducing narrative devices that are usually associated with a traditional "who-done-it," and reserving Part 2 for the more *Fugitive*-like story of a man who is forced to confront his demons and decide once and for all what kind of person he is going to be.

There is no hint of that man's existence as Part 1 begins. Kimble has seen a newspaper account of a one-armed man who had just about destroyed a bar in Los Angeles and is now in jail. Gerard has seen the same account, and with the help of LA police captain Ralph Lee (played by Joseph Campanella), he devises a plan to lure Kimble out of hiding. It works.

Kimble quits his job as a driver for a trucking firm in Tucson (the location of the series' first episode; everything comes around) and heads for Los Angeles.

But Jean Carlisle (Diane Baker), a court stenographer who happens to be from Stafford, overhears Gerard and Lee talking about Kimble; she intercepts Kimble as he arrives in town and takes him to her apartment. The two draw closer together as they talk about Stafford. Carlisle recalls the unhappy experience of being the daughter of a convicted embezzler who was also a friend of the Kimble family. Her mother, she says, stayed in Stafford because the town wanted her to continue "paying a debt she never owed."

As the relationship between Kimble and Carlisle develops, Gerard is interviewing Fred Johnson, the one-armed man. In the course of the questioning, Johnson trips himself up, and we see Gerard beginning to wonder whether, perhaps, Johnson may be Helen Kimble's killer after all. Kimble, meanwhile, has decided that his best bet is to turn himself in now that Johnson is incarcerated and can be questioned.

But then a new element is introduced and with it a mystery of a kind we do not usually meet in *The Fugitive*. Johnson has been bailed out. The bail bondsman, Arthur Howe (played by Michael Constantine), doesn't say who is supplying the funds. Carlisle, who learns Johnson has been freed, again intercepts Kimble before he gets to the police station. Meanwhile, Johnson and the bail bondsman walk into the zoo so they can talk privately and evade electron-

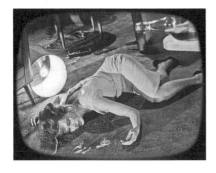

ic surveillance. Howe tells Johnson that the man who sent him wants him to skip bail and is offering Johnson one thousand dollars to do so. But, Howe says, there is even more money to be had; if this guy is willing to pay one thousand, he will be willing to pay fifty. Johnson asks for Howe's client's name.

The bail bondsman asks why this person would be so eager to help Johnson get away from the police. He knows it has something to do with Kimble, and asks directly: "Did you kill Kimble's wife?" Johnson answers, "No, but I was there and saw the man who did."

This is misdirection not only on Johnson's part but on the part of the writers. It is we who are sent down a new (garden) path, tantalized by the possibility that the true perpetrator is someone we know nothing about. The bail bondsman gives Johnson the name of the man he represents, and as a reward he is beaten to death. Kimble and Carlisle find the body, and they also find a note containing the name Johnson has been given: Leonard Taft, Kimble's brother-in-law. Another surprise and, as it turns out, another misdirection—one that makes Kimble think he must go to Stafford. But when he tries to catch a cab, Gerard (who has figured out that Jean Carlisle is helping Kimble) is waiting. "It had to happen some day," Gerard says. "You know that. I'm sorry, you just ran out of time." (The "I'm sorry" is significant; it telegraphs the turn Gerard will soon take.)

So ends Part 1, with everyone heading back to Stafford—Johnson so he can blackmail the man he believes is Leonard Taft, Jean Carlisle so she can be close to Kimble, Gerard and Kimble so the fugitive can finally meet the fate the law has ordained for him. The pair, once again handcuffed to each other, ride back on a train. Full circle.

As Part 2 begins, Kimble begs Gerard for twenty-four hours, and after a brief conversation, Gerard relents. At this point, the tension between the two, so central to the story, had been dissipated. Although Gerard is on camera for most of "The Judgment," he is not a part of its true drama; he is a function—the lawman with a gun—not a protagonist with a fissured psychology.

Neither man thinks Leonard Taft bailed out Johnson, but Kimble believes that if he can find out who did, the truth about the fatal evening will be revealed. We meet him (although we do not know it at first) in the very next scene when Lloyd Chandler (J. D. Cannon) stops by the house of Donna Taft, Kimble's sister (Taft's and Chandler's children are playmates), and talks about the dreams he has never quite realized. Donna responds by praising his accomplishments as the city planner. Then she tells him that among the crank calls she has received since her brother became a fugitive was one from a man who said he had seen her husband, Leonard, at the Kimble house the night of Helen's murder; the man wanted to meet with him at 7:30 at the old Mitchell stables. I said yes just to get him off the phone, she tells Chandler, who later goes to meet Johnson himself. Chandler takes a gun (he gives rifle lessons to the young boys of the town), but before he can use it, Johnson hits him over the head from behind. When Chandler gets up, he asks. "What do you want from me?" The answer: "Fifty thousand dollars, because you're the one I saw that night." Johnson gives him until noon the next day. They are to meet at the old amusement park.

This is more misdirection designed to make us think Chandler may be the killer. He spends the day desperately trying to raise the money, but no one will help him. He is bitter and goes so far as to

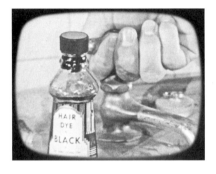

put his house up for sale, asking his wife (Louise Latham), "Where are all those people who said after the war that they'd do great things for me?" She asks him what's wrong. "You've always told me everything." Not everything, he replies. "Five years ago I did something terrible and it's not over with."

This is the last misdirection, and it lasts only a second, as the true story finally comes out. First Chandler reflects on his life: "A kid gets put down in the battlefield and he's scared, and he does something he would never do, *because* he's scared. So they give him a silver medal, and call him a hero, but he's no hero." His wife protests—"Of course you are"—but Chandler goes on, reminding her of the night they and the Kimbles talked about adoption at the country club. (In case you had any doubt about what class Kimble represents.) Two nights later, after Richard Kimble has stormed out of the house because Helen will not consider adoption, she calls Chandler and asks him to come over. He finds her in the bedroom more than a little drunk and fearful that Richard will not come back. Helen hears a noise downstairs, thinks it is her husband, and rushes downstairs to find Johnson in the act of robbing the house. The two struggle, and Johnson begins beating Helen over the head. Chandler is on the stairway, frozen. He does nothing, says nothing. As his eyes meet Johnson's, he nods, almost imperceptibly, but there is no doubt about what the nod means: "I won't say anything if you don't."

Why did you keep silent? Chandler's wife asks, and he mumbles something about protecting her. But she isn't having any: "You weren't trying to protect me. You couldn't bear the thought of a war hero huddled on the steps like a beaten puppy, and as a woman called out for help, you watched her die." And then she issues the challenge usually issued by Kimble. "It's not too late to make it right . . . . You can still be a man."

"Maybe I can," he says, but what he does next shows he still hasn't learned what being a man means. He grabs a gun (he is a crack shot) and goes out to kill Johnson. In other words he is going to be a hero again, and perform an extraordinary action in the (false) hope it will cancel out his failure to act earlier. Chandler doesn't understand that heroism, of the kind he involuntarily displayed in the war, is just the flip side of the cowardice he involuntarily displayed on that terrible night. Both are departures from the everyday heroism of just meeting one's obligations, including the obligation to come to the aid of a friend.

Meanwhile, Kimble and Gerard have figured out that Chandler is involved somehow, and they learn about the meeting at the amusement park. Everyone converges on the site, and everyone starts to shoot at everyone. Johnson hits Gerard in the leg. Gerard gives his gun to Kimble. (Nothing more clearly marks the change in their relationship). Kimble goes after Johnson. They end up climbing a tower (which makes no sense at all), and when Kimble has a chance to shoot Johnson he (always in character) can't do it. Johnson stumbles, almost falls to his death, but Kimble pulls him up. They fight some more, and Johnson gets the gun and points it at Kimble. "You killed my wife, didn't you?" "Yes, I killed her . . . . Now I'm going to kill you." But before he can, Gerard, still on the ground, takes Chandler's rifle and shoots Johnson.

It's over, but it isn't. The story turns back to its real center: Chandler's moral crisis, now, like Kimble's plight, in its fifth year. Gerard says to Chandler, "You can relax, Chandler. I just did your killing for you. For four years we, both of us, kept an innocent man in hell. You could keep that man alive, but you won't, will you?" Kimble climbs down and tells Gerard, "He confessed up there for what it's worth." "I'm afraid you know what that's worth" is Gerard's answer. But then Chandler finds his voice. "I saw that man Johnson murder Helen Kimble." Now it's really over, both Kimble's nightmare and Chandler's. In a final irony, the man who set Kimble running in the first place stops both his and his own running. Kimble is no longer running from the police. Chandler is no longer running from himself. He is the last of those who, prodded or guided by a fugitive, comes home to the straight and narrow path. Kimble again has done his job—the job of bringing integrity and centeredness to places where they are in danger of being lost.

In the epilogue, everyone is emerging from the courthouse where justice has finally been done. Reporters ask Kimble, "Doctor, what are your immediate plans?" He says, "See some of my family and get back to work." Or, in short, I'm going to be the ordinary man I always was, and there is no reason for you to be covering me.

He and Gerard then shake hands (maybe they'll have a drink later in the week), and Kimble and Jean Carlisle stride off.

There is one last great *Fugitive* moment. A police car pulls up to the courthouse, and Kimble involuntarily reacts with apprehension and fear. Jean says, "Hey," meaning, "Remember, no one's after you any longer." He replies, "Hey," and flashes a smile that is almost, but not quite, real.

The reporter's question—what are your plans?—is formulaic and obligatory, but one can ask it in a sharper tone. What exactly will a no-longer-hunted Richard Kimble do? In a way vindication is the worst thing that could have happened to him. In Stafford he will settle into his old life, a respected doctor, a devoted brother, a pillar of the community, a member of civic organizations—a suburban bore burdened by the same attachments he was able to shed because of the fortunate fact that

he could never stay long enough to accrue them. The title of the series after all is *The Fugitive*, and once that identity is no longer his, he is a totally uninteresting person.

No one saw this more clearly than *Chicago Sun-Times* columnist Mike Royko who, in a piece published the day after the series ended, imagines himself visiting the post-*Fugitive* Kimble in Stafford. He finds him mowing the lawn in front of his "large tree-shaded house," the antithesis of the all the small spaces in which he ministered to a succession of fragile men and women. He's willing to talk, but he says that he must continue to mow because "we've got a dinner date at the country club and she'll blow her stack if I don't finish the lawn." "She" turns out to be his wife, Jean Carlisle, who, he says, is a bit of a shrew and "a little plump."

The reporter asks, "Well, Doctor, how do you like being free?" And he replies with scorn and self-hatred: "Listen, I got this house to pay for, two cars and an expensive country club membership. I spend my days listening to hypochondriacs and my evenings attending civic meetings, medical association meetings, neighborhood improvement meetings. You call that being free?" He complains he's getting fat: "I was really in shape. Hard as a rock, lean . . . I'd rather be a young adventurous fugitive than a fat old doctor."

But at least, the reporter persists, you have peace of mind. "Who has it? Before, all I worried about was a few cops and brushing off some girl who fell for me. Now I read the papers and look at TV and I worry about Vietnam, air pollution, and college campus riots." (All the things that never made it to the center of *The Fugitive*.) Finally the reporter asks, "But isn't there some happiness in your life—something to look forward to?" The answer is brief and to its bitter point. "Another one-armed man." By this he could mean either "I hope someone comes along and kills *this* wife" or "I hope something happens that puts me on the road again." Either way, the message is clear. Success in his quest has brought the fugitive nothing except the loss of what he cherishes, the freedom of cherishing nothing.

But this is all fanciful speculation. In real—that is TV—life, it's over for good with William Conrad's final words: "August 29th. The day the running stopped."

The Fugitive Lives to Run Another Day

Except it didn't. ABC reran the series in 1967 and 1968. The A&E network showed it twice a day (at 11 and 4) from 1990 to 1993. The blockbuster major motion picture starring Harrison Ford was also released in 1993. And in 2000, CBS tried to revive the series, but the new *Fugitive* was canceled at the end of the season.

The movie succeeded because, despite the title and the retention of some proper names, it was nothing like the original. Richard Kimble, played by Ford, is still a doctor, but he is a vascular surgeon rather than a pediatrician. The change is significant because in the series Kimble's professional identification is tied first to the disagreement he has with his wife about adoption (he is for, she is against), and second to the role he typically plays when he wanders into some small town: he helps, or tries to help, men and women leave their childish ways behind and grow into the adulthood he offers them as a model. In the movie the Kimbles are a perfectly happy couple; they make a "date" in anticipation of his return home after an emergency operation to which he has been called as they leave a professional gathering. (Kimble's wife, played by Sela Ward, is killed in the interim.) Although Kimble is again on the run as the result of an accident involving a bus and a train (more about that in a moment), he does not wander into any small towns. He does not wander at all, but stays in Chicago, a city that is the antithesis of Stafford and a third protagonist—along with Kimble and Tommy Lee Jones's Sam Gerard—in the drama. The opening credits alternate between grainy shots of Helen's murder and panoramas of the Chicago skyline. Although Chicago is much larger than the hamlets Kimble typically enters in the series, its prominence in the film has the effect of narrowing the focus to the events that occur within its theatrical precincts. It's because it is Chicago that there can be an extended scene in which Kimble evades capture by moving in and out of a St. Patrick's Day parade. Chicago's hospitals and medical laboratories provide the resources for Kimble's investigative efforts (in effect he becomes a private eye) to identify the one-armed man he fought with as his wife lay dying. It is Chicago's vast Hilton Hotel, with its many spaces and levels, that provides the grand stage for the final confrontation between Kimble and the person responsible for his wife's murder.

That person is not the one-armed man. This is the other significance of the change from pediatrician to vascular surgeon. The movie's Kimble has discovered that a much-touted drug causes liver damage. Although he doesn't figure it out until the last act, his best friend, Dr. Charles Nichols (Jeroen Krabbé), has been substituting healthy tissues for the diseased ones revealed by Kimble's experimental research. It is Nichols who hired the one-armed man (an ex-cop working for the pharmaceutical company that has developed the deadly drug) to silence Kimble by killing him; his wife was an unintended casualty. It is Nichols who passes himself off as Kimble's strongest advocate and loyal supporter, and fools everyone, including the movie audience, until the last fifteen minutes. It is Nichols, in short, who is the linchpin of the film's plot.

With that word, "plot," we arrive at a key difference between the movie and the series. In the TV show, the plot exists only as a device that gets Kimble in and out of places before and after his moral and educational work is done. In the movie there is no moral and educational work to do. No one is changed, no one is redeemed; the only thing that happens is that facts are clarified. Everyone's efforts are directed at solving a puzzle, and when the puzzle is solved, when Nichols is revealed to be the criminal mas-

termind, the action is over, except for an extended and thoroughly conventional action sequence complete with an epic fight, falls
through glass skylights, and a last-second rescue of Gerard by the
man he has been pursuing.

Since there is nothing psychological or philosophical going on
in the film, there has to be something that fills up the intervals between stages in the unfolding of the plot, and that something is
spectacle. Andrew Davis, the film's director, has said that one of
his aims was to come up with "the best train crash ever seen on
film." He succeeds. The scene is an extended one that begins with
Kimble's fellow prisoners (he has been tried and convicted) stag-
ing an escape from the bus that is transporting them to death row.
The escape falls apart; the bus careens down a bank and comes to
rest on a railroad track. An oncoming train (rigged, Davis tells us
in a commentary that comes along with the DVD, with explosives)
crashes into the bus at the instant Kimble jumps to safety. (Can
anyone say Indiana Jones?).

A few (screen) minutes later, another slam-bang sequence unfolds. Kimble, driving a stolen ambulance, has been trapped in a
tunnel and, pursued by Gerard and his minions, finds his way to
the catacomb-like spaces below. After a few twists and turns, he
and Gerard confront one another at a point where a huge drain
pipe juts out above turbulent waters. Gerard, who has a gun, orders Kimble to get on his knees and place his hands on the back
of his neck. Kimble appears to comply, but suddenly he launches
himself out into the void and plunges into the cascading streams.
(*Butch Cassidy and the Sundance Kid* is the obvious film reference
here.) The appropriate and sought-for response to both these moments is admiration for a technical achievement; there is more to
come when, in another lengthy sequence, Kimble and Gerard play

cat and mouse in the county jail before Kimble barely escapes as an automated door almost closes on his foot. And of course there is the scene on the El where, in rapid succession, Kimble is recognized by a fellow passenger, the one-armed man assaults him and kills a transit cop, and, in a dramatic reversal, Kimble overcomes the one-armed man, chains him to a guardrail, and kicks open a window. And we haven't even gotten to the big finale in the Hilton.

The phrase for this is "nonstop action," and it is easy to understand why a movie that has nothing to say but a lot to show wouldn't want to stop. In the series, however, stopping is the norm; the little action there is recedes into the background, the noise level (never really high) lessens, and two or three people try to work out the imperatives of the moral life. In the series spurts of action interrupt extended dialogue; in the movie dialogue is either purely instrumental—it advances the piecing together of the puzzle—or it is the occasion for a display of Gerard's wit. After Ford's Kimble jumps, a colleague says, "He's dead," and Jones's Gerard replies, "That ought to make him easy to catch." You can't imagine Barry Morse's Gerard saying anything like that; it would be totally out of character. Jones's Gerard doesn't have character; he *is* a character: his mannerisms and witticisms entertain his troops, but they have no relationship to anything but their own production.

There is one exception. Before Kimble jumps, he says to Gerard, "I didn't kill my wife," and Gerard replies "I don't care." This is an allusion to the series-long dynamic between Kimble and his pursuer and to the obsessive nature of Gerard's pursuit, a pursuit he refuses to abandon even at the possible cost of his marriage and his humanity. All Jones's Gerard means is that pursuit, not criminal investigation or prosecution, is his job. Morse's Gerard also insists on the limited nature of his responsibility; but he does so in the spirit of a zealot—"let others ponder; I obey"—and it is his zealotry, bordering on fanaticism, that gives the relationship between him and Kimble psychological depth. Psychological depth, or depth of any kind, is lacking in the movie, although there is an attempt in the last scene to make something of this moment. As the hunter and his former quarry get into a police car, Gerard removes Kimble's handcuffs. Kimble says, "I thought you didn't care." Gerard replies, "I don't," and then chuckles, "Don't tell anybody, okay?" Suddenly, and for an instant, we are watching a romantic comedy with a plot Eve Sedgwick might relish. Boy meets boy under unhappy circumstances; boy and boy circle each other and exchange hostile messages from afar through intermediaries; but in the end boy and boy get together and ride off into the sunset.

Don't get me wrong. *The Fugitive* is very good movie. It just has nothing to do with *The Fugitive* despite the fact that Roy Huggins is credited as executive producer. Andrew Davis is known as a director of action films. He has made the best Chuck Norris movie, *Code of Silence*, and the best Steven Seagal movie, *Under Siege* (which features an over-the-top maniacal, wisecracking Tommy Lee Jones). *The Fugitive* is *Under Siege* with a bigger budget.

The gang that made the movie also produced CBS's short-lived revival in 2000. You can tell where the new *Fugitive*'s heart is twenty minutes into the first episode. Running once again from Gerard, Kimble escapes by jumping from an overpass onto a moving truck. He avoids being decapitated by executing a leap-and-grab maneuver that would have earned him gold at the Olympics. Twenty minutes later he is again cornered by Gerard on a high ledge of a building under construction. He jumps off the ledge and falls into a net that begins to rip apart beneath him. He staves off certain death by grabbing what is left of the net and using it Tarzan-fashion to swing himself back onto the ledge of a lower floor.

It goes without saying that neither of these "highlights" would have graced an episode of the original series. First of all, Kimble the pediatrician displayed no athletic abilities (although Janssen himself was a star athlete in high school). He was in many fights and lost most of them, suffering, by Bill Deane's count, "twenty-four serious injuries.[4] His moments of trial find him not in some precarious physical position, but crouching behind a door in a small, windowless room, or refusing one of the easy outs offered by the many men and women eager to possess him, or waiting passively while some troubled person—sometimes a child—decides whether to betray him or to remain silent and allow him to begin running again. By the end of an episode, none of those with whom Kimble interacted would be what they were when he first entered their lives. Each learns a lesson or fails to learn it, with future consequences that are clear to viewers even if they are not spelled out. The characters who populate the remade *Fugitive* series learn nothing. Hastily sketched-in stereotypes—the crooked construction foreman, that attractive woman with a winsome little girl, the venal clerk in a seedy hotel—they are utterly dispensable and serve only to ferry Kimble from one moment of physical danger to the next. In the original, at the end of an episode, we feel that we know this town and its inhabitants better than we know Kimble, who works very hard at withholding himself from everyone, including us. When the new show returned Kimble to the road, we knew and cared about nothing, because everything we were shown was one-dimensional and forgettable.

---

4. Bill Deane, *Following "The Fugitive"* (Jefferson, N.C.: McFarland, 2006).

This was true of Kimble himself as played by Tim Daly (brother of Tyne and son of James, who appeared in two episodes of the original). It's not simply that Daly was just another pretty face. Janssen was even prettier, especially in the early years before the legendary hard living that led to his death at the age of 48. It's what the face does or doesn't convey. When Lois Nettleton (one of the great character actresses who made repeat appearances in the original's four-year run) says to Janssen, "You sure have a face," she means not only that he is physically attractive, but that she sees in his visage a complex mixture of fear, anxiety, outward turmoil, and inner peace. When a woman tells the new Kimble that he is different and much more than he appears to be (a lowly day-laborer), all she means is that he is the star, for nothing at all separates him from the other dark-haired, wiry younger men who populate the television landscape. As Kimble is about to escape for the third time in a single hour, Gerard declares, "I will never stop," and the fugitive replies, "Neither will I." But where similar exchanges in the original are energized by complicated patterns of interdependence and obsessiveness that bind the two together, in the later series the urgency of these statements is energized by the hope that next year they will still have jobs.

There were any number of tips of the hat to the old show in the later one, but they were undercut by the changes the remake's producers made. In the original Kimble's wife was alone on the fateful evening because the couple had had a big fight about adopting a child, and this fact (which came out at the trial) complicated and shadowed his claim of innocence. In the 2000 remake, the doctor and his wife are rapturously happy as they run and clown along Chicago's lakefront. It is only because he stumbles and suffers a minor injury that she gets home ahead of him. The newer Kimble is straightforwardly innocent of even a bad thought and is suspected largely because a bystander to the physical horseplay between him and his wife has mistaken it for abuse. No bystander saw Janssen's Kimble, and no one could back up his account of what he did after the quarrel. We viewers know that he drove angrily away from his house, sat alone in a deserted spot in a car (another *Fugitive* enclosure), and looked out at a boy fishing alone from a boat. The scene is significant as an emblem of the individual isolation and loneliness the series embraces and dissects. There is no significance whatsoever to the man who misinterprets the camaraderie between the young marrieds. It doesn't go anywhere.

I fear that had the remade series continued, another change would have gone somewhere. The new Gerard was black, and while it may have been that the producers just wanted to employ an African-American actor, it is more likely, I'm afraid, that they had something more in mind, and that in a future episode Kimble would have wandered into a minority community pursued by a Gerard who would have been confronted with the contradiction of his being a black enforcer of the white man's law. It was the resolve to avoid social relevance that accounted for the old *Fugitive*'s power, and that refusal was possible (and even easy) because the producers and writers actually had an idea—something the series is actually about—in relation to which the plot of a fugitive running from the law and running after the real villain is just a framing device. In the remade series, which seemed to be without an idea, that device (puffed up by spectacular stunts) was everything, and it proved not to be enough.

Part 3

Fugitive
Variations

The Fugitive Is Born

I AM AWARE THAT IT MIGHT
seem that in the preceding pages I have asked a piece of pop culture to bear a weight of moral and philosophical significance foreign to the intentions of those who actually worked on it. But in
fact, the meanings and structures I tease out of the series were
placed there by the writers, directors, and producers who thought
of themselves (with good reason) as intellectuals. When I visit-
ed Roy Huggins, *The Fugitive*'s creator, I told him that although I
taught poetry for a living, all I did in my nonworking hours was
watch television. He replied that although he wrote and produced
TV programs for a living, what he did in his nonworking hours was
read poetry. In fact before the Harrison Ford movie came out, Huggins had never watched the series for which he was famous in the
industry (along with *Maverick*, *77 Sunset Strip*, *Bus Stop*, and *The
Rockford Files*). He feared the finished product would not be up to
his concept (of which more in a minute). It was the concept, not

the production details (although he knew them too; he directed a film before he moved to television), that interested him because he was basically an academic, as were many of the others who brought *The Fugitive* to the small screen.

Huggins was a summa cum laude graduate of UCLA who began graduate work in political science and wrote novels before he became a TV producer and writer. When his idea of a series chronicling the life of a fugitive unjustly convicted of his wife's murder was repeatedly rejected, he decided to return to his studies, "get my Ph.D., and go on with the career I had originally planned, which was being a college professor".[1] Alan Armer, who produced some of the series' best episodes, did become a college professor at California State University, Northridge, where he taught and wrote books on directing and screenwriting. Stanford Whitmore, who wrote the pilot and several other episodes, got an M.A. from Stanford and based some of his ideas (he told me) on Tolstoy's *War and Peace.* George Eckstein, another key writer (he wrote the two-part finale and eight other episodes), was a theater major at Stanford; he later got a J.D. from USC Law School and worked as an entertainment lawyer for William Morris. These very literate men all knew, as Walter Grauman (director of the pilot and ten other episodes) put it when I interviewed him, that *The Fugitive* "was about something." What it was about was authoritatively and precisely set down in the remarkable "original treatment" Huggins wrote in 1960 and used as the basis of his pitch to ABC in 1962.

The six-page treatment begins with a fully detailed account of what was to be the famous opening shot of each episode. "A pas-

---

[1] Quoted in Mel Proctor, *The Official Fan's Guide to "The Fugitive"* (Stamford, Conn.: Longmeadow Press, 1994), 4.

senger train, its enormous headlight glowing in the distance, is racing [TOWARD CAMERA] through a dark and lonely country." It's all there: a world of darkness and isolation illuminated only by the single and intense light of Kimble's relentless effort to clear his name and receive justice. The shot then switches to the train's interior where we see Kimble, his eyes "turned toward the dark window where broad farmland, with its occasional solitary glow of light, swiftly passes." The train is the first of the small, dimly lit enclosures in which Kimble and those he encounters will work out their respective fates. But there is an enclosure even more central to the series' obsessions, and it too is named here: "We sense from his inward air that he is seeing little of this, that whatever beauty there may be in the swift passage of quiet, moonlit countryside had no meaning for him." His meanings, the ones that absorb him, are all internal.

The pattern of semidarkness punctuated briefly and intermittently by light is repeated when "the police officer beside him, using his left hand, offers a cigarette to Kimble and takes one himself." He "lights both cigarettes with a lighter, using the same left hand" because his right hand is covered by a topcoat which also covers Kimble's left hand. The two men are handcuffed to each other, although Huggins wants this fact to be inferred rather than shown: "The camera does not single this out because the action itself suggests that the unseen wrists are joined by handcuffs." To the casual observer passing through the aisle, two men sit side by side companionably. The truth—it is always the truth about the world in *The Fugitive*—is that the surface tranquility barely hides the unhappy reality of restraint and confinement.

In the next instance that surface is torn away by the impact of the train's crashing as it takes an "unintended turn" onto a spur that should not have been open. What follows is silence ("the night sounds are distant") until a man—Richard Kimble—stumbles into "the moonlight" (the same play of light and dark again). He is "bewildered," and we, as observers, are unenlightened. "We see nothing. We hear nothing but the sounds of the crickets and an occasional night bird." All we see is Kimble, facing "the almost terrifying fact of freedom." And then, in the signature moment of the series, he "begins to run," and as "his figure recedes we see an odd configuration in the distance." That configuration grows and fills the screen with "two sharply violently formed words": "THE FUGITIVE." The music climaxes and the screen fades out.

The fact that this setting of the initial scene (and I have only reproduced a small portion of it) fills up three and a quarter pages out of six should itself indicate how carefully Huggins has thought his concept through. In the paragraphs that remain, he provides the thematic counterpoint to the images that structure the prologue, which is to be repeated each week so as to "restate the premise and reset the mood of the series." That mood is not lighthearted. Each episode, Huggins tells us, "will deal with a week, a month, a day, or an hour in the life of Richard Kimble as a fugitive, a life which involves flight, search, moral dilemma, friendship, love, laughter, all underlain with unfulfillment, danger and tragedy."

Huggins does not see his creation as being in competition with the other series vying for the public's attention. He sees it rather as being in competition with the many literary and philosophical efforts to define the American experience. "At the heart of the series," he writes, "is the preoccupation with guilt and salvation which has been called the American Theme." Huggins acknowledges that a typical American respect for law might make a fugitive an uneasy object of audience affection, but he argues that the "idea of natural law is too deeply embedded in the American spirit for anyone to question Kimble's right, after all recourse to law has been exhausted, to preserve his own life."

Natural law is the law that is prior to and finally more compelling than any system of laws formally set down. It is natural law—the law written not on tables of stone but on the fleshly tables of the heart—that leads some men and women to know immediately, and in defiance of the formal evidence and judgments on which Gerard relies, that Kimble is innocent. It is natural law that justifies the lies told by those who help Kimble even when they are aware that the justice system (in which the fugitive himself believes) has condemned him. It is natural law, not so much religious as it is internal, that provides the touchstone and the measure of the actions every character in the series takes or declines to take. Natural law is the source of a higher authority in whose name one can flout the historically limited and challengeable authority of manmade law—an authority, Huggins reminds us, recognized even by Hobbes, "the great philosopher of authoritarianism," who "acknowledged one circumstance in which a man has a right to resist Leviathan: when an attempt is made to take his life on mistaken grounds."

Given these pronouncements, it may not be too much to say that for Huggins *The Fugitive* is the Ph.D. dissertation he never wrote, a working out of the political and philosophical ideas that led to his wanting to do graduate work in the first place. But political and philosophical ideas, however exciting they may be, cannot be presented directly in a popular medium. What is required is a dramaturgy that gives them narrative life, and Huggins finds it in two places: first, in Victor Hugo's *Les Misérables*, "the story of Jean Valjean and his Javert," which, he says drily, "had not remained a classic for insignificant reasons"; and second, "in the character and mode of life of the Western hero." That hero, as Huggins describes him, "is a man without roots, without obligations." He "avoids commitment to one locale, or one occupation or one woman," and "he actually seemed *compelled* to change his dwelling place, his occupation, his human attachments." To be sure Kimble's avoidance of attachments can be explained as a function of his situation. He knows that he cannot stay too long in one place, lest his pursuer catch up with him. ("As a fugitive he is compelled to live in a drifting alienated way.") But the avoidance he acts out again and again is deeply embedded in his nature and would be part of his "mode of life" even if no one were chasing him. Like the Western hero, Kimble is "without anxiety about his place in the order of things." At times the order of things can become disorder—a man is unjustly accused or finds himself thrust into circumstances that threaten him—and while in these moments (which may last for years) everything is in flux, he remains always what he is, untouched by the vicissitudes he moves through.

This is so even when he "must change his appearance" and his name, and everything else. What Huggins calls this "purposeful loss of identity" is not a negation of character but a paring of character down to its essence, and that essence, Huggins announces, is the "absolute freedom" celebrated by "the traditional Western," the freedom not to be defined by values and allegiances one does not freely choose. He finds the "great example" of that freedom in the movie *Shane*, the story of a mysterious drifter who comes into town, solves its problems, and rides away with women and children calling after him. We know that he is pursued, "but by what we are not told." We do know by what Kimble is pursued, but for the space of his sojourn in a place he must leave, it doesn't matter. What matters is a protagonist (Huggins is now talking about both Shane and Kimble) who is "apart from society" even when he lives within it, "rootless" even as he tries to get back to his roots in Stafford, Indiana (where he may once again disappear into anonymity), and "immune to permanent human commitment" even as he falls into commitments from which he must, time and again, extricate himself.

If Shane is the laconic embodiment of this ethic, Yul Brynner's Chris Adams gives explicit voice to it in *The Magnificent Seven* (1960), which Huggins doesn't mention but may well have seen. Explaining to the young novice who wants to join them what the life he aspires to is like, Chris asks and answers a series of questions: "Places you are tied to? None. People with a hold on you? None." Later, when the seven have to decide whether to return to the village that has betrayed them, Chris says to Lee (Robert Vaughn), you can leave, "You don't owe anything to anybody." Lee replies, "Except to myself."

Huggins calls this way of living "willed irresponsibility"—a resolute detachment from conventional obligations except those the free man himself names. Willed irresponsibility is forced on Kimble by the accident of his plight, but it is also what he desires. The only difference between Kimble the fugitive and the Kimble who in the last episode returns to the bosom of Stafford is that the former hides by running and the latter (if we can imagine him in a post-series future) will hide in plain sight, or, as Mike Royko predicted, start running again.

The degree to which Huggins has worked out the implications of his great idea is little short of astounding. More than two years before production, he already knows that "this will be a series that will be brought to a planned conclusion." And he knows too that because "the thematic basis of the series is so explicit," the writers and directors will be able to count on "a sympathy for the protagonist" (we will not be worrying about the state of his mind or soul) and will therefore be free to build the episodes "around character." In short, he knew everything that I have been telling you.

Those who brought to realization what he had written knew it too. A *Fugitive* script, Grauman said to me, "had a quality beyond just the bare bones of the guy on the run and being pursued and fearing discovery. It had a quality either of philosophical depth or an emotional depth in relationships or both." George Eckstein echoed him: "The series wasn't a chase. That's not what the series was about." Indeed, Eckstein observed, the plot device was a problem because you couldn't let it control the episode and that "ran contrary to every rule of drama; . . . you have a leading man who should in no way get involved in the story we have to involve him in." His involvement is in a sense accidental; he doesn't seek it, but once it finds him, he doesn't shirk it. He is, as Eckstein explained, "a catalyst rather than a positive reformer" (a bearer of negative, not positive, liberty). He doesn't come into town with a mission; he interacts with the missions (some good, most not) of those he encounters, and when he's done what he can, which is not always enough, he gets out.

It is this ability if not compulsion to disengage that makes Kimble so attractive a hero. He doesn't have to stay. (In one episode, "The Good Guys and the Bad Guys," he is put into a faux prison on Wild West day, and an inhabitant of the town says to him, "It could be worse; you could be sentenced to live here for life.") As Stanford Whitmore put it, "Here is Richard Kimble, who goes from city to city, he meets a good-looking woman every week, he gets involved in something, and he gets out of it." That was the great appeal: "The guy didn't have any job to go to, he showed up in town and got a job, . . . and he took off," leaving those who did live there for life with a new understanding of who they were and what they must do. Every episode tells their stories, not Kimble's story, which because it was a given—William Conrad retold it at the beginning of each episode—could recede into the background and be brought in when it was needed. "Early on," Eckstein recalled, "we came to the realization that there had to be some internal story that would resolve . . . so the audience could have some sense of fulfillment," given that "the protagonist could not reach his goal, he had to be unsuccessful." So that "became our pattern for the series, to use the Gerard-Kimble plot as an umbrella and within the framework of that suspense build an internal story . . . that would get him involved with real people and perhaps find some kind of successful conclusion that would help them with their lives even though he could not help his own." With that in mind, Eckstein continued, "Gerard was committed for 3 out of every 13 [episodes], so 3 out of 13 would be heavier on the melodramatic or suspense elements, the chase elements." (Needless to say the proportions of internal story to melodrama were quite different in the movie and in the CBS revival.)

The subordination of plot to the internal story of "real people" goes along with the subordination of themes or messages. When Stanford Whitmore and Quinn Martin got together to brainstorm an episode, they never began, Whitmore told me, by asking, "What's the problem?" (Racism, the Vietnam War, corruption, immigration, whatever.) "It was like, okay, what does he do, and then he meets this woman, and then Quinn would say, 'What's her problem? What's *her* problem? What is *his* problem?'" Those problems—existential problems of character—once identified, would take over the episode; Kimble would be playing against them rather than agonizing about his own problem, which was cut and dried. Yes, we know all about that. Let's get on with what is really interesting. Let's build this, as Huggins planned, around character.

Those like Armer, Eckstein, Grauman, and Whitmore who were centrally involved in the series expressed distaste for what television drama had become when I interviewed them in 1993. On this point Whitmore was the most eloquent. He divided the world into those who were born before 1950 and those who were born after 1950. The first group, of which he and his colleagues were members, "gained a sensibility . . . from reading or listening to the radio, both of which are active acts." Those, he said, "are the sort of people that wrote and produced *The Fugitive*." We were just "coming out of ideas," and not out of the narrow demands of "show business." But now, he went on, "this town strikes me as a place where people of bad character can become very powerful." Although they might "have a talent" and "ambition," what they don't have are "moral qualifications," and therefore, "they would do *anything* for money." If you asked, "'Would you write something sympathetic to Hitler,' they would do it." "I don't see a commitment," he said. With *The Fugitive*, on the other hand, "there was a dedication on the part of everybody who was in it. . . . It wasn't like, 'Well, I'll knock off a *Fugitive*, and then I'll go do something else, and I don't give a damn about it.'" In a round table discussion at the Museum for Radio & Television in 2000, Huggins said, "I wanted to do an existential show." Well in advance of *The Sopranos, Deadwood*, and *The Wire*, he did exactly that with the help of the writers, producers, and directors who understood his vision and dedicated themselves to realizing it.

The Fugitive Receives Its Due

The initial reviews of *The Fugitive* indicated that the critics did not understand Huggins's vision. In the September 18, 1963, *New York Journal American* (*The Fugitive* has outlasted it), Jack O'Brian declared that "it does seem improbable that the running story of an innocent fugitive could sustain a full season of shows, and such a dramaturgical block also seemed to strike the program's creators, and so they virtually ignored it." That is, the show's putative dramatic premises seemed to play a minimal role in the unfolding of the story. Exactly. What O'Brian saw as flaws—he points to the refusal of plot interest (the opening "states flatly at the start that he was an innocent victim")—were markers of the producers' intentions. Armer observed that "if you just have Kimble escape at the end, you're right back to where you were when the episode began." He and the other producers decided to "fill the body of the show with an anthology story that Kimble would become involved with, so that along the way, something positive would be achieved." In the September 18, 1963, *New York Post*, Bob Williams made fun of the pilot and of Barry Morse as the Javert of a "pallid *Les Misérables*"; he speculated that Janssen's earlier TV incarnation, Richard Diamond, "would have nabbed himself the first time out." John Horn in the *Herald Tribune* called the show a "stumbling vapid melodrama" in which "many a cliché reared its tired head." Barbara Delatiner of *Newsday* chimed in to say that "of all the things missing from the new series, the most obvious is suspense": "A suspense show without suspense. Really!" (You bet!) The *Daily News* commiserated with the series' writers who would be "straight-jacketed" by a format that leaves Kimble "no place to go but to the next town and the next involvement." Right as a description, wrong as a criticism.

As the series flourished, more reflective critics began to tumble to what was going on. John Horn did a *mea culpa* and acknowledged that *The Fugitive* is "an interesting morality play" that continually "underscores the theme that morality is the law's foundation"

(*New York Herald Tribune*, October 21, 1964), Cleveland Amory (*TV Guide*, January 11, 1964) recognized the interest of a leading man who has often "gotten the worst of it" in a fight, but who "consistently comes through with a consistent portrayal of a consistent character—and these days, considering the inconsistencies elsewhere on your screen, that makes him practically alive." Marian Dern (*TV Guide*, February 22, 1964) saw the appeal of the kind of life the fugitive embodies: "The fugitive, like the Western hero, has the appeal of the foot-loose, restless wanderer, whose commitments to jobs, women or society are temporary, and who is never tied down by those nagging responsibilities like paying for the new refrigerator." She also saw that the fugitive "is not a tragic figure at all" because "his problems arise from no agony within his own soul." It is a series "about an ordinary human being," Dwight Whitney declared (*TV Guide*, November 2, 1963), and added that Janssen was precisely the actor to portray him. In an interview Whitney found him "an intelligent, well-read, considerate and apparently egoless man." "There is so little self-consciousness," he added, "that one is prepared to believe that Janssen is trying to please no one but himself." (Sound familiar?) Ten years after the series' run, David Thorburn commented on the same happy matching of actor to role. "The smoldering physical authority of most film stars would have been an impediment in this role, which required a hero of modest dimension, an ordinary fellow able to lose himself in crowds and able to move and speak inconspicuously. Not physical energy or size, then, but psychological nuance was what the role demanded, an actor able to create a sense of character through the rhythm of his speech, the way he cocked his head or shrugged his shoulders, an actor alert to all the minute physical and vocal maneuvers that define our ordinary individuality" (*New York Times*, August 14, 1977).

When the Harrison Ford film came out, commentators had the opportunity to reassess the original, and generally they liked what they saw. Marvin Kitman (*New York Newsday*, August 16, 1993) said *The Fugitive* on television was not about violence: "It was about relationships." It is interesting, he added, "to ponder how a show without a lot of killing, fighting, gunfire and car chases managed to sustain dramatic tension and keep a nation glued to its seat for many years." Poet-essayist Georgia Jones-Davis knew the answer:

> The old television series was an Edward Hopper painting in motion, film noir for the small screen. It echoed Thomas Wolfe's poetic monologues about America at night, the loneliness of small towns under the prairie moon, train whistles, bus rides into empty town squares.
>
> *The Fugitive* wasn't about glamorous aerial shots of city lights, amoral doctors, train wrecks, hovering helicopters and guys shooting each other. It was about the loneliness at the core of the American heart.
>
> And David Janssen—he of the big ears and basset-hound eyes, surely the saddest face in America; he looked even *more* depressed when he smiles—captured in Richard Kimble a quiet, gentle man of dignity, the misunderstood Western drifter for our own times. (*Los Angeles Times*, 1993)

Jones-Davis's essay (titled "Keep on Running") was sent to me by Stanford Whitmore, who included in his letter a copy of remarks written by Paris-based journalist William Pfaff in 1990. (Pfaff was not talking about *The Fugitive*, but Whitmore thought that he could have been.) Pfaff began by observing that "Fifty years ago there was a clear moral and civic identity" that was "Anglo-Saxon in cultural inheritance, Protestant and Puritan in religion." He went on to note that "Immigrants, blacks, Catholics, Jews, Asians—all those who did not belong to this majority, were made powerfully aware of [its] effect and submitted to intense pressures to conform and assimilate." It was, he declared, "a parochial America, an intensely limited one, but connected." All that changed "somewhere between the start of World War II and the Vietnam War," and "it will never be recovered." What changed it, according to Pfaff, was "the migration of blacks from farms to cities, non-European immigration, affluence, television, the decline of the churches, the successful self-assertion of minorities." Add to these developments the ideological efforts of liberals who contributed to the old America's demise "by attacking its values, despising its conformism and subordinating the demands of community to those of individual liberty." In the process, Pfaff concludes, "much good was done for many," but "out of this . . . has come an America of morally isolated people, no longer connected to a culture deeper or more responsible than that provided by the mass entertainment industry."

And yet it was that same industry that in *The Fugitive* gave us a compelling portrait of this transition from community to individuality, with all of its attendant gains and losses—a sustained and even profound meditation on what America was and was becoming, a landmark of popular entertainment, and, according to Stephen King, "absolutely the best series done on American television."

Index of Episodes

The following
episodes are discussed
at some length:

Season 1

"Fear in a Desert City"
(Episode 1), 21–27

"The Other Side of
the Mountain"
(Episode 3), 53

"Never Wave Goodbye"
(Episodes 4 and 5), 41–47

"Decision in the Ring"
(Episode 6), 66–68

"Nightmare at Northoak"
(Episode 11), 36–40

"The Girl from Little Egypt"
(Episode 14), 28–30

"Home Is the Hunted"
(Episode 15), 84–89

"Angels Travel
on Lonely Roads"
(Episodes 22 and 23),
94–98

Season 2

"Man in a Chariot"
(Episode 1), 90–93

"Dark Corner"
(Episode 8), 111

"Ballad for a Ghost"
(Episode 15), 60–61

THE DEATH

THE DEATH OF SOCRATES

EMILY WILSON

Harvard University Press
Cambridge, Massachusetts
2007

First published in the United Kingdom by
Profile Books Ltd
3A Exmouth House
Pine Street
London EC1R OJH

Printed in the United States of America

Library of Congress Cataloging-in-Publication Data

Wilson, Emily R., 1971-
The death of Socrates / Emily Wilson.
p. cm. -- (Profiles in history)
Includes bibliographical references.
ISBN-13: 978-0-674-02683-4 (alk. paper)
ISBN-10: 0-674-02683-7 (alk. paper)
1. Socrates. I. Title.
B317.W55 2007
183'.2--dc22
2007008183

For Imogen, who always asks, 'Why?'

CONTENTS

Introduction

THE MAN WHO DRANK
THE HEMLOCK

'The more I read about Socrates, the less I wonder that they poisoned him.'

Why should we still care about a man who did little in his life except talk, and who drank poison in an Athenian prison in 399 BC – over 2,400 years ago?

Some stories shape the ways people think, dream and imagine. The death of Socrates has had a huge and almost continuous impact on western culture. The only death of comparable importance in our history is that of Jesus, with whom Socrates has often been compared. The aim of this book is to explain why the death of Socrates has mattered so much, over such an enormously long period of time and to so many different people.

The death of Socrates has always been controversial. The cultures of Graeco-Roman antiquity remain relevant not because we share the beliefs of the ancients, but because we continue to be preoccupied by many of their questions, worried by their anxieties, unable to resolve their dilemmas.

The trial of Socrates is the first case in recorded history when a democratic government, by due process of law, condemned a person to death for his beliefs. Athens, one of the

world's earliest democracies, raised Socrates, educated him
and finally sentenced him to death, having found him guilty
of religious unorthodoxy and corrupting the young. The trial
and its outcome represent a political problem with which all
subsequent democratic societies have struggled: how to deal
with dissent.

Socrates is, for many people in the twenty-first century,
a personal, intellectual and political hero, one of the most
obvious 'good guys' of history. His death is often considered a terrible blot on the reputation of democratic Athens;
Socrates is seen as a victim of intolerance and oppression,
a hero who struggled and died for civil liberties. We look
back to John Stuart Mill's classic argument for toleration, *On
Liberty* (1859), which uses the death of Socrates as the first
example of the damage that can be done by a society that
fails to allow full freedom of speech, thought and action to
all individuals. Martin Luther King declared on two separate occasions (in 1963 and 1965) that 'academic freedom is a
reality today because Socrates practised disobedience'.

It is tempting to imagine Socrates on trial as precursor to
a series of great heroes who stood up for their religious or
scientific beliefs, and for conscience, against unjust governmental oppression and restriction. We may be in danger of
forgetting that it is possible not to admire Socrates.

Socrates comes to us mediated through the work of
others. He may be the most famous philosopher in world
history, but he wrote nothing – except some versifications
of Aesop's fables, while waiting in prison for the death sentence. He did not write a word of philosophy. The twentieth-
century French theorist Jacques Derrida defined Socrates as
'the man who does not write'. Plato's *Phaedrus* implies that
Socrates had theoretical objections to writing philosophy,

since writing is always less truthful than the direct medium of speech. Socrates probably never gave official public lectures or founded a philosophical 'school'. He seems to have imagined philosophy as something close to conversation. The fact that we cannot read Socrates is one of the main reasons for his enduring fascination.

To us, the most familiar ancient accounts of the life and death of Socrates are by Plato, Socrates' student and friend. We also have the Socratic works of another student, Xenophon, whose version of Socrates is very different (as we shall see). Both Xenophon and Plato wrote Socratic dialogues – imaginary or semi-imaginary conversations between Socrates and other real people, on philosophical topics. These dialogues bring Socrates to life with almost novelistic detail and intimacy.

Plato tells us that Socrates compared himself to a gadfly, whose stings are necessary to keep a sleepy horse awake. The image is so familiar that we may fail to notice that it is fundamentally self-justificatory. A tiny gadfly could never seriously harm the horse it provokes, though the horse may, in annoyance or by clumsy inadvertence, squash the fly or throw the rider. By analogy, Socrates suggests that he provides helpful stimulation but no actual threat to the city. If we accept Plato's image of Socrates as a mere gadfly, we must also share his view of Socrates as harmless – and ultimately beneficial – to the community that chose to kill him. Plato emphasises the devastating, tragic grief suffered by the master's followers at 'the death of our friend, who was the best and wisest and most just man of all those of his time whom we have known'.

But not everybody in Athens at the time was a friend or student of Socrates. Many people surely felt that the jury reached the right verdict. The earliest book ever written about the death of Socrates was not a homage by a friend, but a fictionalised version of the case for the prosecution: the *Accusation of Socrates* by Polycrates, composed only six or seven years after the trial (393 BC). This work is lost, so any account of it must be speculative, but Polycrates seems to have denounced Socrates as an enemy of democracy, a man who – as the original prosecution had claimed – 'corrupted the young', taught his pupils to question the existing government and tried to overthrow the laws and customs of Athens. For Polycrates, Socrates was something much more dangerous than a gadfly. He was a hostile parasite, or – to use a more modern simile – a virus, tainting the whole body politic. He represented a massive threat to democracy and all civil society. Modern visions of Socrates might be very different if more work by his enemies had survived.

Many writers and thinkers in the twentieth century have tried to disentangle the supposedly good, liberal, individualistic Socrates from the distorting lens of his wicked, mendacious pupil Plato, who has often been seen as a totalitarian, an enemy of free speech and a proto-fascist. A book published in Britain at the beginning of the Second World War (R. S. Stafford, *Plato Today*, 1939) implied that siding with Plato over Socrates would be like fighting for Hitler's Germany: 'It is Socrates, not Plato, whom we need.' To attack Socrates came to seem, in the twentieth century, like a political heresy. It was equivalent to defending fascism, or attacking democracy itself.

But this vision of Socrates as a martyr for free speech is very different from the ways in which he has been viewed in earlier ages. My task in this book is a kind of archaeology in the history of ideas. I hope to show where the modern vision of Socrates came from, and how it differs from other stories which have been told about him. I do so on the understanding that the presence of multiple voices, including dissenting ones, including the voices of the dead, can only make our whole intellectual community stronger. If gadflies are to be beneficial, we must be able to feel real pain at their bite.

I will argue that even Socrates' admirers – including Plato himself – have almost always articulated doubts, distance and irritation as well as love for their dead master. The dying Socrates is multi-faceted in a way unparalleled by almost any other character, either fictional or real. He was a new kind of hero, one who died not by the sword or the spear, but by poison, without violence or pain. His death embodies a series of paradoxes. It is a secular martyrdom, representing both reason and scepticism, both individualism and civic loyalty. This new story about how a hero should die was provocative to the ancient Greeks, and should continue to challenge and puzzle us today.

When I contemplate this death, I find myself torn between enormous admiration and an equally overwhelming sense of rage.

I revere Socrates as a man who spoke truth to power, who was fearless of his reputation, who believed in a life devoted to the search for truth and who championed the idea that virtue is integral to happiness. In a world where prejudices seem to be taking ever firmer and firmer root, I respect Socrates as a man who left no traditional idea unchallenged, and felt that asking intelligent questions is valuable in itself, regardless of what conclusions one draws – if any. I believe strongly in the importance of Socrates as a reminder that the majority is not always right and that truth matters more than popular opinion. I am inspired by Socrates as an example of how the life of the mind can be playful, yet not frivolous.

But then doubts, resentment and annoyance begin to set in. Socrates' self-examination – at least as depicted by Plato – was conducted by questioning other people. Having been told by an oracle that he was the wisest of men, he tested those around him who seemed to be wisest – and discovered that they were even less wise than himself, because he was at least conscious of his own ignorance. Socrates seems to stand one step outside his own investigations. His own beliefs are never called into serious question.

I find Socrates' family life – or lack of it – particularly difficult to admire. It is hard to respect a man who neglected his wife and sons in order to spend his time drinking and chatting with his friends about the definitions of common words. When Socrates chose to risk death by the practice of his philosophy, and when he chose to submit to the death sentence, he was condemning his wife and young children to a life of poverty and social humiliation. From this perspective, his willingness to die starts to seem not brave but irresponsible.

Socrates died for truth, perhaps. But he also died in obedience to his own personal religious deity. He died for faith, even superstition. I am suspicious of the Socrates who believed in an invisible spirit – a *daimonion* – that whispered in his head.

Socrates' false modesty – in Greek, his 'irony' or *eironeia* – may be the most annoying thing about him. He was – it often seems – both arrogant and dishonest. I am infuriated by the Socrates who pretended it was all free discussion but always had an unstated goal – to prove the other person wrong.

I wonder whether it is really admirable to die so calmly,

so painlessly and, above all, so talkatively. One of the deepest niggling anxieties about the death of Socrates, which runs through the tradition from the time of antiquity, is that he was always too clever by half.

My mixed responses to the death of Socrates reveal my own preoccupations. As a teacher, academic, would-be intellectual and aspirant to a good life, I am interested in whether I can take Socrates as a model. I wonder whether I should, like Socrates, put the quest for the truth before everything else – including my family, my material well-being and the wishes of my community.

I sometimes wonder whether Socrates was even a good teacher. The question hangs on whether the central goal of education in the humanities is to prompt students to examine their own lives, or whether we have a responsibility to teach students some specific things – skills, facts, a canon or curriculum. Socrates claimed that he never taught anything, because he did not know anything of any value. But if a student asks for factual information, it is unhelpful to say, with Socrates, 'What do *you* think?' I suspect that a weak version of the Socratic method has become all too common in university classrooms.

I sometimes feel that Nietzsche was right when he blamed the decadent dying Socrates for the later decline of western civilisation. We still live in the shadow of what Nietzsche called Socrates' 'naive rationalism'. Perhaps Socrates has held sway over our culture for far too long.

You, the readers of this book, will bring your own special interests to the contemplation of its subject. I hope it will help you to understand the death of Socrates as a historical event that happened a long time ago. But I also hope it will show you how this event has been recycled, reinterpreted and re-evaluated by generation after generation. You too must find your own vision of Socrates.

THE HEMLOCK CUP

Some scholars – such as Alexander Nehemas – have claimed that the death of Socrates took on cultural importance only in the eighteenth century, when it became an image of the enlightened person's struggle against intolerance. Others – most notably the Italian scholar Mario Montuori – have claimed that, up until the eighteenth century, the dying Socrates was always viewed sympathetically: he was 'the just man wrongly killed'. Only the development of academic historical method – it is claimed – allowed scholars to recognise that the Athenians might have had good reason to want him dead.

In this book, I will argue against both these positions. There have always been people who thought Socrates hardly died soon enough; and Socrates' death, for good or ill, has played an essential role in the stories told about him.

Plato makes the hemlock central to Socrates' character and philosophy. He describes Socrates as a man who can control even the ending of his own life, who understands his death even before it happens.

Ever since Plato, the hemlock has represented Socrates. Writing at the end of the fourth century AD, John Chrysostom alluded to Socrates without feeling the need to name him. 'People will say that among the pagans also, there have been many who despised death. Such as who? The man who drank the hemlock?' Socrates does not need to be mentioned by name, any more than we need to name 'the man on the Cross'.

Many other Athenian prisoners must also have been executed by this means. But the hemlock is so important in the story of Socrates that it has become his symbol, his identifying mark. We have descriptions of Socrates' life, death and philosophy from two pupils: Plato and Xenophon. Both present Socrates' death as not merely the end but the culmination of his life. Socrates said, according to Xenophon, 'I have spent my whole life preparing to defend myself.' In Plato's *Phaedo* Socrates claims that, 'Those who pursue philosophy properly study nothing except dying and being dead. And if this is true, it would be strange to desire only this one's whole life long, but then complain when that very thing which they longed for and practised for so long has finally arrived.' Socrates claims that he was born to die, in precisely this way.

Socrates' life and death were dominated by two oral activities: talking and drinking. Monty Python's 'Philosopher's Drinking Song' is a hilarious celebration of the philosophical greats – Aristotle, John Stuart Mill and others – not for their thought, but for their capacity to down large quantities of alcohol.

Heidegger, Heidegger, was a boozy beggar
Who could think you under the table.

In most of the stanzas in the song, the idea of the boozing philosophers is funny because it is absurd: Nietzsche was more or less teetotal, and in the wine-drinking culture of ancient Greece, Plato would presumably not have had access to 'half a crate of whisky every day', even had he wanted it. But Socrates stands out in this group, a climactic figure who is mentioned emphatically both in the middle and in the end:

Yes, Socrates himself is particularly missed,
A lovely little thinker,
But a bugger when he's pissed.

Socrates is different from all of the rest not merely because
he was the first ethical philosopher in the western tradition,
but also because he really is famous for drinking as well as
for thinking.

Plato's *Symposium* or *Drinking-Party* presents Socrates as
the heaviest drinker of all, but the one who is best at holding
his liquor: he keeps talking cogently even when almost all his
friends have gone to sleep. As Socrates' friend and admirer
Alcibiades comments, 'The amazing thing is that nobody
ever saw Socrates drunk'.

Hemlock, just like alcohol, seems hardly to affect him,
however much he knocks it back. An epigram on Socrates'
death by the ancient biographer Diogenes Laertius (third
century AD) celebrates the hemlock as only the most literal
of Socrates' many drinks:

Drink now, O Socrates, in the kingdom of Zeus.
Rightly the god declared that you are wise,
Apollo, who himself is perfect wisdom.
You drank the poison which your city gave,
But they drank wisdom from your god-like voice.

The poem suggests that there was an intimate connection
between Socrates' oral philosophy – the 'wisdom' that he
gave to the city – and the poison by which he died. The
means of Socrates' death defined the meaning of his life.

On a mundane historical level, we might be tempted to
say that the philosopher died by hemlock simply because he

was a white-collar criminal who had some rich friends. In Athens in the late fifth century BC, the most common means of execution was so-called 'bloodless crucifixion'. (The term 'crucifixion' is used for any kind of death where the victim is strung by the arms to a post, tree or stake.) In bloodless crucifixion the prisoner was strapped down to a board with iron restraints round limbs and neck, and strangled to death as the collar was drawn gradually tighter. The advantages of this method were that no blood was spilt (and thus no blood-guilt was incurred), and it was much cheaper than hemlock, because the same materials could be recycled again and again.

Hemlock, a natural plant-based poison, had to be imported from Asia Minor or Crete; hemlock was not native to Attica. The prisoner or his friends may have had to pay for his own dose. Plato – whose family was rich – may have been the author of Socrates' death in more senses than one.

One obvious advantage of hemlock over other methods, including those popular in modern societies (such as hanging, beheading, knifing, stoning, shooting, the electric chair or lethal injection), is that it felt clean – even more so than bloodless crucifixion. Hemlock poisoning hardly looks like execution at all. The prisoner brings about his own death: he kills himself, but without committing suicide. This final paradox becomes an essential element in the myth of Socrates' death.

For most of us, death is something that comes upon us. We cannot predict the day or the hour when we will die. Socrates, by contrast, died in complete control, and his death fitted perfectly with his life. If Socrates had been crucified, then the whole later history of western philosophy and religion might have looked very different.

Socrates was, we are told, delighted that he had the opportunity to die by hemlock. According to Xenophon, he cited at least three advantages to dying this way. 'If I am condemned,' said Socrates, 'it is clear that I will get the chance to enjoy the death which has been judged easiest or least painful (by those whose job it is to consider these things); the death which causes the least trouble to one's family and friends; and the death which makes people feel most grief for the deceased.' Socrates avoided all of the indignity usually associated with death. He died at the peak of his powers. His friends did not have to see him convulsed or racked by agonising pain. They did not have to empty bedpans, mop up vomit or nurse a senile old man. He left only good memories behind him.

Socrates – surrounded by a group of friends – drank the poison in prison. Plato gives us a detailed and tear-jerking description of what happened as the hemlock took hold of him.

He walked about and, when he said his legs were heavy, lay down on his back, for such was the advice of the attendant. The man who had administered the poison laid his hands on him, and after a while examined his feet and legs, then pinched his foot hard and asked if he felt it. He said, 'No'; then after that, his thighs; and passing upwards in this way he showed us that he was growing cold and rigid. And again he touched him and said that when it reached his heart, he would be gone. The chill had now reached the region about the groin, and uncovering his face, which had been covered, he said – and these were his last words – 'Crito, we owe a cock to Asclepius. Pay it, and do not forget.' Crito said,

1. *Jacques-Louis David's* Death of Socrates *(1787) shows the philosopher dying in his sexy, six-pack prime, an Enlightenment hero of reason and revolution (see chapter 6). Through the archway we glimpse Xanthippe going away up the stairs, while Plato, as an old man, sits at the foot of the bed remembering the scene.*

'It will be done. But see if you have anything else to say.' To this question, he made no reply, but after a little while he moved; the attendant uncovered him; his eyes were fixed. And when Crito saw it, Crito closed his mouth and eyes.

This was the end, Echecrates, of our friend, who was, as we may say, of all those of his time whom we have known, the best and wisest and most just man.

The manner of Socrates' death fits perfectly with the life he has chosen to live. The numbness which overcomes him is presented as a gradual liberation from bodily life. Socrates dies with all his faculties intact, talking all the while, in no particular physical discomfort. The body need not intrude on the final work of the soul as it prepares to depart. Although the friends are all finally reduced to tears, Socrates remains calm, his attention devoted to philosophy until almost the last minute of life. This is the image of the death of Socrates which has most deeply influenced later generations.

Several late-twentieth-century scholars argued that Plato's account of the death of Socrates cannot possibly be accurate. It seemed too good to be true. Hemlock poisoning, they claimed, produces drooling, profuse sweating, stomach pains, headache, vomiting, rapid heart rate, dry mouth, fits and convulsions. A passage from an ancient didactic poem about poisons and their remedies (the *Alexipharmaca* of Nicander, from the second century BC), describes these horrible symptoms:

> A terrible choking blocks
> the lower throat and the narrow passage of the
>   windpipe;
> the extremities grow cold, and inside the limbs the
>   arteries,
> strong though they are, get contracted. For a while he
>   gasps
> like somebody swooning, and his spirit sees the land
>   of the dead.
>
> (186–94)

This does not sound much like the death of Socrates according to Plato's *Phaedo*. If Plato sanitised the real symptoms of hemlock poisoning, this would suggest that his version of Socrates' death is largely fictional, albeit based on a real event.

But the sceptical view has been convincingly challenged in a brilliant article by Enid Bloch. She shows that Plato gives a perfectly accurate description of Socrates' medical symptoms in the last hours of life. The hemlock family of plants is a large one, including water hemlock, poison hemlock and 'fool's parsley' or lesser hemlock. They all look almost identical. Whereas water hemlock attacks the central nervous system, producing seizures – as described by Nicander – poison hemlock works on the peripheral nervous system. Consequently, those who take it are affected just as Plato describes: they go gradually numb and then die – painlessly – once the paralysis affects the respiratory system or the heart.

The effects of poison hemlock are relatively unfamiliar to the modern medical profession, but they were much studied in the nineteenth century, when it was hoped that hemlock might offer a cure for cancer. One case closely paralleled the medical symptoms described in the death of Socrates. In 1845 the children of a poor Scottish tailor called Mr Gow kindly made a sandwich for their hungry father. They used what they thought was fool's parsley growing wild. But they had gathered poison hemlock by mistake. The man grew gradually numb, losing the use of his legs, then his other limbs. His intellect remained unimpaired up to the very end. A few hours after eating the fatal sandwich, he was dead.

Poison hemlock (*Conium maculatum*) still grows wild in parts of Europe and many states of North America, such as Ohio and Wyoming. It continues to cause difficulties for farmers, who have to try to keep their sheep and cattle from enjoying a Socratic death.

The Greeks did not have separate words for these botanically distinct plants, and there is no way of knowing, a priori, whether poison hemlock or water hemlock would be meant by the Greek *koneion*, or Latin *cicutum*. In any case, Plato avoids using a specific term: in the *Phaedo*, he always calls Socrates' poison simply *to pharmakon*, the 'drug', the 'poison' or the 'medicine'. The Athenians often mixed their poisons: it is quite possible that Socrates took some strain of poison hemlock cut with crushed opium from poppies, which would have increased the sedative effects of the poison.

There is, then, no reason to doubt the medical facts of Plato's description of Socrates' last hours. But even if true, it is still a good story. Thanks in large part to Plato, Socrates' death by hemlock has come to seem not merely the means by which he happened to be executed, but essential to the meaning of his life.

OVERVIEW OF THIS BOOK

In the first chapter, I describe Socrates' philosophical teaching. I show why his beliefs seemed so dangerous to his contemporaries – and why his philosophy remains challenging for us today. I suggest that the Athenians may have had good reasons to put this strange, radical thinker to death.

But Socrates' philosophy cannot give us a complete explanation for his execution. I turn, in the second chapter, to the social context of the trial. In order to make sense of Socrates' death, we need to know about the history of his time, his friends, his family, his enemies and his lovers. Socrates was killed not only for his beliefs, but also because of the people he knew.

In the third chapter, I move back to the question of sources. All our knowledge of Socrates is filtered through the words of others: we can have no unmediated access to the event itself. It is through his pupils Plato and Xenophon that the death of Socrates became a legend.

In the remaining four chapters, I evoke the later reception of the death of Socrates, showing how this pivotal cultural event has been linked with significantly different sets of problems at different moments of our history.

First, I discuss the Romans and Greeks living under the Roman Empire. For them, the most pressing question raised by the death of Socrates was whether imitation of his calm, philosophical death was either possible or desirable in a world of violence and imperial power. Some Romans suspected that Socrates was just a Greek show-off, and many in this period wondered whether intellectuals have the moral right to cut themselves off from political engagement.

In the fifth chapter, I concentrate on parallels between the death of Socrates and the death of Jesus. This comparison has been made repeatedly, throughout the Christian tradition. But the analogy was particularly important at two turning points in Christian history: in the second and third centuries AD, when the new cult was first establishing itself as the official religion of the Roman Empire, and in the Renaissance, when humanist scholars began to revive 'pagan' learning. At both these moments, debates about the relative moral values of paganism and Christianity were articulated through comparisons between Socrates' peaceful, painless, confident death, unblessed by Christian revelation, and Jesus' agony on the Cross.

The eighteenth century is a climactic moment in the story of this book. It was a period of particularly intense interest in the death of Socrates. The philosopher who talked to his friends as he sipped hemlock seemed to resemble a fashionable French intellectual or *philosophe* discussing the issues of the day in his salon or the coffee house. The death of Socrates became an image of the shared life of the mind, and provided a locus for debates about the power and limitations of reason.

My final chapter takes the story into modern and postmodern times, describing the persistent contemporary interest in this ancient story. I suggest that there was a radical shift in perceptions of Socrates's death after the Enlightenment. It now represented not the pleasures of intellectual friendship, but the solitude of the intellectual who resists social conformity. In the twentieth century, Socrates facing his judges was viewed through the lens of modern totalitarianism.

At the turn of the twenty-first century, our perspective seems to have changed again. The dying Socrates is assumed to be a hero for our times, but he is often found acceptable only in a radically simplified guise. Contemporary responses often show particularly deep discomfort with his actual death.

For example, Ronald Gross's *Socrates' Way: Seven Keys to Using Your Mind to the Utmost* (2002) provides a 'step-by-step' programme for self-improvement and worldly success, through such 'keys' as 'Know Thyself' and 'Speak the Truth' – mottoes supposedly inspired by Socrates. But the book deliberately underplays the end of its hero's story. Presumably people who are searching for greater success with colleagues and friends are not often willing to risk death to get it. One Amazon review of Gross's book warns us that Socrates failed to observe his own 'precepts' properly, 'as his ultimate demise demonstrates'. All the more reason to hurry up and master those seven 'keys' as quickly as possible: otherwise you too could find yourself in a dank prison cell, sipping hemlock. In our times, a Socratic death seems to have become not something to aspire towards but something to avoid for as long as possible.

The relative lack of interest in Socrates' death in the past generation or so may be a symptom of our increasing discomfort with death in general. We no longer look for models of the ideal death. We hope, ideally, not to have to die at all. Failing that, we would rather not think about it. Our society may also be increasingly suspicious of ideology in general, as well as of many of the '-isms' with which the dying Socrates has been associated – including rationalism, liberalism, individualism and secularism.

This is all the more reason to turn back to the tradition and think again about why the death of Socrates has mattered in the past, and what meanings it might still hold for us today.

Throughout the book I aim to evoke the diverse, multiple voices of those who have struggled with the dying Socrates. I imagine all these voices as participants in an ever-growing set of new Socratic dialogues or conversations which are not over yet.

1

SOCRATES' PHILOSOPHY

The charges against Socrates vary slightly in different sources but went roughly like this: 'Socrates is guilty because he does not respect the gods that the city respects. Instead, he introduces new deities. He is also guilty of corrupting the young.' The prosecution convinced the jury that Socrates' teachings threatened the religious traditions of the city and were morally damaging to the young.

But how exactly was Socrates' teaching incompatible with the religious traditions of the city? What were these 'new deities'? What made his teaching seem liable to corrupt young minds?

We can try to answer these questions only by turning to the accounts of his friends, pupils and enemies. We can never be certain that we have got it right. Socrates' character, his life and his ideas come to us filtered through other writers – above all, through Plato.

In this chapter, I try to reconstruct Socrates' teaching and consider why Socratic philosophy seemed so radical, and potentially dangerous, to his contemporaries. But Socratic philosophy is a highly controversial field among contemporary academics. Several of the claims I make here for Socrates' beliefs about religion, ethics and politics, as well as my assessment of the relative value of the ancient sources, will not command universal agreement from specialists in the field. I refer interested readers to the bibliographical suggestions at the end of the book.

THE FIRST DEATH OF SOCRATES: ARISTOPHANES' *CLOUDS*

The most extensive surviving discussions of Socrates' philosophical teaching are by his pupils Plato and Xenophon. But the reader of either Plato or Xenophon may be left puzzled about a fundamental question: how Socrates' philosophy got him killed. Were the people of Athens really such fools as to kill their wisest citizen?

If we want to explain how Socrates' philosophy led to his death, we should begin with our earliest surviving description of the philosopher, a text that was composed during his own lifetime. Aristophanes' comedy the *Clouds* includes the first account in literature not only of Socrates' teaching, but also – surprisingly – of Socrates' death. The comedian created a fictional 'death of Socrates' some twenty years before the trial. Plato later suggested that Aristophanes' play was an important factor in the actual condemnation of Socrates. The *Clouds* shows us, with shocking clarity, why an ordinary citizen of Athens might have thought Socrates needed to be killed.

It is a comedy about a middle-aged man called Strepsiades ('Mr Topsy-Turvy') who has run up enormous debts because of his aristocratic wife's thriftlessness and their young son's penchant for horses. Strepsiades decides that he should enrol as the pupil of a teacher of wisdom – a 'sophist' – in order to learn 'how to make the weaker argument appear the stronger' and hence be able to evade his creditors. The sophist he chooses is a boffin called Socrates, who keeps his head literally in the clouds. He rides aloft in a basket and talks to his pet deities, the Clouds, who appear in person, presumably clad in fluffy white costumes, as the Chorus of the play.

Strepsiades is happy to parrot Socrates' view that he should reject the old gods in favour of new-fangled deities like Whirlwind and Tongue and Vapour. But he proves too stupid and senile to do well at the absurd linguistic pedantries peddled by Socrates. Eventually the philosopher gives him up as a bad lot.

Strepsiades' son, Pheidippides, seems much more capable of being taught – and hence more subject to the corrupting influence of Socrates. He takes over his father's place as a student in the school. Socrates delegates the education of Pheidippides to the Worse and Better Arguments themselves, who appear on stage to fight it out. Better Argument turns out to represent the old-fashioned Athenian values of an earlier generation, while Worse Argument articulates the more cutting-edge ideas brought into the city by the sophists. Better Argument insists on the importance of self-control, gymnastics, military training and cold showers – the foundations that helped the Athenians beat the Persians at the Battle of Marathon in 490 BC. Worse Argument favours rhetorical cleverness and mocks the idea that self-control could be valuable in itself: 'Have you ever seen anybody get any benefit from self-discipline?'

Strepsiades is emboldened by Socrates to do what he had been intending to do all along. He refuses to pay his creditors, fobbing them off with specious puns and nonsensical meteorology. Becoming like his own headstrong son, he treats the creditors as hard-driven horses: he clinches his case by setting his slave on them with a whip.

But his pleasure is short-lived, since Pheidippides immediately starts beating his father, and threatens to beat his mother too. At this, Strepsiades at last sees the error of his ways and realises that he should never have listened to Socrates or rejected the old gods. He climbs up on the roof of the school with a lighted torch and sets fire to it. One pupil protests in horror, 'You'll murder us, you'll murder us!' But Strepsiades replies, 'That's exactly what I want to do!' Socrates is presumably killed in the fire, along with his remaining pupils. Anyone who escapes the flames will be hacked to death by Strepsiades, who is armed with an axe.

Socrates' last words are a desperate cry: 'Ah no, poor me, it's terrible! I am going to suffocate!' Suffocation seems, within the play, an appropriate death for one who has relied so heavily on various forms of hot air. Socrates, who spouts windy nonsense, who worships the Air and the Clouds themselves and who explains thunder as a cosmic fart, finally gets the death he deserves. Strepsiades shows no sympathy for his plight. Indeed, he urges his slave to attack the inhabitants of the school all the harder as they try to escape the flames: 'Pursue them! Hit them! Hurl your weapons at them! For all number of reasons, but especially because you know that they did wrong to the gods.'

From the perspective of many modern readers, the end of the Clouds makes for disturbing reading. It suggests that we should cheer – or, worse, laugh – when new ideas are suppressed. Those who challenge received wisdom deserve to be lynched.

Equally worrying is Aristophanes' failure to distinguish those aspects of Socratic philosophy that might be dangerous from those that are merely silly. The play mixes up at least four distinct stereotypes about intellectuals. Socrates is a word-chopping academic, interested only in trivia such as (false) etymologies and how to measure the jump of a flea. He is also a materialist, atheist scientist who gives purely physical explanations for cosmic phenomena like rain, and who rejects the worship of Zeus. He lives a life of asceticism and semi-deliberate poverty, forcing his pupils to sleep in beds riddled with bugs (although he also seems to steal other people's cloaks, on occasion). Finally, he is a master of 'spin' who poses a serious threat to traditional morality. It is striking how persistent all these clichés remain in our own cultural imagination.

The Clouds suggests that there is a slippery slope from pedantic academic investigations and petty theft, through cosmology and scientific speculation, straight on to blasphemy and moral corruption. The implication, then, is that no intellectual pursuit at all – even those that ostensibly have no ethical or social consequences – can be practised without threatening the fabric of society.

But although Socrates and his school are primarily responsible for the breakdown of moral values in Athens, Aristophanes seems to condemn traditionalists almost as fiercely. In the debate between the Better and Worse Arguments, the former is, if anything, more ridiculous than the latter, being obsessively interested in sex, with a particular fondness for young boys' buttocks. The debate suggests that the 'good old days' of Athenian culture were not so great after all. Society has become less decorous than it used to be, and more heterosexual, but the old days were no better than the new.

The inclusion of the Arguments in the play suggests that not all current social problems can be blamed on Socrates alone. The philosopher is tainted by his association with these shady characters, who seem to play a prominent part in the work of his school. But the triumph of Worse Argument happens without Socrates' direct intervention, while he is absent from the stage. It seems that the dangerous powers of rhetoric to foster moral corruption have taken on a life of their own. Socrates is by no means the only person who can teach young people how to cheat and disobey their parents. He is just the most famous example. The *Clouds* suggests, then, that the death of Socrates might not solve anything – although it would give satisfaction to his personal enemies and those suspicious of the new ways.

While the play hints that Socrates could be a corrupting social influence, it does not actually show him corrupting anybody. In fact, none of the characters needs to learn moral corruption from Socrates. They know all about it already. Strepsiades did not need Socrates' guidance to come up with the idea of cheating his creditors; he had been meaning to do that all along. Even Pheidippides, who seems a worryingly apt pupil of the Worse Argument, does not undergo a fundamental change as a result of his education. He has been disobedient towards his father all his life. The teaching of Socrates' school allows both father and son to give voice to the unpleasant desires that they have always had. Socrates offers his students only a reflection of themselves – just as the Clouds, his friends and guides, have no shape of their own, but mirror the shapes of those around them.

But from another perspective, the woolly-headedness of Mr Topsy-Turvy, and the hot-headedness of his son, only bolster the case against Socrates. If most citizens are idiotic and fundamentally amoral, society will be destroyed without firm moral leadership. Most people, the play seems to suggest, will behave abominably if they think they can get away with it. Belief in the usual gods is needed to enforce social order. The *Clouds* is a bracing reminder that unfettered intellectual enquiry and freedom of thought will seem like good things only if one believes that human beings are capable of behaving well and discovering truth for themselves, without carrots or sticks.

Aristophanes often seems to ascribe the views of other contemporary sophists to his Socrates. It was really Anaxagoras, not Socrates, who claimed that Mind created and rules the world. Apparently Socrates studied with Anaxagoras in his youth, but rejected his materialist philosophy in later life. Aristophanes' portrayal of Socrates contrasts sharply with those of our other main contemporary sources, Plato and Xenophon. According to them, Socrates was mostly uninterested in science; and he was positively hostile to the new-fangled techniques of rhetoric that were recommended by Aristophanes' Worse Argument. Plato and Xenophon suggest that Socrates' main interest was in ethics: he wanted, above all, to learn how to live the good life.

Where the sources diverge, many modern scholars dismiss Aristophanes' description of Socrates and his philosophy as just comic slander – and unsuccessful slander at that. The *Clouds* failed to win first prize at the dramatic festival at which it was performed, in 423 BC; the text we have is a partially revised version. The original ending was different, and the scene between the Better and Worse Arguments was added in the revision.

But the play's failure with the judges hardly undermines its value as evidence of contemporary opinions about Socrates. The *Clouds* shows us how Socratic philosophy seemed to those outside his immediate circle, and helps us understand why the jury condemned Socrates to death.

As one recent editor remarks, 'In the absence of unbiased information about Socrates … we must accept *Clouds* as a valid expression of what public opinion believed, or might be expected to believe, about him in the Athens of 423–*c*. 416 BC.' To most Athenians at this time, Socrates' philosophy was almost indistinguishable from that of any other contemporary wisdom-monger. Socrates was simply the most famous practitioner of the dangerous new learning.

SOCRATES' PROFESSION

Socrates was the founder of philosophy as we know it. His interests – in morality, value, language, happiness, truth and the human mind – are all recognisably 'philosophical', from our perspective. We must remind ourselves that in the fifth century BC nobody could have known that Socrates' limited set of interests would be identified with all true wisdom or 'philosophy' ('the love of wisdom'). It was Plato, writing after Socrates' death, who redefined the master's work in this way, separating the 'philosophical' study of ethics and metaphysics from the 'sophistic' pursuits of science and oratory.

The first Greek wise men – dubbed 'philosophers' by later tradition – were primarily interested in the composition of the universe – 'cosmology', or the study of the world and of nature. Thales, the earliest of them, believed that the world was made of water. Later theorists devised a version of atomism. Their enquiries look, to modern eyes, like a strange mixture of metaphysics, theology and speculative chemistry. They mostly came not from Athens, but from the coast of Ionia in Asia Minor.

During the fifth century a wave of foreign intellectuals began to visit Athens. They included orators and rhetoricians as well as sophists. These three categories are distinct but overlapping, and we tend to describe most of the intellectuals of the fifth century as sophists. 'Sophist' was not originally a term of abuse, merely a description; Protagoras, Gorgias, Hippias and their friends would have not been offended to hear themselves referred to in this way. Many of these men turned their attention away from physics towards more recognisably philosophical topics, including language, culture, politics and human society. Protagoras taught a version of moral relativism: 'Man is the measure of all things', he famously declared.

If Socrates' contemporaries had had to describe his profession in one word during his lifetime, they would presumably have called him a sophist. The trial of Socrates can be seen simply as a gesture of the city's dissatisfaction with sophistry.

But we still need to explain why it was Socrates, not any of the other sophists, who earned the hemlock, even though many others brought startling new ideas to the city.

SOCRATIC IMPIETY

Socratic philosophy was particularly radical in two main areas: theology and human psychology. I begin with the first, which was apparently most important for the prosecution.

Three accusations were brought against Socrates at his trial: a failure to respect, worship or acknowledge the city's gods, the introduction of new deities and corrupting the young.

It is unlikely that there were specific laws on the statute books against any of these. Some have argued that Socrates was condemned under a decree which allowed for the impeachment of 'those who did not believe in religion or who taught cosmology' (the Decree of Diopeithes). But since Socrates had little interest in cosmology (if we believe Plato and Xenophon), it is unlikely that this was the main point at issue. There was a general law against impiety, *asebeia*, and probably all three charges were aspects of one central accusation of religious impiety. The prosecutors claimed that Socrates corrupted the young by teaching them not to respect the city's gods, but instead to acknowledge his own, new deities.

There was no precedent for the death of Socrates in Athenian history. We hear of one instance of intellectual censorship: when Protagoras wrote a book which began, 'I have no way of knowing either that the gods exist, or that they do not exist.' The Athenians expelled him from the city and sent a herald round to collect up all copies of the book, burning it in the marketplace. The lyric poet Diagoras was supposedly condemned as an atheist; he too perhaps went into exile. Anaxagoras is said to have been exiled. But none of these people was actually killed. And it is quite possible that all these stories were made up or exaggerated by later writers hoping to find precedents for the death of Socrates at the hands of the Athenian state. Ancient historians, like modern ones, saw the execution of Socrates as a strange anomaly.

BELIEF IN THE CITY'S GODS

The charges against Socrates seem to focus on his religious beliefs ('He does not believe in the city's gods'). From a post-classical perspective, it is tempting to define Socrates' crime as heresy. But it is quite unclear whether the main issue was religious belief or religious practice. The prosecution used a verb whose meaning was shifting in this period: *nomizein*. This word could mean 'to follow a custom' or 'to respect'; but it could also mean 'to believe'. The charge against Socrates could be read as a claim that he 'does not worship' the city's gods, or that he 'does not believe' in them. Most likely, the prosecutors and the jury did not distinguish sharply between the two. Greek religion was very largely a system of shared religious traditions and shared myths. The Athenians had no equivalent to a Christian creed.

Xenophon assumes that the prosecutors were accusing Socrates of lax religious practice, not unorthodox religious beliefs. He retorts that Socrates 'was always to be seen offering sacrifices, both at home and in the city temples'. In fact, we have no evidence that Socrates' religious *practice* was in any way strange. In Plato's *Phaedo*, his last words are an injunction to make a traditional blood sacrifice to a named god: 'Crito, we owe a cock to Asclepius. Pay it, and do not forget.'

But it is very likely that Socrates questioned many of the traditional Greek myths about the gods. In Plato's *Euthyphro*, Socrates says he does not believe that Zeus chained up his father, Cronos, for eating his children, or that Cronos in turn had castrated his own father. Socrates is talking just before his trial, outside the courthouse, and he suggests that his religious doubts are the reason for the prosecution. He asks, 'Is not this the reason I am being prosecuted, because when people tell these stories about the gods, I find it difficult to believe them?'

It is possible that Socrates' prosecutors meant to accuse him of actual atheism. If so, the case would have been highly unusual. Almost nobody in the ancient world doubted the existence of any gods at all. The word *atheos* usually meant 'a person hated by the gods' – not 'atheist'. According to Plato, Socrates frequently referred to 'the god', who guided his whole career.

But it is also possible that the prosecution objected to Socrates' religious views, because he questioned the old traditional Greek stories about the gods. We tend to assume that Socrates was condemned to death unjustly. But this assumption depends on believing in the effective rhetoric used by the Platonic Socrates, who persuades us that it is more pious *not* to believe in anthropomorphic gods who eat, castrate, chain up, fight and cheat on one another. We should try to remember that this was a paradoxical position, not an obvious one. The changing currents of belief since Plato's time have helped make some of his religious ideas seem self-evidently true. Paganism is dead, and Socrates' refusal to accept traditional Greek religious beliefs has made him seem like a monotheist or even a Christian *avant la lettre*. History sided with Socrates.

But if Socrates did question the old myths, then the charge that he failed to respect 'the city's gods' was perfectly true. He was guilty as charged.

Scholars disagree about how radical Socrates' views were in the context of his time. Questioning the traditional myths about gods was nothing new for the Greeks. As long ago as the sixth century BC, Xenophanes had claimed that men make gods in their own image. In the fifth century BC rationalist approaches to religion were common among the sophists. Anaxagoras rejected the traditional account of the creation of the world by anthropomorphic Titans and gods, and substituted his own more scientific narrative, in which Mind brought about and rules the cosmos. By comparison, Socrates' doubts about the old stories seem relatively mild.

But Socratic religion may have seemed even more liable to corrupt the young, because it was more insidious. Socrates presented his own rationalised, highly moralised conception of the gods as the 'true' religion of Athens. Socrates may have been seen as more impious even than Xenophanes and Anaxagoras, because he presented his religious radicalism as an ideal form of piety.

INTRODUCING NEW DIVINITIES

The prosecutors claimed not only that Socrates 'does not believe in the city's gods', but also that he 'introduces new divinities' (*daimonia*). This is a clear reference to the fact that Socrates believed in a special divine power (a *daimonion*), that guided his actions, warning him if he was on the point of doing something wrong and perhaps also (according to Xenophon) giving positive advice about what he ought to do.

Daimonion was a vague term that could be used to refer to the work of an unknown god or to some inferior spiritual power. Socrates' *daimonion* was a startling innovation in terms of traditional Athenian religion.

Xenophon tries hard to make the Socratic *daimonion* seem normal. He has Socrates ask, 'How could I be guilty of introducing new deities just for saying that the voice of a god appears to me and shows me what I should do? Surely those who practise divination with birdsong or human utterances are also using voices ...'

But the analogy does not hold. Ancient soothsayers, prophets and priests interpreted divine signs that were visible or audible to everybody – such as the flights or songs of birds. They interpreted public natural phenomena as signs of divine will. This is quite different from the claim that one can hear a divine voice inside one's own head that is accessible to nobody else. Socrates' belief in a personal deity was extremely unusual in the context of his time.

It is easy to see why the idea of a personal *daimonion* might have seemed dangerous. The deity authorised Socrates to cross-question even the most highly respected citizens of Athens. Any number of other people might hear divine voices too – or pretend to hear them. A city in which every citizen followed the instructions of his own divine sign could easily slip into anarchy.

For the Athenians, believing in the gods was – as one scholar, Mario Vegetti, has remarked – 'not so much a spiritual act of faith or theological respect as a concrete sense of belonging to the political community'. It was shocking, in this context, that Socrates separated religion from communal life.

Plato presents Socrates as a man who believed that tradition can never be a sufficient guide for moral action, since different elements in a tradition may come into conflict with one another. In such a case, we need to be willing to use our own minds to try to resolve the dilemma. Euthyphro, for example – the man to whom Socrates talks outside the courthouse before his trial – seems to assume that tradition is sufficient to guide his moral conduct. He remembers the old Greek precept 'The guilty person must suffer', and he is therefore prosecuting his own father for murder. But Euthyphro seems to be unaware that an equally authoritative traditional precept suggests that you should 'Honour your father'. The two precepts, on their own, cannot possibly explain what a man should do if he believes his father guilty of murder. What is needed, Socrates suggests, is a much more thorough understanding of the principle that should underlie all pious action ('holiness'). For Socrates, the only way to begin to behave in accordance with the will of the gods is to keep on thinking and talking about questions of principle. He is willing to continue the conversation indefinitely, or until death comes.

As one recent scholar (Mark McPherran) has argued, Socrates' religious views threatened many traditional religious practices, since he believed that we cannot buy the gods' favour by means of cult offerings or ritual. We cannot, and should not, expect the gods to be magically influenced on our behalf by prayer, burnt offerings or sacrifice. This aspect of Socratic theology may have been even more shocking than Socrates' views about the moral character of the gods themselves – since the latter were, as we have seen, paralleled by other thinkers of the time. In questioning the value of ritual and the power of prayer, Socrates threatened the whole structure of religious practice in Athens.

Strepsiades in the Clouds feared that if traditional religious beliefs were lost, morality would also, inevitably, be eroded. Socrates' position in Plato's Euthyphro suggests a strong but subtle response to this non sequitur. He insists that the gods love what is good, but its goodness is independent of their approval. Allowing an external religious authority to guide all decisions is lazy and morally irresponsible. It is even impious, in so far as God or the gods have set us on the quest for ethical truth. If we believe that any action may qualify as holy or good simply because God or the gods approve of it, then God or the gods are morally arbitrary tyrants, and we live in a world where the only right is might. If we imagine that people only ever act 'morally' out of reverence for tradition and fear of divine retribution, then we have already denied the possibility of true moral choice.

Religion, Socrates insisted, must be treated as an inspiration for independent moral thinking, not as a substitute for it. It is easy to see why his vision of religious authority should have been inspiring to his pupils. It is also easy to see why it would have seemed abhorrent to anybody who thought of religion as the glue that binds citizens, families and communities together.

KNOWLEDGE AND IGNORANCE

Socrates' views about human knowledge, ethics, psychology and happiness were if anything even more radical than his beliefs about religion.

He believed that thinking and talking about morality were of the utmost importance: virtue was, for him, the central goal of human life and human happiness. But Socrates did not think that simply following traditional moral principles could ever be sufficient to achieve a virtuous life, a good life – or even a properly human life.

He declared, 'The unexamined life is not worth living by a human being.' Students undergoing final exams may sometimes believe the opposite: the examined life is not worth living. But the Socratic concept of self-examination is directly opposed to that of the test-taking culture of contemporary Anglo-American education. Academic exams test how well a student remembers and understands the assigned material. A Socratic examiner would want to know why the student valued the assignment at all, and how getting an 'A' would contribute to a life of virtue. For Socrates, 'examining' one's life had nothing to do with the achievement of goals set by society. It meant questioning and testing one's most fundamental beliefs. He argued that a failure to look honestly at one's own life was to betray one's very humanity.

Socrates appropriated the words that were written over the temple of Apollo at Delphi: 'Gnothi seauton' ('Know yourself'). He showed his contemporaries what a difficult task this might be.

Socrates' life-work was inspired by an oracle given by Apollo at Delphi. A friend of Socrates had asked the god, 'Is there anybody wiser than Socrates?' The oracle said that there was not. Socrates was puzzled and asked himself, 'Whatever does the god mean, whatever is his riddle? For I know that I am not wise, neither very wise, nor even a little bit. So whatever does he mean by saying that I am the wisest?' (Plato, *Apology*, 21b). In order to solve the enigma, he went to question all those who had a reputation for wisdom: the politicians, the poets and the tradesmen. If he could find even one person who was wiser than himself, he would be able to prove the oracle wrong. But he found no such person. Instead, as he cross-questioned people, he discovered inconsistencies in the things they claimed to know. The process has been dubbed by scholars 'the Socratic *elenchos*' (the word means 'refutation'). The Socratic quest was, paradoxically, a search for ignorance rather than for truth.

Socrates eventually decided that there was more than one different type of wisdom (in Greek, *sophia*). Many people have 'wisdom' in the sense of technical expertise: they can write poems, lead an army, address an assembly or make a pair of boots. But all such wisdom is not merely inferior, but worse than useless. Expertise, Socrates suggested, is morally dangerous, because it gives people a false, inflated idea of their own knowledge. People think their capacity to practise a particular art also gives them wisdom in other areas where in fact they know nothing. Socrates drew a stark contrast between this 'worthless' human wisdom (which is not really wisdom at all), and 'true' wisdom, which belongs only to the god. His final interpretation of the oracle was, 'The god is truly wise, and by this oracle he is saying that human wisdom has little or no value' (Plato, *Apology*, 23a). This might suggest that human wisdom is a contradiction in terms: only the god is truly wise.

What, then, of Socrates' own claims to know anything? Socrates is sometimes accused of being self-contradictory or paradoxical in saying that he 'knew' that he 'knew nothing'. But it is quite possible that Socrates included himself in his condemnation of all merely human wisdom. In Plato's version, the oracle never said that Socrates was wise; it said, rather, that 'There is nobody wiser than Socrates.'

Alternatively, Socrates believed that human beings can count as 'wise' in a third, limited sense: if they understand their own ignorance in comparison with divine enlightenment. Socrates, in this interpretation, viewed himself as the only person in the world who came anywhere near to divine wisdom.

Perhaps, as Robert Nozick has argued, Socrates genuinely did not know how to define many evaluative terms, such as courage, holiness, or justice. But he knew more than most people, because he had at least rejected some common false beliefs about these concepts, such as the idea that holiness simply means making the guilty suffer, or doing the things the gods like. He knew that most people are wrong or misguided in thinking they know anything about their own systems of belief and value.

SOCRATIC IRONY

Socrates embodied a series of paradoxes. He questioned religious traditions and myths, but out of religious piety. His wisdom was his ignorance. His death was happiness and victory, both unknown and certainly good. The last words he spoke at his trial – according to Plato's account – were an assertion both of supreme confidence and of radical uncertainty: 'But now it is time to go away, for me to die, and for you to live. But which of us goes to a better thing is unclear to anyone except the god.'

The tension between Socrates' insistence on his own ignorance and his assertion of positive (and peculiar) beliefs about ethics and religion is particularly evident in Plato's *Defence Speech of Socrates* – which is more commonly known as the *Apology.* The usual title in English may be misleading since Socrates certainly does not 'apologise', in the usual sense, for any of his actions. Quite the opposite: he justifies his whole career, and indicts the city of Athens for his conviction.

It is difficult to reconcile Socrates' claim to know 'little or nothing of any value' with his confident assertions about ethics. We may well wonder what status any positive claim by Socrates can have, if no human being is capable of true wisdom.

This is a controversial area in modern scholarship about Socrates and I cannot hope to reproduce all the nuances of the scholarly debate. I also doubt whether it is possible to find an entirely satisfactory solution. Socrates the radical sceptic undermines Socrates the moralist, and vice versa. Either we must see Socrates' renunciation of knowledge and wisdom as just a rhetorical gesture or we must view his claims about morality as mere guesses or beliefs, albeit perhaps true ones, but not knowledge.

If the problem has a solution, it might seem to lie in the concept of 'Socratic irony'. Socrates' irony is one of his most famous attributes. But it is difficult to define, because the term is used to mean a number of different things.

In antiquity, Socrates was known for his *eironeia*. But this ancient Greek term does not correspond exactly to the modern concept of 'irony'. In English, 'ironic' utterances may be those where a speaker says the opposite of what he means to convey. I might, ironically, claim that they have lovely weather up in Glasgow. But 'irony' can have a much wider range of meanings than this. In 'dramatic irony', for example, the words of the speaker are more true than he realises. So Oedipus says that he will fight for Laius as if he were his father – not realising that he really is his father. 'Irony' is used to describe any kind of gap between appearance and reality.

Eironeia is more specific. It is a mode of behaviour – a kind of mock modesty or hypocrisy. *Eironeia* involves speaking in understatements, describing oneself as less good than one really is – or perhaps as less good than one believes one really is. Uriah Heep in Dickens's novel *David Copperfield* is a classic modern example of a person characterised by a kind of *eironeia*. Heep claims, ad nauseam, to be 'very 'umble'. But the reader always knows that Heep is a snake: we can hear in the name 'Uriah Heep', 'you are a creep'. His self-professed humility is a not very successful mask for his ruthless avarice and social ambition. In fact the mask acts as an advertisement: the claim to humility underlines Heep's desire for power.

When other characters in Plato's works accuse Socrates of 'your usual *eironeia*', they often seem to mean something like Uriah Heep's fawning false modesty. In the *Republic*, for example, when Thrasymachus accuses Socrates of *eironeia*, it is because he is enraged by Socrates' sly deceitfulness, his refusal to fight fair.

Mock modesty, in the case of either Socrates or Uriah Heep, can be seen as a form of inverted boasting. It is clear – as we shall see in more detail in the next chapter – that many of Socrates' contemporaries felt he acted in a superior or arrogant way towards his fellow citizens.

In general, Socrates' professions of ignorance are not explicitly described as *eironeia* in our ancient sources. But one might well connect Socrates' disavowal of wisdom with his arrogant mock modesty. Socrates pretended to think he knew nothing in order to take the moral high ground against his interlocutors. His modesty was a form of pride. On this interpretation, 'Socratic irony' is a way of being fake. It need not be seen as actually deceptive: Uriah Heep, for example, does not fool anybody into thinking that he really *is* humble. Instead, Socratic *eironeia*, like Heep's humility, might be a supposed claim to inferiority that really functions as a claim to superiority.

But many of Socrates' admirers have been troubled by this way of understanding his 'irony' – for obvious reasons. It makes him sound so thoroughly horrible.

There are several possible ways to make Socratic mock modesty sound less obnoxious. The central question here is what Socrates' motives were for speaking and acting in a way that seems, on the face of it, dishonest.

Aristotle suggested that Socrates was self-deprecating out of genuine dislike for showing off – not out of arrogance. He presents Socrates' *eironeia* as a gentlemanly refusal to blow his own trumpet. But Aristotle lived a generation after Socrates and never knew him. Contemporaries certainly did not see him this way.

Modern interpreters struggle to understand Socratic irony. One approach to the problem, favoured by Leo Strauss among others, is to regard irony as a mechanism to protect a hidden, unspoken truth from the uninitiated mob. According to this view, Socrates – or rather, Plato – uses 'irony' in order to express his secret doctrines to a set of initiated students, while keeping them secret from those who do not and cannot understand. Plato's Socrates does indeed have definite moral beliefs, but he chooses at times to speak 'ironically' or to distance himself from his own doctrines, so that stupid or frivolous people will not have access to his true meaning. Here, 'irony' is still a mark of extreme arrogance, but it is arrogance harnessed to a political mission.

Alternatively, irony may be seen as a tool for teaching everybody – not just those who are already initiated. An important champion of the ironic Socrates as a devoted moral teacher was the philosopher Gregory Vlastos. He insisted that Socrates never tries to deceive anybody, or tell anything other than the truth. Instead, his ironic utterances are true in one sense, although obviously false in another. Vlastos dubbed this possibility 'complex irony'. According to Vlastos, when Socrates says, 'I am not wise', he means that he does not possess certain knowledge, but he does possess 'elenctic' or 'fallible' knowledge, derived from refuting the claims of his interlocutors.

It remains a little unclear why Socrates did not spell out his position clearly, without any irony at all. Perhaps, as other commentators suggest, Socrates wanted to make his students figure out the answer for themselves. Speaking in an ambiguous or opaque way about, for example, knowledge could be seen as a means to force students to analyse the different types of knowledge for themselves. Another, related possibility is that Socratic irony typically depends on an unspoken conditional – which, again, students or interlocutors must work out for themselves. If Socrates' profession of ignorance is an example of 'conditional irony' (as suggested by another scholar, Iakovos Vasiliou), the implied conditional could go in one of two directions. He could mean, 'I know nothing of any value (if valuable knowledge is the stuff which generals, poets and politicians know – but of course it is not).' Or he could mean, 'I know nothing of any value (if valuable knowledge is the property of the god alone).' It seems possible to understand Socrates' irony in both of these two ways. On either reading, he is extraordinarily self-confident in relation to his fellow human beings and extraordinarily humble in relation to the god.

One final possibility is that Socratic irony should be understood as a kind of radical ambiguity, or unknowability. Perhaps – as Alexander Nehemas suggests – Socrates' paradoxical statements have no 'hidden doctrine' behind them, and no specific pedagogical purpose. Rather, Socrates' irony is a fundamental unknowability. We cannot tell whether he is arrogant or humble, whether he is wise or not, or whether his provocative attitudes should be seen as claims to truth or simply philosophical gestures.

None of these approaches provides an entirely satisfactory solution to the problem with which we began. The scholarly debate on the topic is extensive and more complex than I am able fully to indicate here. But whatever we think of Socrates' irony, it remains difficult to reconcile his claim to know 'little or nothing of any value' with his confident assertions about ethics. We may still wonder what status any positive claim by Socrates can have, if no human being is capable of true wisdom.

WISDOM IS NOT FOR SALE

Socrates' views about the limits of human knowledge had important implications for his status as a teacher of wisdom, a 'sophist'. It would be hypocritical for a person who doubts the value of any human wisdom to teach other people to be wise.

In fact Plato suggests that Socrates did not even pretend to be a teacher of wisdom. 'I have never set up as any man's teacher', he declares. 'But if anyone, young or old, is keen to hear me talking and carrying out my own mission, I never refuse to let him do so; nor do I charge a fee for talking to him, or refuse to talk without one' (Plato, *Apology*, 33a). In this respect, Plato's Socrates is sharply distinguished from the sophists, who claimed to have wisdom and to be able to impart it to the young – for a hefty fee.

Sophists taught teenagers who had finished their basic training with a tutor. Like an education at a good American college today, a course of study with a well-respected sophist did not come cheap. The most famous (like Protagoras or Gorgias) could charge around 100 *minae* for a complete course of study. This is roughly equivalent to $500,000 – more than the current cost of a bachelor's degree from Harvard or Yale, which is around $300,000. Less famous teachers could be hired for a much lower fee. Euenus of Paros charged only five *minae* for a whole course.

High fees were justified by the importance of the product for sale. As one contemporary commentator put it, 'We value what is expensive more than what is free.' Those who were 'reassuringly expensive' treated their financial success as evidence for their value: 'The proof of wisdom is the ability to make the most money', as Plato's Socrates sarcastically put it. Inevitably, fathers who paid such large sums worried about whether they were getting their money's worth. Would these self-professed teachers of wisdom equip their sons well for society? Or did they only make young people question the ways of their fathers? As we have seen, Aristophanes' *Clouds* articulates many of these anxieties.

Unlike all other freelance wisdom-mongers in the city, Socrates did not charge private fees for his teaching. Sophists were often seen as intellectual whores who would sell their minds to all comers. By contrast, Socrates asked (in Xenophon's account), 'Who do you know who is more free than I am, since I accept neither gifts nor wages from anybody?' Presumably the claim never ever to accept gifts is a flattering exaggeration. Socrates certainly accepted dinner invitations, and it may well have been his rich friends who ensured that his wife and children did not starve. But the main point is clear enough. Socrates was a poor man who could behave like an aristocrat through his indifference to worldly goods. His refusal to charge fees allowed him to choose his associates freely – although, as we shall see in the next chapter, Socrates' strange ways with money earned him enemies as well as admirers.

For Plato, Socrates' refusal to charge fees was philosophically significant. His Socrates often declares that the sophists are well worth the money they charge, if indeed they are able to teach people to be wise. If there were a person capable of teaching wisdom, Socrates would advise any father to spend his life savings on an education with such a man, and count it cheap at the price. But if the sophists do not really know the things they profess to teach, and if wisdom is not really the kind of thing that one person can teach another, then the whole enterprise of sophistic education is wrong-headed. Socrates rejects the idea that wisdom can be gained through commercial exchange.

Plato describes Socrates discussing wisdom at a party with a pretentious tragic poet called Agathon. Socrates says:

> Oh, Agathon, it would be wonderful if wisdom were the kind of thing that would flow from us, from the fuller one to the emptier, if we just touch one another, like water which runs from a fuller cup to an emptier one on a piece of wool. If wisdom works that way too, I would feel enormously privileged to sit next to you. I reckon I would soon be filled up with a beautiful big river of wisdom.

But Agathon recognises that he is being teased. 'Socrates,' he says, 'I know you are making fun of me.' Wisdom is precisely not the kind of thing that can be transferred from one person's mind to another's, like water on a piece of wool. A wise person can interact with a foolish one and leave him none the wiser.

In modern American colleges, and increasingly in Britain, students and parents want to get good value for the large cost of a higher education. You do not pay $75,000 a year to learn that you know nothing. Plato's Socrates suggests that money taints the whole educational process: you cannot be entirely open-minded about the value of a product that you have bought. All consumers fear buying 'a pig in a poke'. We want to get what we pay for and we want, therefore, to be able to examine the product before we buy. But buying an education cannot fit this model, because the evaluation can take place only retrospectively and will itself be affected by the experience that has been bought.

Modern societies are increasingly built on the exchange

of cultural or intellectual capital for economic wealth. Plato's Socrates challenges this system, suggesting that the search for truth should be entirely distinct from commercial exchange. You may be able to buy social advancement, political connections or better job prospects for your children by sending them to Yale, but you cannot buy them access to the truth.

If wisdom is not the kind of thing that one person can teach to another, then the sophists' fees are obviously a waste of money. But, even more than that, the fees of the sophists may be morally dangerous, if they lull people into the false belief that they can pay somebody else to do their thinking for them. Wisdom, Socrates insists, is not a commodity. This is a radical claim, both for the Athenians and for us today.

HAPPINESS, CHOICE AND BEING GOOD

Socrates' views about knowledge and wisdom were deeply paradoxical by any standards. He thought that nobody could teach another person to know the truth. And yet knowledge was more or less the only thing worth having, since knowledge alone can make us both happy and good.

Socrates set knowledge at the centre of human behaviour. He claimed that 'Nobody willingly does wrong' and argued that whenever people behave badly – to each other or to themselves – it is because they do not know the truth about what they should do.

This is, on the face of it, an absurd idea. We all see people acting against their own best interests all the time and often they seem to know quite well what they are doing. For example, everybody knows perfectly well that smoking cigarettes is bad for your health. It tells you so right there on the

pack: SMOKING CAUSES CANCER AND OTHER DISEASES. If we
extend 'doing wrong' to cover immoral as well as imprudent
action, the Socratic position seems even more ridiculous.
People behave badly all the time. Some murderers are crimi-
nally insane, certainly. But many more people act in cruel,
unjust, dishonest ways, even though they seem to be quite
well aware that what they are doing is wrong.

One obvious explanation, which both Plato and Aristotle
adopted (with variations), is to suggest that people are
divided into several different parts, including both rational
and irrational elements. Perhaps your rational self knows
that cigarettes may make you die a horrible early death. But
another part of you – which Plato names *to epithymetikon*, the
'desiring part' – has a nicotine craving to satisfy. Similarly,
your 'desiring part' might want money more desperately
than your superior moral part wants to avoid committing
murder. Reason often seems to fight with desire; our rational
knowledge of what we ought to do is overwhelmed by our
passions.

Socrates' position, then, was extremely surprising, and
on the face of it extremely implausible. He believed that in
so far as we know the good, we act upon our knowledge.
This leaves an obvious problem. How can a philosophy that
denies the existence both of wilful imprudence and of deliberate crime make any sense of the world we live in?

Socrates' account of human behaviour will seem plausible only if we revise our notion of what it means to 'know'
or 'understand' that something is good or bad. According to
Socrates, people always act in accordance with their actual
knowledge or beliefs. A smoker may claim to 'know' that
she shouldn't do it. But in a Socratic account, she must be
deceiving herself. Maybe she does not really understand the

health risks involved; she can read the health warning on the label, but she has not thought through what it means. Or perhaps she really believes that the pleasure and consolation outweigh the dangers – in which case, she is acting in accordance with her beliefs after all. Similarly, murderers, rapists, thieves and other wrongdoers must always act under the belief that their crime is justified. The murder committed by Raskolnikov in Dostoevsky's *Crime and Punishment* – he kills an old woman for her money, but believes, at the time, that he is acting for the greater social good – might serve as an example of Socratic crime.

We can see, then, why talking about moral questions should have been the central activity of Socrates' life. Recognising good behaviour turns out, according to Socratic philosophy, to be much harder than we normally think. It is not enough merely to recite the principles we have been told in our childhood – that, for example, murder is wrong. Parroting received opinion is not the same as knowledge. We will 'know' that murder is wrong only when we feel absolutely no temptation to commit it.

Socrates seems to have been interested in the definitions of common evaluative terms. He asked his interlocutors if they knew how to define qualities like courage, or holiness, or friendship. Usually it turns out that they do not understand these terms as well as they thought at first.

But Socrates may also have believed that all virtues are fundamentally the same. All good behaviour stems from knowing the right thing to do. In this way, being brave is really no different from being kind or just or holy: they are all just different words for the person who knows what is right.

I have, up to this point, treated prudential and ethical considerations as if they were entirely comparable. But normally we assume that prudence and ethics present two entirely distinct and perhaps incommensurable sets of values, and that fulfilling one's moral duty will, fairly often, be incompatible with satisfying one's own best interests. Surely it would be in my best interests to steal a million dollars from the bank, if I could be certain of getting away with it – even if, morally, stealing is wrong. If this could be true, then prudence must be distinct from morality.

Socrates again opposed all our common-sense intuitions by suggesting that there is absolutely no distinction to be made between prudence and ethics. Being good and being happy are the same thing. Doing wrong hurts the perpetrator, by deforming his or her moral character. There is no such thing as 'my interests', as distinct from my duty. It is always imprudent to behave badly.

If I robbed the bank, I would assume that having the money would be good for me. But Socrates denies that any material possession could benefit me at all. Even more surprisingly, he sometimes seems to deny that any of the things we normally consider bad for us – such as poverty, pain, enslavement, humiliation or death – are actually evils at all. None of these is bad because none of them hurts your soul. The only thing that is bad for you is acting wrongly. This is at least one possible interpretation of Socrates' famous claim, 'To the good man no harm can happen'.

This position is an extreme one and some modern scholars doubt whether Socrates held it. Certainly, there are moments (for instance, in the *Crito* and the *Gorgias*) when the Platonic Socrates seems to acknowledge that extreme physical suffering might make one unhappy, and might even make life no longer worth living. It is possible to argue that Socrates did not believe that *only* damage to the soul is relevant to human happiness, but rather that the soul is far more important for happiness than the body. This is a difficult issue to resolve; for more extensive scholarly discussion, see my suggestions for further reading. I will simply note here that even the modified position is quite surprising from the perspective of common-sense attitudes towards human happiness – either in ancient Athens or today.

Socrates' idea that sin is more harmful than physical suffering helps to explain his astonishingly cheerful attitude towards his own death. It was the prosecution, not Socrates, who had behaved badly. It was they, then, who suffered from his trial and execution. Wrongdoing harms the perpetrator more than the victim. Socrates suffered condemnation, imprisonment and death. But he suffered less than his prosecutors, because he died without doing anything wrong. Death could not threaten his integrity or his virtue. This is why it hardly mattered to Socrates whether he was executed or not. He declared to the jury, 'Either acquit me or do not acquit me, but do so in the knowledge that I will never behave differently, not even if I were going to die many times over' (Plato, *Apology* 30b–c).

It should now be clear why Socrates' views about human behaviour are extremely shocking for any society that depends on an ordinary judicial system – including modern Britain and America as well as ancient Athens. Socrates presented his own work as the most important form of social service. Only a gadfly could save his fellow citizen's souls from the worst evil of all: moral ignorance. He denied the existence of crime as we normally understand it. The infliction of merely physical harm might have no effect on the victim's well-being. The city's instruments of punishment and political control – such as execution, exile or imprisonment

– were feeble, since they primarily affected the body, not the soul. It may seem like a slippery slope from here to anarchy.

Socrates was not interested in making sure that governments punish wrongdoing or in social justice. In his philosophy, by far the most important thing in life is whether you, as an individual, understand how to behave well. One may be appalled by this radically individualistic view of ethics, or thrilled, or a bit of both. But it is impossible not to find it challenging.

As we shall see in more detail in the next chapter, however, it was his views about politics and society that shocked many of Socrates' contemporaries the most.

2

POLITICS AND SOCIETY

DEMOCRACY THREATENED

Politics was a touchy subject in Athens in the year 399 BC, for good reasons. The lives of most of the population had been dominated by a war with Sparta which had gone on for over thirty years, a whole generation: the Peloponnesian War. Hostilities had broken out in 431 BC.

Sparta was, unlike Athens, not a democracy. It was a militaristic society that had two kings but combined this double monarchy with oligarchy. An assembly of twenty-eight men, drawn from the elite members of the population, ruled the country and used force to keep down the mass of the people – the *helots*, who were treated as slaves.

The Athenians were initially confident of victory in the war. But the war dragged on, and more and more powers in the Mediterranean became involved on one side or another. The Athenians made a number of strategic mistakes, including a disastrous expedition to Sicily in which most of their navy was destroyed; there were enormous casualties, from disease, thirst and starvation as well as battle. Many of the surviving Athenian citizens were enslaved. The city became demoralised and increasing numbers of people lost faith in the democratic government. In 411 BC democracy was briefly overthrown, and a group of Four Hundred elite citizens formed an oligarchic government.

The oligarchy lasted only a few months. But its formation showed the deep political divisions within Athens in the later years of the war. The oligarchs hoped that a non-democratic Athens might negotiate a peace treaty with Sparta. But talks failed and people who favoured oligarchy or opposed democracy looked increasingly like traitors to the city of Athens itself.

As the war continued, Athens – despite some military successes – was starved of resources. In 404 BC, after yet another naval defeat, the city surrendered to Sparta. Aided by Sparta, a group of Athenian citizens formed a military dictatorship. This group was dubbed the Thirty Tyrants. They instituted a rule of terror. In less than a year, at least 1,500 citizens were killed without trial. If we include non-citizens, such as permanent resident aliens (called 'metics'), women and slaves, the numbers may be much higher. Anyone who seemed likely to pose a threat to the regime was summarily assassinated. People were encouraged to inform on one another to protect themselves and their families. The militia removed all civil rights from the majority of citizens, allowing only a small minority the 'privilege' of trial by jury or the right to carry arms.

The seeds of democracy had been sown in Athens in the early sixth century, by the great law-maker, statesman and poet, Solon. Solon introduced trial by jury, set up a representative Council of 400 citizens from the four major tribes of Athens, and granted all citizens (even the poor) the right to vote in the Assembly. The city moved back towards one-man rule, called 'tyranny', in the later part of the sixth century, as Peisistratus and his sons seized power. In 508,

Athens made a further movement towards democracy, when the sons of Peisistratus were overthrown, and a politician called Cleisthenes created a series of reforms which gave more power and equality to all citizens. Cleisthenes called his system, '*isonomia*' – 'equality before the law'. The year 508 BC is conventionally seen as the beginning of western democracy.

It must have seemed to many Athenians, in the early months of 404, that the democratic experiment had at last failed.

But after a few terrifying months, a group of Athenians who had gone into exile in Thebes returned in force to the city and successfully overthrew the Thirty. Extraordinarily, the threat of further civil war was averted and democracy was restored. In 403–2 the Athenians drew up a set of agreements to rebuild civil society in the wake of the war.

The terms of the agreements tell us a great deal about the environment of the city in these years. One important provision was that anybody who felt under threat in the newly restored democracy was allowed to emigrate to the neighbouring city of Eleusis. For those who wished to remain in Athens, there was a general Act of Oblivion or Amnesty: all except the Thirty and their immediate henchmen were exempt from any further recriminations. It became illegal to 'remember past wrongs'. The old laws were totally revised and codified: no law that had not been reinstated by the commission was active any longer. It was a period of anxiety and feeble hope – comparable, in modern times, to Germany after the Second World War or South Africa after Apartheid. Like those societies, Athens was left poor and shaken by the hostilities, even once they were over. Citizens were conscious that many of the neighbours with whom they must now be friends had probably, only a few months earlier, been willing to turn them in to the militia.

It is not surprising that people who had so recently lost a protracted and impoverishing war, and who had so narrowly escaped from a military junta, should feel wary of anybody who might threaten the brand-new democratic government. It would also not be surprising if people in such a situation were on the lookout for scapegoats.

The Act of Oblivion made it illegal to prosecute anybody for political crimes committed during the rule of the militia. But it seems at least initially plausible that politically motivated prosecutions might have taken place, disguised under another kind of charge – such as the crime of impiety. It is therefore tempting to believe that the 'real' charge against Socrates was lack of support for democratic government – or even sympathy with the militia. As we shall see, Socrates had some reservations about democracy. He certainly associated with both aristocrats and oligarchs.

It would be reductive to suggest that all religious anxieties can be translated directly into political terms. But politics played an essential part in religious prosecutions of the time. The Athenian population was particularly eager to appease the gods, in the aftermath of the recent troubles. Religion and politics were bound up with one another.

Most Athenian private houses owned at least one 'herm' – a statue representing the head and phallus of the god Hermes. Herms were believed to provide divine protection over a household. In 415 BC, immediately before the Athenian navy set out on the Sicilian expedition, all the herms in the city had been mutilated. The vandals hacked at the face and phallus of the god. Since Hermes was the god who presided over journeys, the attack was clearly a bad omen for the fleet. There were also rumours of another sacrilege. A set of particularly holy, secret religious rites, called the Eleusinian Mysteries, had been profaned. A small group of citizens, including the notorious playboy Alcibiades – of whom more later in this chapter – had apparently acted out a perverted form of the secret ritual, performing the Athenian equivalent of a Black Mass.

The troops went to sea nonetheless, but with a sense of foreboding. Their fears were fulfilled. In retrospect, it seemed as if the destruction of the herms and the profanation of the Mysteries had caused the Athenian defeat in Sicily, and perhaps were responsible for the ultimate Spartan victory in the war as a whole.

One of those accused of this sacrilege was an orator called Andocides, who escaped punishment by informing on his more famous companions. Afterwards Andocides wisely got out of town. A condition of his freedom from harsher penalties was that he was forbidden to enter temples or participate in the rites of Eleusis in the future: he was, as it were, excommunicated.

Andocides returned to Athens after democracy was restored, taking advantage of the forgiving new political climate. But around the turn of the year 400–399 BC, he was finally brought to trial, on the grounds that he had violated the terms of his bail: he had been seen participating in religious events from which he had been banned. Although the explicit charge was religious, there were clear political overtones to the trial. Those who attacked the herms had been members of an oligarchic drinking club. They were not, as is sometimes said, simply high-spirited young men having a laugh, but a group with a clear political purpose: to undermine the decision of the democratic government to send ships to Sicily. The trial of Andocides was an opportunity for the prosecution to blame undemocratic, oligarchic citizens for everything that had gone wrong for Athens in the past fifteen years. In his defence, Andocides cited the new amnesty laws, suggesting that it was time to forget old wrongs in the spirit of new civic harmony. He defended himself successfully and was acquitted.

The trial of Andocides illuminates the trial of Socrates in several important ways. It reminds us how closely religion and politics were connected. It also shows very clearly that the city was torn in two different directions at this moment of the rebirth of Athenian democracy. On the one hand, citizens hoped to avoid endless recriminations. On the other hand, they were – inevitably – interested in looking back at recent history, and trying to find a reason why things went so badly wrong for Athens.

The trial of Andocides took place in the year 400, or perhaps early in 399 BC. The prosecution of Socrates followed a few months later, in the spring – probably some time in May 399. In the context of Andocides' trial, we should be particularly mindful of the charge that Socrates 'corrupted the young'. The Athenian court had just decided that the damaging antics of the vandals in 415 BC should indeed be forgotten. Perhaps they did not act out of natural depravity, but as a result of bad teaching. Socrates was already in his fifties when the Sicilian expedition began. If he was seen as the instigator of the sacrileges against the Herms and the Mysteries and as the ultimate moral source for the city's political undoing, his contemporaries might well have felt less inclined to let him off. The ideas and teaching of this (supposedly) wicked, anti-democratic old man could be seen as the true cause of the Athenian defeat.

SOCRATES' POLITICS

Athenian democracy was in many ways more fully participatory than the mixed political systems of most modern western societies. Democracy was not combined with republicanism or monarchy, as in the US and the UK. It was not a representative democracy: citizens voted directly for important decisions, rather than delegating their authority to a senator or an MP.

Athens was not, in a strict sense, a 'radical democracy': not all ultimate authority lay with the people, since the law-courts (*dikasteria*) also had significant powers. Some scholars argue that the courts, not the popular assembly, should be seen as the 'ultimate sovreign' in Athens. But authority for much important city business did lie with the Assembly (the *ekklesia*), a gathering of at least 6000 people, composed from all qualified adult male citizens. Among other things, the Assembly had control of all foreign policy decisions.

For the daily running of government business, there had to be smaller executive groups. The Council of the Five Hundred was selected by lot every year and subdivided in turn into ten smaller groups (the Ten Tribes established by Cleisthenes), so that at any one time most political decisions were taken by a set of fifty citizens (the *prytaneis*). Out of this fifty, another lottery selected a single man as leader – an office that would last only a day or so and could be held just once.

From a democratic perspective, the system of random selection had some important advantages. It ensured that, in so far as the lottery was fair, anybody could take on a position of huge political importance, regardless of money or birth.

Athens was not, of course, a society untouched by social divisions. There were slaves, women were rarely allowed outside the house, and resident aliens – even free-born males – had significantly fewer rights than Athenian citizens. Some citizens were much richer than others. Some were aristocrats, others peasants. Military rank, especially in wartime, took on great political significance: charismatic generals won the people's hearts and votes.

But the degree of equality between members of the adult male citizen population was remarkable by modern standards. Even those who could not run a long, expensive election campaign could still become governors of the city. If the US switched over to random selection for the presidency and the senate, it would no longer be a disadvantage if a candidate was too ugly for television, gay, black, Hispanic, female, non-Ivy League-educated or poor.

But from Socrates' perspective, the practice of selecting officials by lot was problematic, because it took no account of a person's competence for the job. One of Socrates' core beliefs was that in order to do something well, you have to know how to do it. He objected, then, to the idea that no specific qualification or competence was required of those chosen to rule the city. Socrates thought that every person should do the job they were most suited to do. Those who knew how to govern should govern.

Not all modern scholars agree that we should see Socratic philosophy as essentially anti-democratic. It is possible to argue that Socrates would have favoured democracy over other political systems – even if he had specific objections to Athenian democratic practice. If we remember that Socrates doubted whether 'human wisdom' could exist at all, it seems possible that he would have thought nobody was truly qualified for government. None of us knows anything of any value, least of all how to run a city.

Socrates probably did not favour any conventional form of government that had been realised in his time, be it oligarchy, monarchy, tyranny, aristocracy or democracy. But in so far as he cast doubt on election by lot and on election by the (uninformed) citizen body, and in so far as he questioned the people's power to recognise their own best interests, it is easy to see how his philosophy might have seemed dangerous for the democracy, to those outside his own intimate circle. As we shall see, contemporaries suspected Socrates of sympathising with oligarchs and aristocrats.

AUTHORITY AND SUBMISSION

Socrates' attitude towards authority is one of the most complex and hotly disputed aspects of his political thought. He insisted on the importance of submission to one's superiors, at certain times. He himself fought for the city of Athens in no fewer than three military campaigns during the Peloponnesian War. He believed that a soldier in war ought to obey his military commander.

But at home in Athens, Socrates sat on only one council and he had not set foot in a courtroom as a litigant before the day of his own trial. Socrates had a different vision of his political obligations from that of most of his contemporaries. He believed that he could best serve the city not by sitting on committees or talking in the assembly, but by doing exactly as he did: by walking the streets of Athens, talking and thinking about the good life. He redefined 'politics' so that he, not the politicians, was the most truly political member of the community. 'I am one of the few Athenians – not to say the only one – who undertake the real political craft and practice of politics', he declared (according to Plato in the *Gorgias*).

Socrates made some important interventions in the conventionally-defined political life of the city. One such moment happened after an Athenian naval victory towards the end of the war. The Athenians won the battle (at Arginusae in 406 BC), but afterwards twenty-five ships were wrecked in a storm. The ten generals in charge of the expedition failed to recover the bodies of the dead or rescue the wounded. The knowledge that the bodies of all those Athenians were lying without honour in the sea was horrible for a society that placed enormous importance on the proper burial of the dead (as evidenced by, for example, Sophocles' *Antigone*).

When the survivors returned, it was proposed that the ten generals responsible should be executed en masse, and that they should not be allowed to defend themselves individually. This was illegal under Athenian law, which required that anybody charged with a capital offence should have an individual hearing. It was also – of course – unjust, regardless of the guilt or innocence of the prisoners. The right of prisoners to a proper hearing has been a key tenet of almost all democratic or semi-democratic governments in western history (only recently violated, in America, in the case of the Guantánamo Bay prisoners). This happened to be the one moment in Socrates' life in which he was sitting on the council. He spoke out against the arrangement, and continued to vote against it, even when all the other members of his tribe, which then held the chairmanship, were swayed by the general will.

Again, during the rule of the Thirty Tyrants in 404 BC, Socrates showed considerable personal courage in refusing to submit to political authority. A member of the militia tried to make Socrates bring a man called Leon of Salamis to them to be killed. The Thirty would then have succeeded in killing off one prominent citizen, Leon, and making another, Socrates himself, accessory to his murder. But Socrates refused. He would not do something he believed to be wrong simply because a government leader or an authoritative political group told him to do it. This is the clearest case in Socrates' biography of civil disobedience: he refused to obey the injunction of a ruling government because he knew it was wrong.

We might, however, want to criticise Socrates for not doing more – in fact, for not doing anything. He did not taint his own hands in Leon's murder. But he also did nothing to stop it, either by warning Leon, or by confronting the Thirty directly. Socrates' sense of his own integrity was probably more important to him than any issues of social justice.

Socrates believed that we each owe our final allegiance to the gods and the truth. These matter much more than any merely human authority. He claimed, according to Plato's *Apology*, that he valued his duty to obey 'the god' over his ties to his fellow citizens, declaring, 'Men of Athens, I respect you and I love you, but I will obey the god rather than you, and as long as I live and breathe, I will never stop doing philosophy, not even if I were to die many times over' (Plato, *Apology* 29d). The will of the god trumps any merely human power. These lines lie behind many later reinventions of the dying Socrates as a proponent of freedom of conscience and freedom of speech.

But Plato's *Crito* presents a Socrates who is strikingly different from the speaker of the *Apology*. He is far less agnostic about the proper course of action for himself or others, and far more willing to identify his own interests with those of the city.

The *Crito* is an account of a conversation in prison

between Socrates and an old friend, Crito, two days before the execution. In this text, Socrates seems like the answer to a riddle about how to die deliberately, but not by one's own hand. The philosopher submits to death, longs for it, lives for it and dies entirely on his own terms, and yet does not commit suicide.

Socrates' death was delayed for some weeks after the sentence had been passed, because the trial happened at the time of a religious festival, when no public executions could be carried out. The delay is significant in that it gave Socrates enough time to escape from prison. Crito comes to Socrates with a promise of help. He has gathered money from some foreign friends of Socrates. Crito himself has friends in Thessaly who can offer Socrates protection. There is no need for him to await his sentence. But he chooses to be executed: the paradox is an essential element in the story.

Socrates explains his decision not to allow his friends to ferry him to safety by emphasising his duty to obey the city's laws – regardless of whether they are just or unjust. In contrast to the *Apology*, Socrates is now a figure who insists on conformity with the will of the city, even when the city makes a mistake.

Crito offers several inducements to Socrates to leave, some of which are extremely compelling. Crito admits that he is concerned for his own reputation: he worries about what 'the many' will say if they learn that he could have saved his beloved friend from death and did not do it. But he also argues that Socrates himself will behave wrongly if he submits to death. After all, he has a wife and young children, who will be left destitute if he dies. Crito argues on principle: 'Either one ought not to have children at all, or one should stay with them, and bring them up, and educate them.'

2. In this moving lost painting, by an unknown follower of Caravaggio from the early seventeenth century, we see Xanthippe and her sons leaving Socrates in prison, preparing to philosophise and drink the poison in the company of his male friends. He has already got rid of the leg fetters, which lie on the ground between husband and wife. One of the touchingly fat-legged toddlers reaches longingly back to his father, who does not notice him. Socrates' pose here must have been an influence on David.

Socrates pays little heed to his parental duties. Instead, he attacks those who pay attention to the opinions of society. He insists that death is not to be feared by the person dying. But it is hard not to feel that Socrates has missed the most important point in what Crito was saying. He does not discuss his children's fear of their father's death. Instead, he redirects the whole conversation, and begins to ventriloquise the Laws of Athens, who will challenge him if he should attempt to escape from prison once he has been condemned to death by the court. They will say, 'What are you doing, Socrates?

Are you attempting anything other than the destruction of us, the Laws, and the entire state, in so far as you can do so?' Socrates turns from the family as the primary locus of responsibility, to the abstraction of the laws.

In the *Apology*, Socrates had insisted on the duty of all adult human beings to think for themselves, deferring only to the gods. But Socrates in the *Crito* suggests that he must conform to the city's decisions, whether they are just or not. Children and slaves, the Laws suggest, are property, and all citizens are like children or slaves before the law. This analogy provides an implicit answer to Crito's question about Socrates' own living children. The Laws imply that he owes no more responsibility to provide for his sons than he does for his sandals, cloak, or any other item of property.

Scholars call the conflict between the apparent conformism of the end of the *Crito*, and the gadfly Socrates of the *Apology*, 'The *Apology–Crito* Problem'. There are various ways to try to resolve the contradiction. Some insist that the situation in the *Apology* is quite different from that of the *Crito*. When Socrates says to the jury in the *Apology*, 'I will obey the god rather than you', he need not be talking about actual civil disobedience. One could believe that opposition to unjust laws is sometimes justifiable, without believing that it is right to escape from a punishment imposed by a legitimate jury in a democratic city-state. No society can function if every law can be broken.

But this kind of approach is ultimately unconvincing because the voice of the Laws is so vehement and unrestrained. No distinction is made between yielding to a sentence and obeying a law. The possibility of an unjust law is never discussed by the Laws. Their metaphors suggest that the rule of law is absolute: a slave must obey his or her master, whether or not the master's commands are fair.

A more convincing approach is to remember that the *Crito* includes three quite distinct voices: the voice of Crito, the voice of Socrates and the ventriloquised voice of the Laws. The text juxtaposes three incompatible points of view: the responsibility of human beings to one another, represented by Crito; the responsibility of philosophers to truth, justice and the unknown will of the gods, represented by Socrates; and the responsibility of underlings to their superiors and of citizens to the state, represented by the Laws.

But the *Apology* cannot – in my opinion – be fully reconciled with the views expressed in the *Crito*. In each of these texts, but in strikingly different ways, Plato uses the scene of the death of Socrates to provoke hard questions about how to make good choices in an unjust world.

SOCRATES' STRANGENESS

In historical terms, the trial of Socrates remains puzzling. Plenty of people, in this period of political upheaval, could have been considered guilty of anti-democratic sentiment – whether or not this perception was true. Why, then, was it Socrates who drank the hemlock?

One possible answer is that it just happened to be Socrates: it could have been anyone. He was killed *pour encourager les autres*. Perhaps Socrates was chosen because he was one of the oldest and most famous of the sophists. He was a convenient figurehead for all kinds of free-thinking, standing in for a whole set of current cultural anxieties and fears about the coming generations, and a sense of disruption in the old ways.

In Plato's account, Socrates himself believes he is a typical, exemplary human being. When the oracle of Apollo at Delphi declared that nobody was wiser than Socrates, the man decided, 'He is not referring literally to Socrates, but has merely taken my name as an example, as if he would say to us, "The wisest of you men is he who has realised, like Socrates, that in respect of wisdom he is really worthless"' (Plato, *Apology* 23b). Socrates denied that he was anything special. If we all could recognise our own ignorance, then the world would be full of Socrateses.

The notion of Socrates as a typical man, and of the death of Socrates as merely representative of universal mortality, survived into Aristotelian logic. Here is Aristotle's famous syllogism:

All men are mortal.
Socrates is a man.
Therefore Socrates is mortal.

Socrates died, according to this simple deduction, because he was a human being. Dying is universal, not distinctive.

But some people – and Socrates was one of them – seem to make death their own, and invest the universal with the stamp of the particular. Socrates' own personality plays a great part in the stories told about his death.

At his trial – as all contemporaries agreed – Socrates showed extraordinary haughtiness in his way of talking to the jury. He was initially found guilty by a fairly small majority: 280 voted against him out of 500 (or possibly 501). It is worth noting that the votes were very close; as Socrates remarked, 'If only thirty votes had changed sides, I should have got off' (Plato, *Apology* 36a). After the conviction there was a second round of voting to determine the penalty. This was normal procedure under Athenian law.

We are also told – by a fairly unreliable late source, Diogenes Laertius – that a *larger* number of people voted for the death penalty than had initially voted to find him guilty. This suggests that certain jurors who had thought Socrates innocent of the charges then voted to have him executed.

Diogenes' claim is extraordinary, and may be based on a misunderstanding. But it seems at least possible that it is true. After all, the jury's voting pattern seems to fit well with accounts of how contemporaries responded to Socrates. They were struck – and impressed or alienated – as much by his style of conversation, his strange behaviour and the odd look in his eyes as by any particular philosophical or political belief.

If, then, Diogenes is to be believed, Socrates was not put to death as a direct result of the actual crimes with which he had been charged – impiety and corruption – nor even for his political beliefs, which can hardly have altered between the time of conviction and the passing of the sentence. Rather, he was executed for his manner. It is certainly true that he infuriated his contemporaries, and carried on behaving in a supercilious and enraging way even under the threat of death.

When given the option of proposing what sentence he believed he deserved, Plato tells us that Socrates conceded that he would be willing to pay a fine: his rich friends could put up the money. But before this concession, he claimed that if he were to get the reward he really deserved, he should get free meals for life in the city dining hall – a privilege reserved for foreign dignitaries and the most celebrated citizens, such as victorious Olympic athletes. If Socrates really said this, the jury would certainly have been shocked. The

3. *Socrates was known for his snub nose, his bald head, his goggly eyes, and his thick lips. His notorious ugliness belied the beauty of his soul.*

city did not subsidise education. Nor did it pay to support those who wanted to spend all their time discussing philosophy. Socrates' impenitent smugness may have influenced the final vote that he should drink the hemlock.

Socrates' behaviour – always peculiar, often arrogant or aggressive or underhand – enraged enormous numbers of those with whom he came into contact in the course of his long life. Part of the irritation can be tied to his 'philosophy' in a loose sense. As we have seen, he adopted a method of philosophical practice that was guaranteed to upset a large number of people. Socrates spent his life proving to his contemporaries that none of them knew anything about anything, and doling out moral advice. He criticised many of the city's most prominent people, claiming that nobody in Athens – not poets, not politicians, not craftsmen – was really wise in any important way. This must have hurt the pride of a city that boasted of its wisdom. It is hardly surprising that he made rather a lot of personal enemies.

Before we turn to the specific people with whom Socrates associated, we should consider why he seemed so strange and so extraordinary in his own time – not in his philosophical beliefs, but in his appearance, his way of speaking and his way of life. Socrates was not good-looking. As many ancient sources tell us, he was bald, fat and snub-nosed – a far cry from classical and neo-classical ideals of beauty. He had big, wide-set, goggly eyes.

To modern viewers, Socrates' supposed ugliness may make him seem cuddly and more approachable than most philosophers. Like Shakespeare's Falstaff, whom Harold Bloom calls 'the first human being in literature', he was a highly individualised, convivial old fellow. The Hostess' moving account of Falstaff's death (in Shakespeare's *Henry V*, II. 3) seems to recall that of Socrates in the *Phaedo* – although Falstaff is no philosopher, and dies babbling of green fields and calling for more sack. Falstaff's limbs, like those of Socrates, grow gradually more and more numb, until 'all was as cold as any stone'. In both cases, the pathos of the death scene is all the greater, since these two old men have been so vigorous, and so youthful up to the very end.

Socrates had something childlike about him. Aristophanes and Plato tell us of his fat belly, fearless gaze, disarming simplicity and waddling walk – all babyish or toddler-like characteristics. His expression was beguiling in its apparent lack of guile.

To the beauty-loving Athenians, however, Socrates was known for his ugliness. The master's appearance was a challenge for Socrates' ancient admirers. How could such an unattractive person have such a beautiful soul? The Greek word *kalos* means both 'beautiful', 'noble' and 'good'. It was a paradox for Plato and Xenophon to find Socrates *kalos* in a moral sense but far from *kalos* in his looks.

Socrates was often said to look like a satyr. Satyrs, in Greek mythology, were creatures like men, but with snub noses, bald heads, furry tails and permanent, huge erections. They were associated with Dionysus, god of wine and excess, and enjoyed sex, getting drunk and playing silly tricks on people. But Socrates, despite his appearance, was known for his self-restraint. According to Plato, he could go a long time without food or sleep, but could also drink more than anyone while staying sober. Xenophon, whose version of Socrates is importantly different from Plato's (as we will see in more detail in the next chapter), gives an alternative explanation for why Socrates never seemed to get drunk: it was because he never drank too much.

Palmistry experts say that the left hand is the hand we were born with; the right is what we make of it. Similarly, according to one ancient story, Socrates' face represents what he was born with; his soul is what he made of it. The sharp distinction between the two, in the case of Socrates, represents the power of good self-discipline. A physiognomist asked him, 'How is it that you look so much like a satyr and yet are so temperate?' Socrates explained that the face reveals only the nature we were born with, not the nature we make for ourselves. Born with greater natural lusts than anyone, he has trained himself to desire only the good.

Plato draws a rather different lesson from the ugliness of Socrates. Socrates is like certain statues of the satyr leader, Silenus, which are made so that they open up to reveal gods inside. Similarly, Socrates has a beautiful soul inside an ugly face and body. His appearance does not fit his true nature. It shows the conflict between false appearances and true reality.

Xenophon's interpretation of Socrates' appearance is different again. For him, Socrates' supposed ugliness shows that conventional ideals of beauty are wrong-headed. The 'beauty myths' of classical Athenian culture have created a false disjunction between attractiveness and practical usefulness. Socrates tells a pretty young boy, 'My eyes are more beautiful than yours, because yours only look straight ahead, whereas mine bulge out and can look to the sides as well' (Xenophon, *Symposium* 5.1–10). Socrates' broad snub nose allows him to sniff scents from all around, whereas elegant straight noses can only smell what is directly below them. Thick lips are more useful for kissing. A broad mouth can gobble up more food. All this is only partly a joke. Xenophon's Socrates is urging us to realise that if we find him ugly, perhaps it is our eyes, or our cultural preconceptions about beauty, that are to blame.

Both Plato and Xenophon hint at the major reason Socrates' strange appearance bothered people so much. He seemed to treat his apparent inferiority (his ugliness) as a form of superiority. Socrates' ugliness seemed to work as a living criticism of ordinary ways of seeing. This implication is explicit in Aristophanes' *Clouds*, which satirises Socrates for looking funny as well as for his philosophical beliefs. The Chorus of Clouds greet their friend Socrates with a detailed description of his appearance:

You waddle in the streets and cast your eyes
   sideways,
and go barefoot, enduring a great deal of suffering,
   but put on
a hoity-toity expression because of us Clouds.

                                      (362–3)

The reference here to Socrates' 'hoity-toity' expression goes
to the heart of the difficulty the Athenians had with his
appearance. His strangeness seemed to present itself as a
criticism of the values of ordinary people.

Some aspects of Socrates' physical appearance, such as his
snub nose, could hardly be considered his fault – although,
as we have seen, an ancient physiognomist might treat the
configuration of a person's features as a sign of his character. But many aspects of Socrates' strange looks were clearly
the result of strange attitudes about what matters in life. For
example, he deliberately dressed poorly, wearing a single
cloak both summer and winter. He went for long periods
without eating or drinking or sleeping: when struck by a
problem, he could happily stay up all night to work it out.
He could bear extremes of hot and cold, without complaint
or even seeming to notice anything wrong. Socrates' asceticism was seen by his friends and followers as a sign of his
willpower, and recognition that money and material comforts do not matter. But to many of his contemporaries, it
smacked of showing off.

Socrates' manner of speaking was, like his manner of
dress, deliberately 'poor' or demotic. He was famous for his
analogies between philosophy and the activities of common
tradesmen – shoemakers, potters or doctors.

As we have seen, Socrates' poverty was not a mere matter

of necessity. It was a deliberate and conscious position, assumed by a man who could have made himself enormously rich. Other sophists earned huge sums by their teaching.

Socrates is said to have been the son of Sophroniscus, a sculptor, and Phaenarete, a midwife. He was not an aristocrat, or rich by birth. Socrates himself, we are told, began life in his father's profession and carved the draped figures of the Graces on the Acropolis. But in later life he certainly had no day job. He seemed to be always at leisure, always willing and able to conduct conversations lasting all day and long into the night. Since he did not charge fees for his teaching, he must have survived on gifts and tips from his rich friends – of whom he had many. In Plato's account of Socrates' trial, the master is willing to accept money from Plato himself and other friends, which he can offer to pay as a fine. The sum involved is fairly substantial: thirty *minae* was equivalent to roughly a year's work for a day labourer. This amount was six times Socrates' whole wealth.

Refusing on principle to earn a regular income may seem morally admirable if you see materialism as a moral failing. But from another perspective, it may seem simply fraudulent to make much of poverty, if you always have rich friends to help out when things get tough. There must have been many low-income Athenians who had no connections in high places, and who would have seen Socrates' deliberate assumption of poverty as Marie Antoinette-ish.

Plato's account (in his *Symposium*) of Socrates' behaviour in the army hints at what many fellow Athenians must have felt about him. In freezing conditions, in which all the other soldiers were bundling themselves up in their warmest clothes, 'This man [Socrates] went out wearing his regular kind of cloak, and even barefoot he walked on the ice more easily than everybody else with their boots on. So the soldiers looked at him with suspicion, thinking that he was looking down on them' (*Symposium* 220b). The passage makes clear that Socrates' gaze – his way of looking at people – implied contempt for many people, and made them, in turn, look back at him with frowning mistrust.

Socrates' asceticism had political implications as well. Aristophanes mocked the followers of Socrates for displaying their hollow cheeks and dishevelled clothes: 'All men went crazy for Sparta: it was considered honourable to grow your hair long and to go hungry, and people gave up washing – like Socrates' (*Birds* 1280–83). In refusing material comforts, Socrates seemed to be echoing the aesthetic of Athens' great enemy, who were also known for their deliberate assumption of poverty. Socrates was Spartan in his hardiness, his arrogant false modesty and his asceticism. Only one thing made him different from the Spartans in his behaviour: his conversation, which was hardly laconic.

Socrates was an Athenian who behaved like a foreigner. Indeed, his whole life's work as a philosopher could be seen not merely as undemocratic, but as fundamentally un-Athenian. Unlike almost all the other sophists and teachers of rhetoric in the city, Socrates was an Athenian, by birth, citizenship and inclination. He looked at his fellow citizens with a gaze that mirrored, but subverted, their own.

Most of the sophists were foreigners from other Greek cities. One prominent teacher of rhetoric, Gorgias, came from Leontinoi in Sicily; Protagoras, a moral philosopher, came from Abdera in Thrace; Anaxagoras was from Clazomenae in Asia Minor; another famous sophist, Hippias, was from Elis in the western Peloponnesus. None of these figures was a citizen of Athens. The norm, then, was that foreigners taught rich Athenians to ask hard questions about physics, rhetoric, religion or politics. The sophists often emphasised their own rootlessness. Gorgias boasted that he 'had no fixed dwelling in any city', as Diogenes Laertius tells us. Another of the sophists, Aristippus, commented on his own situation: 'I am a stranger everywhere.' The sophists were cosmopolitans – citizens of the world.

Athens was beginning to be accustomed to the idea of foreign intellectuals who could contribute to the life of the city by educating the young and stimulating new ideas. If a foreigner questioned the values of the city, he was merely doing what foreigners do. But for an Athenian insider such as Socrates to take on this role must have posed a quite different kind of threat. An Athenian who undermined Athenian values was a traitor to the beliefs of his forefathers.

Socrates appropriated the role and language of foreign outsiders, despite his own position as an Athenian citizen. It is telling from this perspective that in Plato's *Apology* Socrates asks the jury to excuse his ignorance of the rules of rhetoric, just as they would excuse him if he really were a foreigner:

> The fact is that this is the first time I have come before the court, even though I am seventy years old. I am therefore an utter foreigner as far as courtroom speaking goes. So now I make what I think is a fair request of you: disregard my manner of speaking. Pardon me if I speak in that manner in which I have been raised, just as you would if I really were a foreigner. (*Apology* 17d–18a)

The plea makes a complex rhetorical gesture. Socrates claims to be a foreigner in his own city, even to the extent of not speaking the Attic dialect. But even at this moment, he draws attention to his mastery of Athenian oratory – beginning with the clichéd rhetorical trope, 'Unaccustomed as I am to public speaking ...'

Like later public intellectuals, Socrates was both an insider and an outsider in his own society. Perhaps it was for this threat to Athenian civic identity, as much as anything else, that the jury decided to put him to death.

DANGEROUS ENEMIES, DANGEROUS FRIENDS

Socrates spent his whole life in a city that was, even by modern standards, large. In the whole state of Athens, including the countryside that surrounded the centre (and was included in the 'city-state' or *polis*), there were probably about 250,000 people. The number of free-born males who counted as citizens was far smaller – perhaps only about 12 per cent of the total population.

Socrates seems to have been well known to everybody in this bustling community – citizen and non-citizen alike. He was a celebrity, familiar from his reputation, his image and his notorious sayings. But he was also personally acquainted with a vast number of his contemporaries. Aristophanes parodies Socrates and his followers in no fewer than four plays. We should remember that, in an age without television, a joke about Socrates' appearance would hardly be funny for somebody who had not seen him in the flesh. Many Athenians – including those who sat on the jury that condemned him to death – must have seen the living man walking and talking in the marketplace. Many must have had conversations with him. Socrates loved talking, and talked to as many different people as he could. The

Athenians did not have to rely on Aristophanes to form their opinion of Socrates.

At the time of his death, Socrates had never left his home town, apart from his three military expeditions. He rarely travelled even as far as the Athenian port of Piraeus, or to the Athenian countryside. 'I am a lover of learning', he told a friend on a rare trip to the country. 'Trees and open country won't teach me anything, whereas men in the city do' (Plato, *Phaedrus* 230d). The crowded *agora* – the marketplace, which was the hub of the city – was Socrates' life-blood.

In nineteenth-century terms, he was a *flâneur* rather than an academic in an ivory tower. As Xenophon tells us, 'Socrates spent his whole life in the open air. In the early morning he used to go to the public arcades and gymnasiums; around lunch-time he was to be seen in the market; and for the rest of the day, he always used to go wherever there was the greatest crowd of people' (Xenophon, *Memorabilia* 1.10). His students came from all walks of society. Socrates talked to boys, generals, poets, farmers, metics, slaves – even, occasionally, women.

Socrates' death, then, cannot be fully understood without an account of his personal relationships. He may have been killed for his beliefs. But he was also killed because of the people he knew.

Under Athenian law, prosecutions were always brought by individual citizens. There was no such thing as a trial brought by the city – unlike in the US or the UK, where the prosecution is often 'The People' or 'The Crown'. It was a system in which personal grievances might matter a great deal. Socrates had three prosecutors: the main instigator of the trial, Meletus, and two companions, Lycon and Anytus. The three represented three different professions that had cause to hate Socrates: the poets, the politicians and the artisans. These were all groups whose traditional claims to wisdom the philosopher had questioned. It seems likely that all three prosecutors also had private reasons for bearing a grudge against him.

We know little about the main prosecutor, Meletus. He was young and Socrates had never met him before the trial. Plato comments on his dishevelled appearance: he had long hair, a hook nose and a straggly beard. There is a certain amount of confusion about the man's identity, because several other people in fifth-century Athens were also called Meletus – including the prosecutor's father, a poet who wrote drinking songs and plays. It is possible that Socrates had been rude to him. In Plato's account of the trial, Socrates describes how he cross-examined the poets – in front of a crowd of bystanders – and proved that they had no understanding of the meaning of their own best work. It would be unsurprising if a poet who had suffered this treatment felt a little upset, especially if such a public humiliation damaged the market for his work. Perhaps, then, Meletus junior prosecuted Socrates to avenge his father.

We know a little more about Lycon, a politician who vehemently defended democracy. Lycon may have simply condemned Socrates for his political beliefs. But it is quite likely that he had personal reasons for the prosecution too. Socrates knew both Lycon and his son, a body-builder called Autolycus. Autolycus was murdered by the Thirty Tyrants. As we have seen, Socrates made a partial stand against the Thirty on at least one occasion. But he may well have been associated with the overthrowing of democracy. In this way, Lycon might have held Socrates partially responsible for his son's death.

In the case of Meletus and Lycon, the evidence is scanty. With the third prosecutor, Anytus, we are on firmer ground. Anytus was an enthusiastic defender of democracy, but also had personal reasons to hate Socrates. Xenophon tells us in some detail about his grudge. Anytus was employed in a tannery. Socrates warned Anytus not to confine his son's education to leather working and predicted that the son would not continue in the father's trade. Without a good supervisor, he said, the boy would go to the bad. Anytus was understandably bitter about Socrates' intervention.

There may have been any number of similar grudges against Socrates held by members of the jury. Most of his contemporaries would not have agreed with his view that criticism was a kind of social service. Socrates was quite capable of being offensive, abrasive and aggressive.

Socrates' popularity among his own followers may well have contributed to the hostility of those outside the group. Cult leaders, even leaders of a secular cult, threaten the integrity of a society. People may have feared that Socrates' disciples were loyal to Socrates before the city of Athens.

Those outside the circle may have known little about Socrates' beliefs. But they knew who was in and who was out, and Socrates' associates did not bring him credit. His circle included Phaedo, who may have been a foreign aristocrat by birth, but had been captured in war and was working as a prostitute when Socrates asked a rich friend to secure his release; and a woman called Aspasia, the mistress of Pericles, who was commonly, albeit unjustly, said to run a brothel. We are told that she taught Socrates rhetoric and matchmaking. Socrates was associated, then, with rich, morally corrupt toffs as well as with concubines and slaves.

One of Socrates' closest friends was a man called

Chaerophon. It was he who consulted the Delphic oracle about Socrates' wisdom, and whom Aristophanes presents as the deputy leader of Socrates' philosophical school, the Thinkery. He was mocked as creepy, dirty and faddish by the comic poets. Aristophanes compares him to a bat.

Socrates was said to have taught the avant-garde playwright Euripides. Although it is probably untrue that Euripides actually studied with Socrates, people certainly perceived a connection between them. Socrates was imagined to be at the root of all the social and intellectual changes of the latter decades of the century. In his comedy the *Frogs*, composed five years before Socrates' death, Aristophanes associated both Socrates and Euripides with the new-fangled rejection of true expertise, in favour of mere blabbermouthing and rhetoric:

> It isn't stylish to sit
> beside Socrates and blabber away,
> discarding artistry
> and ignoring the most important things
> about the tragedian's art.
> To spend one's time fecklessly
> on pretentious talk
> and nit-picking humbug
> is to act like a lunatic.
>
> (*Clouds* 1491–9 translation by Jeffrey Henderson)

In the fantasy of the play, the old-fashioned dramatist Aeschylus beats Euripides in a contest of words, and his victory signals defeat for Socrates as well as for Euripides. Those crazy intellectuals may be smart, the *Frogs* suggests, but they are not what a country needs in wartime.

Aristophanes' conservative views must have been echoed by many of those who enjoyed his plays.

In some circles, Socrates' reputation as a moral teacher must have been reasonably good. A tantalising quotation from the orator, Lysias, expresses surprise that his opponent in a court case, Aeschines of Sphettos, was behaving dishonourably, despite having been taught by Socrates. Lysias comments, 'I thought that as he had been a pupil of Socrates, and talked so much impressive talk about justice and virtue, he would not have attempted or ventured upon conduct characteristic of the worst, most dishonest people.'

But we do not have the whole speech from which this line comes, and the evidence of this fragment could go either way. Lysias might be expressing genuine surprise, or ironically suggesting that in fact, the followers of Socrates are usually, like Aeschines, all talk and no trousers.

The real test of any moral teacher is how well his students behave, and how beneficial their actions are for the whole community. By this criterion, Socrates failed miserably. His two most famous pupils, Critias and Alcibiades, each in different ways did enormous harm to the city of Athens. Polycrates, in his posthumous *Prosecution of Socrates*, cited the connections with Alcibiades and Critias as conclusive proof that Socrates' teaching had harmed the democratic city.

Critias was the uncle of Plato, a rich and well-born man, probably only about ten years younger than Socrates. Details of his earlier career are scanty, although we know that he committed a crime of some kind and was exiled to Thessaly in the latter years of the war. He returned to Athens in 404 BC and was one of the five leaders who incited the people to bring down democracy. He became a prominent member of the Thirty Tyrants, eager to kill as many of his fellow citizens as he could.

Socrates' link with Critias might alone be enough to explain his prosecution in a city which was still recovering from the abuses and assassinations suffered under the rule of the militia. We have one important piece of evidence that near-contemporaries believed Socrates was killed simply because of his acquaintance with Critias. The orator Aeschines (to be distinguished from Aeschines of Sphettos, the Socratic), in a speech written about fifty years after the trial of Socrates (*Against Timarchus*), asked the jury, 'Did you, O men of Athens, execute Socrates the sophist because he was shown to have been the teacher of Critias, one of the Thirty who put down the democracy …?' Aeschines clearly expected the obvious reply to his rhetorical question to be 'Yes: Socrates was killed for teaching Critias'. Contemporary fourth century Athens should, Aeschines suggests, follow the Socratic example and kill another anti-democratic sophist – Aeschines' enemy, Demosthenes.

Socrates probably fell out with Critias after his return to Athens. Critias was infatuated with a young man called Euthydemus and kept pressing himself on him, even when Euthydemus tried to say no. Socrates said, 'Critias seems to have the feelings of a pig: he can no more keep away from Euthydemus than pigs can help rubbing themselves on stones' (Xenophon, *Memorabilia* 1.2.27–40).

Critias retaliated by trying to create legislation to shut Socrates up. He devised a law forbidding people to teach 'the art of words' and explained that Socrates ought not to talk to anybody under the age of thirty – an absurd provision, as Socrates himself pointed out, since it would prevent him buying a loaf of bread in the market if the baker happened to be under age. Critias failed to devise a law to silence Socrates; he could be silenced only by death. Critias himself was killed by the returning democrats in 403 BC.

It is paradoxical that Socrates should have been blamed for teaching a man who, by the end of his life, hated him so much. One possible explanation is that the enmity between Socrates and Critias has been exaggerated by our pro-Socratic sources. Perhaps the story of the quarrel was made up by Xenophon. But we need not suppose so. It is quite possible that Critias was, in the 430s and 420s, a prominent member of the Socratic circle, but fell out with him in later life. Outsiders to the Socratic circle might very well not have known that Critias and Socrates had quarrelled, especially as Socrates remained on intimate terms with other members of Critias' family. At the time Socrates was prosecuted, several younger relations of Critias were certainly committed students of the philosopher – including his nephew, Plato. There must have been those who feared that, if Socrates was not stopped, he might foster a whole new generation of Critiases.

Socrates' relationship with Alcibiades was more intimate than his relationship with Critias, and if anything, it was even more damaging to his reputation. Alcibiades was a wealthy aristocrat, known as the most beautiful boy of his generation. He was a party person, a heavy drinker and an enormous flirt – in both his personal and his political relationships. He was clearly an extraordinarily charismatic man who inspired desire and admiration in all those who saw him. He was a brilliant leader who made every soldier in his command worship him. He was also an extremely clever military strategist. The Athenian public had a love-hate relationship with Alcibiades: he was condemned but

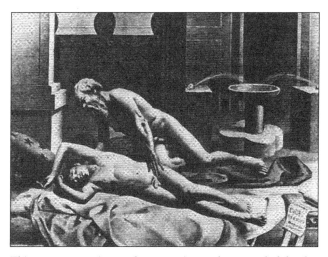

4. This anonymous nineteenth-century image shows a naked, but lusty, old Socrates reaching towards the genitals of the young Alcibiades, who lies back, passive and perhaps half-asleep. According to Plato's account, the relationship really worked the other way around: Alcibiades tried to pursue Socrates, but Socrates refused to go all the way.

then recalled by the city no fewer than three times over. Repeatedly, the Athenians decided that Alcibiades had at last gone too far – only to demand his return when the war took another turn for the worse.

In the course of his brief but intense career, the unreliable Alcibiades served Sparta and Persia as well as Athens. In 415 BC he was involved in the profanation of the Mysteries and perhaps also in the mutilation of the herms. He was absent at the time and managed to escape a formal trial: instead, he defected to the Spartan side. He was assassinated in 404 BC, perhaps by the Spartans, who knew that while Alcibiades was alive the Athenians would always long for him back.

Socrates was a friend and teacher of Alcibiades in his youth. They were also, in some sense, lovers. In fifth-century

Athens a romance between a beautiful male teenager and a paunchy middle-aged philosophy teacher would not necessarily have seemed sordid. Nor would the sexual association, in itself, necessarily have damaged the later careers of either party. It was normal for older men to court and have sex with boys in their late teens, until the age when the beard was fully sprouted. In a society where women were almost entirely uneducated, man–boy relationships offered the opportunity for a greater meeting of minds than was possible within most marriages. The custom was considered good for the boy as well as for the man, since an intelligent lover could teach him how a gentleman ought to behave. A fairly clear set of social conventions surrounded the practice of relationships between boys and men ('paederasty'). An older male slave acted as a chaperon for a well-bred boy, to ward off any unwanted admirers. There was normally a sharp distinction between the lover, who did all the running, and the beloved, who accepted his attentions.

Socrates, like most Athenians, probably had a series of affairs with teenage boys – including one who would later become a well-known tragic poet, Agathon. But his most notorious conquest by far was the young Alcibiades.

Plato assures us that, despite all appearances, Alcibiades and Socrates were not lovers in a full physical sense. They were, rather, the primary instance of that famous ideal of chastity: Platonic love. Plato's account (in his *Symposium*), suggests that the relationship contradicted all the norms of Athenian sexual practice. Alcibiades, the beautiful boy, pursued the older man, Socrates, not the other way around. And even when Alcibiades had manoeuvred Socrates into spending the whole night cuddled up with him, and even when he offered himself to him in the most explicit terms possible, Socrates still refused to go all the way. Alcibiades complained, 'By all the gods and goddesses, it was extraordinary! When I got up in the morning, I had "slept" with Socrates, but in no more eventful way than if I had been sleeping with my father or an older brother.'

Plato implies that Socrates did not object to snuggling under the same cloak as the object of his affections. In the *Symposium*, he carefully engineers things so that he can sit next to Agathon on the sofa. He obviously enjoyed the company of pretty boys and was pleased to offer special private tutorials. But he refused, on principle, to go all the way.

Interesting though it is to contemplate the physical details of Socrates' relationship with Alcibiades, the topic is probably irrelevant for determining the historical causes of Socrates' death. To most contemporary observers, the relationship would surely have looked like any other intense love affair. Socrates had long conversations with Alcibiades, instructing him in moral virtue. They wrestled together in the public gymnasium, naked (as was the Athenian norm) and often at a distance from the other athletes – so there were plenty of opportunities. Alcibiades gradually began to meet Socrates without his chaperon.

The intimacy of the relationship deepened when Socrates and Alcibiades went on campaign together to Potidaea, sharing a number of hardships. Socrates saved Alcibiades' life in an act of extraordinary courage, though Alcibiades himself ended up being awarded the decoration for bravery, because it was thought more fitting that it should go to an aristocrat. Socrates and Alcibiades seem to have remained friends on a fairly flirtatious basis, even after Alcibiades was a grown man and ready to acquire boyfriends of his own.

There is no evidence of a falling-out between student and teacher, as in the case of Critias.

His associations with Alcibiades and Critias may have been the single most important cause of the charge that Socrates corrupted the young. Moreover, Alcibiades' profanation of the Mysteries may well have influenced the charge that Socrates failed to respect the gods of the city. The young Alcibiades had been the locus for many Athenian hopes – which were all devastatingly shattered. The Athenians were unwilling to blame Alcibiades himself for his defections to the enemy, or his failure to secure victory for his city. Easier to blame his teacher and, supposedly, lover who failed to put him on the path to virtue. If Critias and his henchmen had never seized control of Athens, then Socrates would surely not have been brought to trial. If Alcibiades had remained in supreme command of the army throughout the final years of the war, and if he had – miraculously – managed to engineer victory for Athens, then it is possible that Socrates would have died comfortably in his bed.

3

PLATO AND OTHERS: WHO CREATED THE DEATH OF SOCRATES?

THE SOCRATIC PROBLEM

We have seen that Socrates may have been killed partly because of the people he knew: his enemies, acquaintances, students, lovers and friends. But the followers of Socrates also influenced his death in a different sense: by transforming a historical event into a literary legend.

So far, I have relied most heavily on a single contemporary source: Plato. The works of Plato provide by far the most vivid, philosophically interesting, detailed, entertaining and influential contemporary accounts of Socrates' life and death. Plato presents Socrates as an extraordinary character who is both hilariously funny and deeply serious, who seems more charming, more irritating and cleverer than anybody you ever met.

Plato was a pupil of Socrates the historical figure. But he is also the creator of 'Socrates', in his best-known literary manifestation. The French theorist Jacques Derrida once wrote a series of meditations or quasi-novel, *The Post Card*, inspired by a medieval image of Plato and Socrates. This strikingly represents Plato hovering behind Socrates, teaching him to write or dictating to him – not the other way around. Plato is, paradoxically, Socrates' teacher, because it makes sense to

5. In this medieval illustration, a small, fish-faced Plato hovers behind his larger-than-life teacher, Socrates. Plato seems to be telling Socrates what to write. In real life, Socrates probably wrote nothing.

think of 'Socrates' – as we know or imagine him – as Plato's creation.

It is notoriously difficult to be sure of anything much about the historical Socrates, beyond the fact that he was a real person who really was executed in 399 BC. The details of his teaching, his philosophical beliefs, his politics, his social circle, his character and his death are represented in strikingly different ways by our various contemporary sources. It may well be the case that none of the philosophical beliefs I have ascribed to 'Socrates' – on the basis of Plato's dialogues – was in fact held by the historical Socrates. Perhaps Socrates had no fully developed philosophy; perhaps he was just a man who liked asking questions. The difficulty – perhaps impossibility – of reconstructing the historical Socrates is dubbed by scholars 'the Socratic Problem'.

Socrates' words, like his living face, will always be lost to us. Socrates became, even within his own lifetime and still more after his death, a 'mythic' figure, like Odysseus or Achilles. Each writer about Socrates created their own version of the character.

Most Socratic writings of the fourth century do not survive. Some of them, like Aristophanes' mockery in Socrates' own lifetime, were attacks. We know that Polycrates wrote a *Prosecution of Socrates* (393 BC), denouncing him as an enemy of democracy. Polycrates might well have felt concerned that the unpatriotic criminal Socrates would be made into a martyr by his friends – which was indeed what happened. We know too of a fourth-century biography, by one Aristoxenus of Tarentum, that seems to have presented the great man in a sensationalist but unflattering light. He was an impressive speaker, but 'uneducated, ignorant and licentious', and madly passionate about whores and other people's wives. This lust-crazed Socrates is impossible to reconcile with the temperate hero evoked by Xenophon and Plato.

Socrates' followers were probably provoked by such attacks into defending the great man. Each of them seems to have presented his teacher in a different way and to have used him to explore his own philosophical interests. One devoted follower, Antisthenes – who may have been a boyfriend of Socrates – was interested in the master's asceticism and his indifference to wealth. Antisthenes became the founder of the Cynic ('dog-like') sect of philosophy, whose adherents masturbated and scratched themselves in public, like dogs, and lived on scraps of food. The Cynics modelled their own scorn for material possessions on the poverty and temperance of Socrates.

Another student, the sophist Aristippus, was inspired by Socrates to invent hedonism – the idea that the only good thing in life is pleasure. He envied Socrates' painless death, commenting, 'I myself would like to die as Socrates died.' Yet another student, Aeschines of Sphettos, described Socrates as a serious moral teacher, whose homilies on virtue were addressed to the sexually promiscuous people of his time – including Alcibiades and Pericles' mistress, Aspasia. For Aeschines, Socrates' main concern was to persuade people to be more self-restrained in their appetites for sex and power.

The heart of the Socratic Problem, then, is not our lack of sources. If we had more Socratic writings, we might find it even more difficult to reconstruct the historical figure of Socrates.

Many of these texts – including those that survive by Plato and Xenophon – took the form of Socratic dialogues, a new and revolutionary genre which would have an enormous influence on later literature. They were imaginary or partly imaginary conversations, featuring Socrates talking to a range of different people. The characters and settings are 'real' in the sense that they are based on people and places that existed. They are 'realistic' in the sense that they evoke conversations that could have taken place. But they were never intended simply to record Socrates' actual conversations. Rather, they were an enormously flexible instrument to express widely differing ethical and philosophical beliefs. Socratic dialogues anticipated and influenced the development of two genres that had not yet been invented: biography and the novel. Plato's own student Aristotle could find no obvious literary category in which to put the Socratic dialogue; the closest parallel, he thought, was dramatic mime – a theatrical genre.

Phaedo – the slave-boy who features as narrator in Plato's eponymous dialogue – was himself the author of Socratic dialogues. It is from Phaedo that we get the story of Socrates' encounter with the physiognomist, Zophyrus (who was surprised that Socrates' character did not match his face); and Phaedo probably invented the idea of Socrates' conversations with Simon the Shoemaker (who is the forefather of the game, 'Simon Says').

Other Socratic authors included Eucleides of Megara, who wrote at least six dialogues, probably focusing on the idea that the virtues are all the same.

The most prominent writer of Socratic dialogues in the immediate aftermath of Socrates' death was probably Antisthenes – a teacher and relatively senior follower, who was present at the drinking of the hemlock, and whose Socratic writings emphasised the goal of self-sufficiency. He was famously hostile to all pleasure, especially sexual pleasure. 'I would rather go mad than have fun', Antisthenes claimed.

It must have been annoying for the earlier Socratics to see the young upstart, Plato, setting himself up as the real heir to the Socratic tradition. Antisthenes retaliated by writing a satirical dialogue called the *Sathon* – a word which rhymes with Plato's name (*Platon*), but means 'Willy' or 'Prick'.

The enormous imaginative dominance of Plato over the western tradition has made it difficult to think of Socrates except through the eyes of Plato, who created the Socratic character that has been of most interest to later readers – especially, as we shall see, in the past 300 years or so.

But before turning back to Plato, we should remember the one other Socratic writer whose work survives in full: Plato's contemporary Xenophon.

XENOPHON'S SOCRATES

Xenophon was, like Plato, a young follower of Socrates at the time of the latter's death. He was an Athenian from a fairly wealthy, established family. He wrote several books featuring Socrates, including extensive *Memoirs of Socrates*, a comic description of Socrates at a drinking party (*Symposium*) and a short account of Socrates' defence speech at his trial (*Apology*). Xenophon's Socrates is – in sharp contrast to the character created by Plato – not a gadfly. He is a harmless wise man with a fairly conventional, vaguely ascetic mindset. He offers sound advice about diet, exercise, money and family relationships. No topic is too banal for him to discuss. Xenophon's Socrates teaches his followers that one should not eat too much; exercise is important; you earn money by hard work; children should honour their parents. None of these precepts can be much of a surprise to any reader, but we may be glad to be reminded of our duty.

Xenophon himself did not always follow his master's advice. He consulted Socrates when he was considering joining an expedition to Persia as a mercenary soldier. Socrates recommended that he ask the Delphic oracle whether he should go. But Xenophon, who was raring to make the trip, instead asked the oracle *how* he should best go – a clever but evasive move, which annoyed his teacher.

The social milieu evoked by Xenophon is significantly different from that of Plato's dialogues. As we will see, Plato's Socrates subsumes politics, war and the family into the world of male philosophical conversation. Xenophon, by contrast, shows us a Socrates who is interested in giving political, domestic and strategic advice to a wide range of people. He offers advice on dating, for example, gleaned from Aspasia, and he is happy to help couples with their marital difficulties.

Xenophon describes Socrates' own marriage as challenging. Socrates was married to Xanthippe, and they had three sons, Lamprocles, Sophroniscus and Menexenos. Two of these were still little children at the time of his death. According to Xenophon, when the oldest boy, Lamprocles, was angry with his mother, Socrates gave him a good solid lecture about the importance of being respectful and grateful to one's elders. A follower of Socrates, Antisthenes (the Cynic who wrote his own Socratic dialogues), asks him why he puts up with such a truculent wife; why does he not train her into submission? Socrates explains that he chose a high-spirited wife in order to teach himself to deal with people who behave in excitable, uncontrolled ways, just as an ambitious rider would feel unchallenged by too docile a horse.

'If I can put up with her,' he says, 'I shall find it easy to get along with any other human being.'

Apart from Xanthippe, most of the people to whom Socrates talks are very glad of his recommendations and often treat them as great revelations. He suggests to an aristocrat whose household is starving that everybody might be better off if the women worked to earn money for food. The aristocrat is amazed, follows the advice and everyone is happier. Similarly, Xenophon's Socrates offers this profound tip to a man who is worried about making a long journey: 'Don't you know that if you put together the walks you take in five or six days, you can easily cover the distance from Athens to Olympia?' It is good advice, but it is not clear that only the wisest man in Greece could have thought it up. You can imagine Xenophon's version of Socrates running a series of motivational seminars on self-improvement and empowerment through abstinence.

The ordinariness of his hero leaves Xenophon with an obvious problem. How could such an inoffensive man have been put to death by the Athenian state?

Xenophon's political views provided him with an answer. He was a great admirer of the ascetic way of life practised by Athens' great enemies the Spartans. He served the Spartan king after 394 BC, was banished from Athens and wrote a treatise about the Spartan constitution. Xenophon emphasises Socrates' asceticism: Socrates is admirable because he seems to live a Spartan lifestyle, even in Athens. Xenophon's Socrates comments that hunger is the best sauce. His pleasure in shopping is the opposite of most people's. It is anti-retail therapy. When he sees gold and silver in the market, he exclaims with delight, 'How many things I don't need!' Xenophon's love for Socrates can also be connected to his misgivings about Athenian democracy. For Xenophon, the death of Socrates shows the folly and moral decadence of the Athenians.

He combats directly the claim of 'the accuser', Polycrates, that Athens was right to put Socrates to death because of his associations with Alcibiades and Critias. In fact, Xenophon remarks, both these characters were perfectly good as long as they were under their teacher's influence. They were corrupted by later, worse company. Alcibiades was too popular for his own good: 'Just as athletes who gain an easy victory at the Games often neglect their training, so Alcibiades neglected himself.' Xenophon sees Socrates more as a moral trainer than as a teacher. Teachers, one might think, should be able to influence their pupils even *in absentia*; trainers are more hands-on.

Xenophon suggests that, from the Athenian point of view, killing Socrates was a crazy mistake. From Socrates' own perspective, however, death at this precise moment and in this way was the best thing that could have happened to him. When his most emotional friend, Apollodorus, wails, 'But Socrates, what I find hardest to bear is that I see you dying unjustly!' Socrates replies, 'Dear Apollodorus, would you rather see me put to death justly?' He reproaches those who weep for his death: 'Are you only now starting to cry? Do you not realise that I have been condemned to death by Nature from the moment I was born?'

Socrates is willing to die, in Xenophon's version of events, because he has lived a good life, because he is constantly improving himself and because he is conscious of his own virtue. By dying he can exchange the worst part of his life for glory and achieve the most desirable possible death. This is a very over-motivated death. Socrates explains his pleasure in dying at this precise moment with a striking mixture of down-to-earth foresight and self-satisfaction:

> I am enormously pleased with myself, and I know my friends feel the same way, because I know that my whole life has been spent behaving piously and justly. But now, if my life were prolonged, I know that I would have to experience the frailties of age: my eyesight would deteriorate, my hearing would grow weaker, I would become slower to learn and more forgetful of what I have learned. If I see myself becoming worse and feel bad about myself, how can life be enjoyable for me any more? (Xenophon, *Apology* 5–6)

Better to leave a party early enough to be missed rather than waiting until you have made a fool of yourself. Socrates' death, for Xenophon, illustrates his favourite virtue: self-control. You can have too much of a good thing, even of life.

Xenophon's Socrates is, then, a completely different character from that of Plato. For much of the twentieth century, Xenophon's Socratic writings were either neglected entirely or treated as pale shadows of the Platonic ideal. It has often been claimed that Xenophon must be an inferior source for the historical Socrates, because the uninspiring old bore he describes could hardly have attracted the attention of so many bright young men. But in plenty of periods before the twentieth century, Xenophon's Socrates was better known than Plato's. Xenophon's Socrates was an alternative kind of hero, offering a bourgeois, common-sensical ideal, to set against the paradoxes of Plato's philosopher.

As we will see in the final chapter of this book, the twenty-first century seems to have seen a return to a Xenophontic vision of Socrates. Our culture is making a move back to banality, away from the terrifying challenges of Plato.

PLATO AND SOCRATES

Socrates is Plato's central character, the heart of his literary and philosophical achievement. And it was the death of Socrates, in particular, that provoked Plato into writing philosophy.

'Philosophy begins with wonder', says Aristotle. Perhaps Aristotle was led to philosophy that way. But Platonic philosophy – itself the foundation for all later western philosophy, including that of Aristotle himself – begins with grief. Plato was present at Socrates' trial. He was at the time a rich, well-connected young man, originally called Aristocles. He was an aspiring tragic and lyric poet, and a talented wrestler, nicknamed Plato ('Butch', or 'Broad-shouldered') for his skill in the gymnasium. He had probably not written a word of philosophy before his teacher's death.

Plato wanted to find answers to the questions that Socrates – in life and in death – had raised and left unanswered. If democratic Athens could execute the man who was 'the bravest, the wisest and the most just of any in our times', then Plato needed to imagine a new social system in which the philosophers were – as in his *Republic* – not social outcasts but kings. The dying Socrates was not only Plato's mentor, but his subject, and ultimately his creation. Plato's Socrates is the first novelistic character in literature. Plato, founder of western metaphysics and western political thought, was also the originator, through Socrates, of modern western literature.

I use the word 'novelistic' in order to emphasise that the Socrates of the dialogues cannot be identical with the historical Socrates. We know that there are several philosophical positions that Plato ascribes to Socrates, but that the historical Socrates did not hold. Aristotle assures us that Socrates did not invent the Theory of Forms, which became a central concept in Platonic ontology. Socrates was interested in evaluative concepts, such as 'good', 'brave' and 'holy'. But he probably had no general theory about how they came into being. Plato supplied the theory. In the field of human psychology also, Plato's Socrates departs from the teaching of the historical master. The Socrates of Plato's *Republic* argues that people do bad things because their reason is overwhelmed by desire – not because of ignorance.

Scholars have often hoped to use Aristotle's hints to winnow out the pure Socratic grain from the chaff of Plato's work. The enterprise proved particularly tempting in the twentieth century, when – as we shall see in the final chapter of this book – Plato's own politics seemed suspect. The genial, chatty, humane Socrates could be identified as the true founder of western culture, and rescued from the distortions of that horrid old communist-fascist-totalitarian, Plato.

The search for the historical Socrates in Plato's work usually relies on a speculative account of Plato's literary development. When Plato began writing – so the story goes – he was entirely under the influence of Socrates and, in his 'Early' dialogues, Plato's Socrates expresses only the views held by the historical Socrates, and does not mention the Theory of Forms. A few years later, Plato began to develop his own ideas, and mixed these up with those of Socrates: in the 'Middle' dialogues, like the *Republic*, Socrates is beginning to become a mouthpiece for Plato himself. And by the time of the 'Late' dialogues, such as the *Laws*, Plato had all but forgotten about the historical Socrates.

The story is tempting, and it might even be true, but we should notice some important ways in which its methodology is problematic.

The dating of Plato's dialogues is difficult. We often do not have external evidence for which texts are 'early' and which are 'late'. We can make groupings that have stylistic similarities, but we cannot prove that all the dialogues that seem similar must have been written at the same time: generic considerations might have influenced style. In these circumstances, scholars may be tempted into a circular argument: we know that Dialogue Y is early because it represents the ideas of the historical Socrates; we know the ideas of the historical Socrates because we get them in Dialogue Y.

The testimony of Aristotle may well be unreliable; we know that he often gives innaccurate reports of the views of other philosophers. Moreover, even if we believe Aristotle, we have no evidence whatsoever for the idea that Plato only gradually developed the Theory of Forms and his other complex philosophical ideas – beyond the evidence of the dialogues themselves (which is inconclusive) and the presupposition that philosophers always take a long time to invent their big theories (which is, of course, untrue).

Whatever we think about the chronology of Plato's dialogues, it is clear that none of them gives us unmediated access to the historical Socrates. More likely, Plato invented the character of 'Socrates' in a new way in every dialogue he wrote.

Plato's Socrates is extraordinary for many reasons, but

not least for his attitudes towards his own death. He is able – perhaps more than any character in literature, before or since – to take control of death, to own it, and to tell the whole story of his own life, including its end.

Four Platonic works in particular evoke the last days of Socrates' life. The *Euthyphro* is set outside the courthouse as Socrates awaits his sentence and is supposedly a transcription of a conversation between Socrates and Euthyphro. The *Apology* is a version of Socrates' defence speech to the jury at the time of his trial. The *Crito* is set in prison, two days before Socrates' execution. The *Phaedo* is an account of the master's final hours.

These four texts were almost certainly not written at the same time. But read together, they give us an intense impression, plotted almost day by day, of the last weeks of the philosopher's life. Each takes the death of Socrates as an event that raises pressing questions about how we should live and die – which we may still find difficult or impossible to answer. What counts as a truly good, truly wise man? Can such a person teach goodness and wisdom to others? Should we decide what to do by deferring to tradition or by thinking for ourselves? Can we know anything about death before we die? How can we weigh up our conflicting responsibilities to family, friends, religion, work, conscience and ourselves? The central underlying question which haunts all these texts, is whether bad things can happen to good people.

Each dialogue focuses on a different moment in the narrative, offering a distinct vision of the meanings of Socrates' death. The *Euthyphro* suggests that Socrates' condemnation on the charge of impiety is caused by a fundamental misunderstanding of the true nature of holiness. The case of Socrates is an opportunity to examine and question traditional ideas about religion and morality. The text suggests that this process of examination may itself be more truly 'pious' than an unthinking acceptance of any code of behaviour.

The *Apology* is concerned less with religion than with politics and society. It shows us Socrates the gadfly and offers a plea for dissent as part of a healthy political community. It is also a celebration of the quest for truth, even at the cost of death, and even if truth can never be discovered by any living human being.

The *Crito* shows us a different Socrates again – an ecstatic, inspired figure, closer now to death, who has seen a vision of his own end coming to him as a woman dressed in white, and who is bombarded by the invisible voices of the Laws. Socrates' decision to die becomes, in this dialogue, an opportunity for Plato to re-examine the proper limits on human autonomy.

In the *Phaedo*, the meaning of Socrates' death changes again. It is now the supreme example through which to explain and analyse the old, almost stereotypical idea that a good man will not be afraid to die. Plato shows us a Socrates who seems calm, even joyful, at the prospect of death. He proves, both by argument and by example, that death can hold no terror for the true philosopher.

THE DENIAL OF DEATH

We are told that in his youth, Plato composed a tragedy that he destroyed after meeting Socrates. In fifth-century Athens, tragedies were always performed in groups of four – three serious plays, followed by a jollier one called a satyr play. Plato wrote a new kind of tragic tetralogy, in prose, in his account of the death of Socrates. After the struggles of the courtroom and the prison, the text that deals with the master's last hours, the *Phaedo*, is both serious and oddly cheerful.

The text is framed as a second-hand report of Socrates' last day in prison, as described to an absent friend by somebody who was present – Phaedo. The narrative form itself allows Plato to put a kind of bracket around the death of Socrates. We can hear him now only through eavesdropping on other people's conversations: his words come to us from beyond the grave.

The paradox that the philosopher spends his life in preparation for death, and yet may not kill himself, is central to Plato's account of these last hours. Socrates explains that the philosopher will not take his own life: we are the property of the gods and therefore it is forbidden to leave life until they call us away. But the wise man will desire death and will die joyfully, treating death as a great benefit. Socrates devotes most of his final hours trying to prove that his joy is reasonable, because he knows that the soul is immortal and that a good man's soul will be happy after death.

The *Phaedo* offers us a picture of an ideal death. Socrates dies with courage, in complete control, calmly, surrounded by his friends. Death, he shows us, is the wise man's friend. Death is also, we discover, fundamentally unreal: it is only the gateway to the soul's immortal life. The philosopher becomes more and more himself as he approaches liberation from the body. The text represents this death as painless and even pleasurable, a journey away from the burdens of the material world.

The *Phaedo*'s insistence that death can be understood and tamed by means of reason stands in sharp contrast with the end of the *Apology*, where Socrates reminds us that death may be only the final instance of the incommensurability of human and divine knowledge. Plato now presents us with a philosopher whose rational, ethical consciousness always masters his physical and emotional responses. He is not the slave of ordinary desires for food or drink or sex, for honour, love, companionship or even life. The death of Socrates represents total control over the body, the passions and mortality.

The bulk of the dialogue is devoted to a conversation with two Pythagorean friends, Cebes and Simmias. They are convinced by Socrates' claims that the soul is far more valuable than the body and that the wise man dies with equanimity. But they ask for further proofs of the immortality of the soul.

Socrates responds with a series of four arguments, which I will summarise only very briefly.

In the 'cyclical argument', he claims that opposites are always produced one from the other. Sleeping comes from waking, heat comes from cold, the weaker from the stronger, the living from the dead. The dead must continue to exist, because they are reborn as new living souls. We should notice that this is an argument not for the eternal happiness of the good person's soul, but for a constant process of reincarnation – which was a central tenet of Pythagoreanism.

The 'argument from recollection' suggests that our souls must have existed before our births, because certain kinds of knowledge seem to be attained not by learning but by a kind of remembrance. This argument brings in Plato's Theory of Forms: Socrates claims that we can have access to the Forms of the Good and the Beautiful (as opposed to mere instances of goodness and beauty) only because we have known them in our soul's former life.

In the 'affinity argument' Socrates proposes that the soul has more affinity with the immortal, immaterial forms than with the mortal things of this world.

Before the fourth and final argument, Cebes and Simmias raise certain objections to what has been said so far. Simmias points out that there are plenty of things that are immaterial but not immortal: he cites the harmony created when a person plays the lyre. The strings outlast the tune. Cebes in turn points out that even if the soul is stronger and longer-lasting than the body, this does not prove that it is immortal. A man is stronger and longer-lasting than each successive item of clothing he wears and wears out. But his last cloak will outlive him.

Socrates replies with a final argument that again makes use of the Theory of Forms. The soul is the cause of life and can therefore never admit its opposite, death.

It is striking that this set of four arguments includes many of the most influential tenets of Platonism, including the assumptions that the body is less good, less strong and less long-lasting than the soul and the forms, and that the soul is a person's true essence. Plato sets his own philosophical system in the middle of the story of Socrates' death. The *Phaedo* seems to dramatise the idea that the master's death makes way for Platonic philosophy.

But one could also argue that Socrates' death seems to undermine Platonic logic. All four arguments offered by 'Socrates' for the soul's immortality are riddled with logical errors and false premises.

Plato may well have realised that he had not entirely proved his point. Within the fiction of the dialogue, Socrates almost acknowledges that death may remain something of a mystery. He repeatedly hints at a fifth argument, from divine providence or purpose. Socrates criticises scientific or materialistic kinds of explanation and mocks the idea that he could explain why he is in prison by saying, 'because my body is composed of bones and sinews'. The real reasons for his death, he declares, are

> that the Athenians decided to condemn me, and I decided to sit here, thinking it right to stay and undergo whatever punishment they award me; because – by the Dog! – I reckon these sinews and bones of mine would have been somewhere near Megara or Boetia a long time ago, carried off there by the belief that it was the best option - if I didn't think it more just and honourable to submit to any penalty ordained by my country, rather than deserting and running away (*Phaedo* 98e-99a).

Proper explanations must appeal to purpose, not material cause. By analogy, he hints that there must be a 'reason' why we all die, one that has to do not with the destruction of our bodies, but with the divine purpose for which we exist, and the decisions of noble minds.

Finally, bad arguments are followed by good myth. Socrates describes a rich, fantastical landscape of a gem-encrusted upper world, into which the soul is released after death. Even myth fails when he tries to describe the fate of philosophers: 'All who have sufficiently purified themselves by philosophy live without bodies for the rest of time, and come to dwellings still more beautiful than these, which it is not easy to describe, nor do we have time to do so' (*Phaedo* 114c).

The *Phaedo* suggests, then, that the living may not ever get complete access to the world of the dead. Perhaps logic can never fully illuminate the experience of dying. And even story-telling may not be able to show us what it is like to be dead. Socrates gestures towards what may lie beyond death. But he can do no more. The text itself ends when the master is silent.

We might view these arguments less as logical proofs than as magic charms made of words – like the charms intended, as Cebes suggests, to persuade 'the child who lives inside us all' that he need not fear the 'hobgoblin' of death. The philosopher wears logic as an amulet around his neck, which allows him to die like a man, not weeping like a child for his own lost life.

THE LAST SCENE

The final pages of the *Phaedo* evoke, in vivid detail, the last hours of Socrates. Plato creates a sharp distinction between Socrates' death as he himself experiences it, and the scene as it appears to the spectators: the friends of Socrates and the reader. It is a scene that seems to be radically different depending on your point of view. For Socrates' family and friends, his death is tragic; but for Socrates himself, it is the site of calm, joyful triumph.

Socrates, from his own perspective, is not a tragic hero: rather, he resembles Euripides' Alcestis, a woman who triumphed over death, sacrificing herself to save her cowardly husband – in a drama which was performed in place of a satyr play. But there is a sharp contrast between the characters, in that Alcestis acts for the sake of her family. Socrates, on the other hand, seems willing to cause pain to his followers by embracing death and denying them even the opportunity to express their grief in social ritual. He takes upon himself all the parts in the drama: he even lays out his own corpse. The other characters are left with only powerless tears.

'You go to live, and I to die; which is better, the god alone knows', says Socrates at the end of the *Apology* (42a). But in the *Phaedo* it seems fairly clear that Socrates has seized the best thing for himself. Like a swan, he sings with joy at the time of his death, knowing by grace of Apollo, god of prophecy, that he goes to eternal happiness (*Phaedo* 84d–85b).

On Socrates' first appearance in the *Phaedo*, he is sitting with his wife and young son in the prison. When the male friends enter the room, Xanthippe begins to weep and wail:

> When she saw us, she let out a shriek and said all the kinds of things which women usually say on such occasions: 'O Socrates, this is the last time that your friends will see you, and you them.'
>
> Socrates turned to Crito. 'Crito,' he said, 'let somebody take her home.'
>
> Some of Crito's people took her away, howling and beating her breast. (*Phaedo*, 60a)

Socrates makes no further comment. He begins chattering about pleasure, pain and the sensation in his legs, now that the fetters have been taken off. It is clear that Xanthippe is a metaphorical fetter, or 'ball and chain', whom the philosopher has at last got rid of.

This is a shocking moment, made emphatic by its position at the start of the dialogue: these are the first words Socrates speaks in the *Phaedo*. Xanthippe offers a gesture of sympathy as well as of loss. She does not speak of her own grief or her son's bereavement. Rather, she tries to enter Socrates' own mental world, expressing the loss he must feel at departing from his male friends, and their grief for him. Socrates utterly rejects her attempt to engage with him. He offers no reply and does not even say goodbye. He makes no mention of the little boy. We later learn, in a parenthesis, that his sons and womenfolk are brought to him again, for a brief visit before he takes the hemlock.

In Greek society, the work of mourning – marked not by wearing black but by cutting off the hair and performing ritual acts of wailing – was particularly associated with women. In the *Phaedo*, Socrates denies the value of such work. He robs the survivors of their desire for funeral rites. One of the most moving moments in the dialogue comes in the middle of the argument about the soul's superiority and immortality. We are suddenly reminded of the existence of Socrates' living body, which will soon be dead. Phaedo, who worked in a brothel before joining Socrates' circle, must have been a beautiful young boy at the time of Socrates' death. It is, we remember, Phaedo who tells the whole story. Faced with the objections of Simmias and Cebes to his proofs for immortality, Socrates reaches down to fondle Phaedo's hair.

> He stroked my head and gathered up the hair on the nape of my neck in his hand – he was in the habit of playing with my hair sometimes – and said, 'Tomorrow, Phaedo, maybe you will cut off this lovely hair'. 'I suppose so, Socrates,' Phaedo replies. 'Not if you take my advice,' says Socrates. 'You should cut it off today, and I will cut my own hair too, if our argument dies and we cannot bring it back to life.' (*Phaedo* 89b–89c)

Socrates urges Phaedo to trust the power of argument and conversation – *logos* – to discover the truth. The death of Socrates matters less than the truth of his words. If we mourn, we must mourn not our dead friends, but abstractions.

When the sun sinks low, Socrates withdraws to take a bath: 'because I think it is better to bathe before drinking the poison, so that the women will not have to bother to wash my corpse' (115a). He thus appropriates for himself all the tasks traditionally assigned to the surviving family. Death, which had been an event to be experienced and shared by the whole community, becomes now utterly solitary. Socrates regards himself as the only person affected by his death.

The end of the dialogue reminds us that grief and the desire for a funeral are not exclusively feminine preserves. Crito tries to glean from Socrates some instructions about how he would like to be buried. Socrates teases him for thinking that this question could possibly matter: after all, it is not Socrates who will be interred, but only his body. What foolishness, then, to say at a funeral, 'I am burying Socrates.' 'Such words,' says Socrates, 'bring evil to the soul' (115e); they imply, falsely, that the body is the person – not the soul. Instead, Crito must say only that he buries 'the corpse of Socrates' – and do so however he sees fit.

When Socrates takes the cup of hemlock, he refuses to make any clear distinction between this drink and any other beverage. Death is what he has practised all his life. Here is what happens when executioner brings him the cup:

He took it, and very gently, without trembling or chang-ing either his colour or expression, looking up at the man with his usual wide eyes, he said, 'What do you say about pouring a libation to some god from this cup? May I, or not?'

'Socrates,' he said, 'we only prepare as much as we think is enough to drink.'

'I see,' said Socrates. 'But I suppose I may and must at

least pray to the gods, that my journey from here be fortunate. So I do pray this, and may my prayer be granted.' With these words he lifted the cup and very cheerfully and quietly drank it down. (*Phaedo* 117b–c)

Socrates' request to pour a libation from the hemlock cup shows his adherence to traditional religious practices. But it also shows his playfulness, even in the last hour. Usually, a libation is poured from a drink of wine, not poison. People share their best things with the gods. Socrates' request mocks the traditional understanding of death as something bad.

Plato's account of the last hours is intensely moving and again makes a sharp contrast between two different perspectives. On the one hand, there is Socrates, cheerfully setting out on a new journey, a prayer on his lips and a cup in his hands. On the other hand, there are the spectators to the event, who cannot help responding with grief:

And up to that moment most of us had been able to restrain our tears fairly well, but when we saw him drinking, and saw that he had drunk, we could no longer do so, and in spite of myself my tears rolled down in floods, so that I wrapped my face in my cloak and wept – for myself. I was not weeping for him, but for my own loss, deprived of such a friend. Crito had got up and gone away even before I did, because he could not restrain his tears. But Apollodorus, who had been weeping all the time before, then wailed aloud in his grief and made us all break down, except Socrates himself. But he said, 'What are you doing, you strange men! I sent the women away mostly for this very reason, to prevent them from behaving in this excessive way.

For I have heard that it is best to die in holy silence. Keep quiet, and be brave.'

Then we were ashamed and controlled our tears.

(*Phaedo* 117c–e)

Death may mean liberation for Socrates, but it forces on his friends a rigid self-control. In one way, Socrates' death is a slow transition, hardly noticeable at all: he goes gradually numb, without ever ceasing to be himself. But it is also a cause of wild grief to the friends, which must be suppressed if they are to retain their masculine identity. As readers, we are put into the position of the disciples: struggling, and probably failing, to control our emotions.

THE GENDER OF SOCRATES: THE LAST WORDS

Plato puts enormous emphasis on the absence of the women from the scene of Socrates' death. Socrates excludes them because he fears they may spoil the dignity of the moment with their wailing: 'I have heard that it is best to die in holy silence.' This suggests that Socrates hopes not merely to exclude women, but to exclude 'femininity'. He will die in the most absolutely 'masculine' manner.

But as we have already seen, the result of keeping out the women is that Socrates himself must take on many of the tasks that would, traditionally, fall to them at the scene of a death. He bathes his own soon-to-be-dead body and lays out his own body as if for burial. He assures Crito that no trouble need be taken over his funeral, since all mourning rites give the false impression that death is a bad thing. Socrates has appropriated to himself, and so made redundant, one of the major traditional roles for women – the care of the dead.

In the final pages of the *Phaedo*, Socrates also takes on himself – and undermines – the other major social role afforded to women in ancient Athens: childbirth. We read of how a big-bellied figure walks around the room, watched by anxious friends. Plato describes in precise physical detail the progress of the poison. The climax comes when the numbness reaches the lower belly. In a medical description of childbirth, by this point the head of the baby would be engaged, ready to descend to the birth canal. In this narrative, once the chill reaches the area around his groin, Socrates delivers eleven famous last words (in the Greek original): 'Crito, we owe a cock to Asclepius. Pay it, and do not forget.'

A great deal of rhetorical weight is put on the last words. But interpreters have had considerable difficulty making any sense out of them. Crito is clearly unsatisfied with the cock to Asclepius as Socrates' final utterance; he demands, but does not receive, 'something else'.

In citing these last words Plato adduces a final piece of evidence for Socrates' innocence of the charges for which he was dying. Far from failing to acknowledge the gods, Socrates died with the name of a god on his lips.

But the god to whom Socrates owes a debt – Asclepius – was not one of the twelve traditional Olympian gods, but a relatively recent foreign import to the Athenian pantheon. This god of medicine, whose worship involved a magic snake, had been introduced into Athens in 420 BC, only some twenty years earlier; the famously pious poet Sophocles had helped care for the snake. So perhaps the allusion to Asclepius is not a demonstration of Socrates' traditional piety, but a defiant reminder that the Athenians themselves have often introduced 'new' gods into their own pantheon.

Asclepius was the god most closely associated with

doctors, and the last words have therefore been taken to suggest that Socrates has benefited from the cure of some kind of disease. There are several different possible theories about what the disease might be.

It might be a metaphor for life itself. Socrates owes a debt to Asclepius as soon as he has drunk the hemlock, because now he has been 'cured' of the 'long disease' of life. This is the most common interpretation among modern scholars.

But the metaphor of life as disease appears nowhere in the *Phaedo*. Moreover, a similar notion is expressed by Cebes in the *Phaedo* itself: that the soul's entry in the body is 'like a disease'. Socrates adamantly attacks this idea, showing that the soul is immune from any alteration or sickness. It would, as one scholar has noted, be 'strange indeed', if in the last moments of his life, Socrates suddenly adopted a version of a view he had gone to so much trouble to refute earlier in this very text.

Alternatively, perhaps disease is a metaphor for wrong-doing. Elsewhere in Plato's work, bad behaviour is often presented as damaging to the psyche of the perpetrator, just as a disease is damaging to the body. From what wrongdoing, then, has Socrates been saved when he has drunk the hemlock? An obvious answer is that he has been saved from the temptation to evade his sentence and escape from prison – the temptation that was the subject of the *Crito*.

But the possibility of escape from prison and hemlock is hardly a live issue in the *Phaedo*, as it is in the *Crito*. The Socrates of the *Phaedo* shows no sign whatsoever of wanting to escape from prison or delay death. He hardly needs the services of a god to be saved from a sin that he was never in any real danger of committing.

A third possibility, the simplest, is to take the disease

literally. Socrates and his friends owe a debt to Asclepius because someone close to them has recovered from illness.

Only one person is mentioned as ill in the course of the *Phaedo*: Plato himself. We are told laconically, at the start of the dialogue, 'Plato, I think, was ill' (59b): this was why he could not attend the master's deathbed. This is a resonant moment, one of only three times in Plato's entire oeuvre where he names himself. There is a neat ring composition in the *Phaedo*, if it begins and ends with references to Plato's illness. On this interpretation, Socrates has somehow learned that Plato has recovered, and is urging Crito and his other friends to give thanks for it to the god. The last words would then be a claim on Plato's part for his own importance as the true successor and biographer of the great man. If Plato had died of his illness, Socrates' teachings would not have been preserved in their most glorious form.

There are, however, serious difficulties with this reading also. Socrates had no obvious way of knowing that Plato had recovered from his illness. There has been no message to that effect in the dialogue and Plato has not been mentioned since the initial report of his illness. It is true that Socrates claimed to have prophetic knowledge of his own immortality, like a swan who sings for joy before he dies; but he has not claimed to have magical access to the state of his friends' health. It seems strange that Socrates should seem suddenly to be aware of Plato's recovery only after the hemlock reaches his abdomen.

Another possible interpretation, which was current in antiquity, is to say that Socrates was delirious, under the influence of the hemlock. The last words are a pathetic sign that the man who used to be the wisest in Greece is now losing his mind: he babbles about snake gods and roosters, having no clear idea what he is saying. On this interpretation, it seems likely that these really were Socrates' last words; perhaps Plato himself could not understand what they meant.

But in a text as carefully wrought as the *Phaedo*, it is implausible that Plato would have given so much weight to words that he considered incomprehensible or nonsensical. Since all the usual interpretations are flawed in important ways, I propose a different reading, one that has not to my knowledge been suggested before.

Recovery from sickness was not the only reason to invoke Asclepius, the patron god of doctors. Women, at least in the wealthier classes, were almost always attended by male doctors in childbirth. Although Artemis, the virgin hunter goddess, was traditionally the deity who presided over women in labour, we have evidence that women who sacrificed to Asclepius almost always did so in gratitude for his help with fertility and obstetrical issues. It is fitting that Socrates, whose own gender becomes so ambiguous in this text, should call on a male god who had himself taken on some of the role of a traditional female deity.

Socrates gives thanks to Asclepius, I would argue, because he has succeeded – metaphorically – in giving birth to his own death. Life is not a disease, death is not a cure. Rather, dying is like childbirth and death is like being reborn. This reading fits the metaphorical scheme of the dialogue much better than the idea that life is like a disease. Socrates has argued that death and life 'are born' from one another: the whole argument for immortality from opposites is framed in the language of birth and generation.

The *Phaedo* is closely paralleled by another Platonic dialogue: the *Symposium* is set at a drinking-party, while the *Phaedo* is set around Socrates' final drink. Near the end of the

Symposium, Socrates' teacher, Diotima, makes an explicit comparison between the generation of children from the body and the generation of truth from the soul. Elsewhere, too, Plato's Socrates compares himself to a midwife who helps bring to birth the ideas of other people without giving birth himself (*Theatetus*, 148e–151d). In the *Phaedo*, it is as if Socrates the midwife has finally managed to become fertile: he has given birth to his own truth, his own soul and his own death.

One count against this interpretation is its originality. Perhaps the reason that nobody before me has read Socrates' death as a kind of childbirth is because the idea is far-fetched. But it is also possible that this interpretation has never been considered before because most of Plato's readers have been men. There have been, as we shall see, an enormous number of different responses to the dying Socrates in the course of the 2,400 years that divide us from Plato. But almost all these responses assume that the ideal death must be, in some essential way, masculine.

Socrates hardly obeys his own injunction to his friends: 'Keep quiet!' He does not shout, but he cannot stop talking, even in death. His chattering is, one might think, just like a woman. But Socrates' self-control, his calmness, his rationality, his physical courage: all are usually understood as male, not female, attributes. Plato makes the dying Socrates both masculine and feminine; he takes on himself all the powers of a woman, as well as the powers of a man. Later writers have to work hard to claim Socrates' death as an entirely masculine ideal. It is worthwhile pointing to the gender ambiguities in Plato's account of Socrates' death, because the idea that truth is a woman, and that the lovers of truth, 'philosophers', must be men, continues to haunt our own culture – even when we hope to deny the relevance of gender altogether.

4

'A GREEK CHATTERBOX': THE DEATH OF SOCRATES IN THE ROMAN EMPIRE

The Romans had serious doubts about whether the dying Socrates could be a moral example for their own culture. In the middle of the second century BC, one prominent Roman statesman called Socrates 'a big chatterbox who tried to make himself the tyrant of his country, to dissolve its customs, and to entice its citizens into forming opinions contrary to law and order' (Plutarch, *Life of Cato*). The speaker, Cato the Censor (also known as Cato the Elder), was a prominent defender of good old Roman values who felt that the state needed to be defended against all foreign influences – especially Greek philosophers like Socrates.

Romans viewed the dying Socrates within a matrix of specifically Roman cultural preoccupations. The most important of these were political commitment, violence, masculinity, theatricality, and the relationship of contemporary Roman reality to the fantasy-world of Greek literature and philosophy.

The Romans always looked back to the Greeks with a certain amount of wariness. They had no native philosophical tradition of their own and many Romans suspected that

Greek philosophy was essentially unmanly and unpatriotic. These suspicions centred on the figure of the dying Socrates. As Cato remarked, Socrates was a 'chatterbox': he died talking and he died of talking. Rome was a fiercely militaristic and macho culture in which physical violence and physical courage were of the utmost importance. Socrates' tendency to babble was hardly appropriate for any man, let alone a hero. Cato's term hints at a fear that will haunt all Roman responses to Socrates: perhaps he talked just for love of the sound of his own voice. Socrates seemed to represent the pointless prattling which was typical of foreign intellectuals, and which contrasted with real action in the battlefield or the Forum.

Cato praised Socrates for only one thing and even that became a backhanded compliment: he dealt well with his truly horrible family. 'There is nothing to admire in Socrates,' Cato remarked, 'except that he was always kind and gentle with his shrewish wife and his stupid sons.' Plato's gadfly was more threatening to Roman values than the loyal married man depicted by Xenophon.

For Cato, as for many later writers under the Roman Empire, Socrates' actual philosophical beliefs were relatively unimportant. The real issue was not whether Socrates was right – about, say, the nature of human wisdom, virtue or the soul – but whether he represented a good or a bad image of how to live and, above all, how to die. Socratic 'philosophy' and Socratic life become indistinguishable. For that reason, the scene of Socrates' death matters even for writers who are not particularly interested in the arcana of academic philosophy. The death of Socrates, by his own hand but on the orders of the state, seemed to foreshadow the Roman interest in political suicide.

On the other hand, philosophical pursuits became increasingly marginalised in Roman society. Rhetoric and military training took over from philosophy and athletics as the primary means by which young men were educated. Philosophy was no longer a central part of 'real life'. The marketplaces, baths and exercise grounds of Rome were haunted more by orators and politicians than by intellectuals discussing the good life. The dying Socrates, then, often seemed irrelevant to the issues facing real people. Those Romans who admired Socrates had to reinvent him. Since the ironic humour of Plato's Socrates seemed so suspect, Socrates' Roman followers emphasised his courage in the face of death rather than his clever talk. They concentrated on his integrity and his opposition to the 'tyranny' of the Thirty Tyrants – passing over his complex and ambivalent relationship to the democratic government that passed the death sentence upon him. Only on these terms could the Socratic death be seen as an admirable alternative to the machinations of imperial power and military violence.

Imperial Romans used the figure of the dying Socrates to think through the place of the life of the mind in an increasingly violent world, one where political and military loyalties seemed more and more important. Many writers of this period suggest that the death of Socrates might be less inspiring than a more violent and gory death, such as the death of the younger Cato.

THE IDEAL ROMAN DEATH: CATO THE YOUNGER

Romans often compared the dying Socrates with a native Roman non-philosopher: Cato the Younger, also known as Cato of Utica.

Cato was a fierce opponent of Julius Caesar's bid for one-man rule in Rome. He fought with the Republicans (Pompey the Great and Metellus Scipio) against Caesar. But Caesar won a decisive victory at the Battle of Thapsus (46 BC) and slaughtered the entire army of his enemies. There could be no more hope for a free, Republican Rome. Cato responded with apparent equanimity to the news of the defeat. He took a bath, then sat down to supper with a large group of friends. They discussed Stoic philosophy. Cato argued that the good man alone is free – speaking with such vehemence that everyone guessed his intentions. Philosophical talk already had an association, for the Romans, with philosophical death. His son had his sword confiscated from his room.

Late in the evening, Cato retired to his room and began to read the *Phaedo*. Noticing the absence of his sword, he called his servants. When the weapon was not produced, he hit them so hard that he injured his own fist. We might notice the contrast with Socrates, who always behaved kindly to slaves and servants, and who was particularly friendly with his own executioner. Finally, Cato's son appeared. The father demanded, 'Am I a madman, that nobody talks to me about my decisions, good or bad?' The boy went out, weeping. Cato persuaded his friends that it was absurd to keep him alive by force. 'When I have come to a decision, I must be master of the course which I decide to take.' It was already too late to sit around talking, as Socrates had done. The times called for more violent measures.

The friends of Cato, unlike the friends of Socrates, were unable to restrain their tears long enough for more talk about the soul. They burst into tears and left the room. Cato got his sword back and declared, 'Now I am my own master.' At

6. *To the horror of his family and friends, Cato of Utica killed himself by ripping out his own bowels, after his republican army lost to Julius Caesar. He was inspired to his courageous suicide by Socrates' death, as described in Plato's* Phaedo. *In this painting by Pierre Narcisse Guérin (1797), the scroll of the* Phaedo *is visible in the foreground.*

dawn, once he was alone, he stabbed himself. But because of his injured hand, he was unable to strike hard enough. His innards came out of his body, but he failed to die. A doctor was summoned, who sewed up the protruding bowels. As soon as Cato recovered, he pushed the doctor away, tore out the bowels with his own hands and so died.

Cato is like Socrates only in so far as he kills himself – inspired by Socrates' death in the *Phaedo*. In all other respects, his death is not merely un-Socratic but anti-Socratic. It is, for one thing, shockingly violent – in stark contrast to the painless, almost incorporeal death of Socrates in the *Phaedo*.

Moreover, Cato's death is explicitly political: he dies for his city's freedom – while Socrates was condemned by his own newly-liberated city. For many people in the time of the Roman Empire, Cato's violent, political, ultra-macho death seemed far more admirable than that of the foreign gadfly and show-off, Socrates.

BRINGING PHILOSOPHY DOWN TO EARTH: CICERO

An epigram by the learned poet and Alexandrian librarian Callimachus (third century BC) presents the imitation of Socrates' death as a whimsical, frivolous activity.

> Saying, 'Goodbye, Sun!' Cleombrotus of Ambracia
> leaped off a high wall to the Land of the Dead.
> Why? Nothing was wrong. It was only because he
>   had read
> that single text by Plato, on the soul.

This character has no reason for killing himself, other than the inspiration provided by Plato's *Phaedo*. The poem is a tribute to Plato's magnificent artistry; but it is also a comic gibe against taking Socrates' example too seriously.

The great Roman statesman, orator and prolific writer Marcus Tullius Cicero (106–43 BC) struggled with these issues as he confronted the example of the dying Socrates. Cicero himself wrote philosophy and admired Socrates as a philosophical model. He recognised that 'all philosophers think of themselves, and want others to think of them, as followers of Socrates' (*De Oratore* 3.16.60).

But Cicero was concerned about the extent to which non-philosophers should also follow Socrates. On one level,

Socrates provided a model for how philosophy could interact with the real world. He was supposedly the first philosopher to study ethics, rather than cosmology or theology: Cicero noted that Socrates 'brought down philosophy from heaven to earth' (*Tusculanian Disputations* 5.4.10). On the other hand, Socrates seemed still too distant from the realities of life in that he died for an abstraction (truth), not for a concrete political cause.

Cicero speaks against the model of Socrates' defence speech (Plato's *Apology*) for an orator. A Roman defendant called Rutilius Rufus unwisely followed Socrates' example and refused to use appeals to the emotions in his defence speech. He was innocent but, thanks to his foolish insistence on Socratic integrity, he was condemned to exile. Clearly, as an orator, Socrates was a pretty bad example. He did not get himself off (*De Oratore* 1.231).

In his philosophical work, Cicero uses Socrates' willingness to die, and even joy at his own death, to provide the ultimate proof that there is nothing to be feared after life. But Cicero withdraws from Socrates as soon as he seems to get close to him. He comments, 'However, all this is ancient history, and Greek at that. But Cato departed from life with a feeling of joy at having found a cause for dying' (*Tusculanian Disputations* 1.87). Cato's example seems to trump that of Socrates because he was a contemporary of Cicero's – not just a dead Greek. Moreover, Cato died for the Republic. Socrates' motives are far less easy to define. Socrates' life seemed a dangerous model, in so far as he challenged the ways of his city. Cicero warns, 'Let nobody make the mistake of thinking that because Socrates ... did or said anything contrary to the ways and traditions of his city, therefore he too has the right to do the same' (*De Officiis* 1.41.148).

Socrates' death seemed to Cicero rather distant from the real world. He repeatedly compared it with other, more explicitly political deaths. Cato provides one such example. Another is a statesman called Theramenes, who was put to death by Critias in the time of the Thirty Tyrants. Like Socrates, he was made to drink hemlock in prison. As he drank, he made a toast: 'To the health of beautiful Critias', he said. Cicero admires 'this noble man, who joked even with his last breath' (*Tusculanian Disputations* 1.97). Socrates drank the hemlock quietly, but he made no witticism while doing so. Theramenes, not Socrates, offers a good model for how to behave with dignity in that important Roman situation: when forced to commit suicide by a tyrant.

Cicero undermines the idea that Socrates taught us how to die by his own actions in death:

> Let me warn you against allowing any man to rival Cato in your admiration – including the man whom the oracle of Apollo apparently declared to be the wisest of the whole human race. The truth is that the memory of Socrates is honoured for the good teaching he delivered, but Cato's memory is honoured for the glorious deeds he performed. (*De Amiticia* 10)

The passage offers very backhanded praise even for Socrates as a teacher. He can only tell us what to do, not show us the way by example. Better moral teaching is offered by Cato's moral firmness. We can hear in Cicero an echo of Cato the Elder's dismissal of Socrates as a mere 'Greek chatterbox'.

Cicero's own violent death was different from either the calm, philosophical death of Socrates or the suicidal gore of the younger Cato. Cicero was vehemently opposed to

Mark Antony, who seized power after the assassination of Julius Caesar in 44 BC. Cicero's voluminous correspondence during the last two years of his life constantly echoes the central issue of Plato's *Crito*. Cicero worried about whether to remain loyal to his country and its laws, now that bad men were in power; whether it would be a betrayal of principle to escape Rome and go into safety in exile; and whether he should, like Cato or Socrates, kill himself. Cicero dithered long enough to ensure his death. He was caught by a group of assassins, who cut off his head and his hands in revenge for the speeches he had written against Antony.

Cicero achieved a kind of dignity in death, different from that of either Socrates or Cato. He died in transit, on a dusty road, a death not planned or stage-managed, but accepted bravely when it finally came. As Plutarch tells us, 'Stroking his chin, as he used to do, with his left hand, he looked steadfastly upon his murderers, his person covered with dust, his beard and hair untrimmed, and his face worn with his troubles.' Gadflies were treated more gently in the old Athenian days. Those who provoked and challenged Rome's new rulers would get no merciful hemlock.

SENECA, STOICISM AND LEARNING HOW TO DIE

For Roman philosophers, images of Socrates were filtered through third- and second-century Greek philosophy. Two Hellenistic 'schools' in particular affected Roman attitudes towards Socrates: the Cynics and the Stoics. For the Cynics, Socrates was admirable for his lack of interest in worldly possessions. For the Stoics, he represented the ideal wise man who could resist pain, political pressure and the fear of death. More than any of the other Hellenistic and Roman philosophical groups who could trace their origins back to Socrates (including Cynics, Academics, Peripatetics, Hedonists and Sceptics), Stoics emphasised the *death* of Socrates over his life and teaching. Stoics were the main intellectual heirs of Socrates' claim in the *Phaedo* that the life-long task of philosophy is learning how to die. As Epictetus remarked, 'The remembrance of the death of Socrates is more useful to the world than that of the things which he did and said when alive' (*Discourses* 4.1).

Epictetus, an influential Stoic philosopher who lived in the first and second centuries AD (*c.* AD 55–135), treated the dying Socrates as the most important model for contemporary Stoics to follow. He insisted, 'Death is not a bad thing, or else it would have seemed so to Socrates' (*Enchiridion* 5). The model of Socrates' death can make us all brave when our time comes.

A free-born slave, Epictetus was exiled from Rome by the emperor Domitian. He withdrew to northern Greece and set up a school at a safe distance from the centre of the empire. Epictetus saw Socrates as an image of how to behave under political tyranny. He returned repeatedly to the paradox that Socrates' death brought him integrity. The death of Socrates shows us how we can be free, even under oppression. 'The Socrates who resisted the tyrants and held discourses on virtue and moral beauty is preserved by dying instead of running away ...', Epictetus tells us, 'He faced the Thirty Tyrants as a free man.' This is a kind of freedom that is available to any individual but does not precipitate political change.

The Roman Stoic philosopher Seneca the Younger (AD 4–65) anticipates Epictetus in his obsession with the death of Socrates. Like Epictetus, Seneca treats death as the climactic event of Socrates' life. He declared, '*Cicuta magnum Socratem fecit*' ('It was hemlock that made Socrates great') (*Epistles* 13.14). This line suggests that Socrates would have been nothing without his death.

Because Socrates died as he did, he was transformable into a Stoic hero. But Seneca reinterprets the death of Socrates to make it suit Roman cultural expectations. He puts pain into the centre of the story. Plato's Socrates is calm and does not seem to suffer. Seneca's Socrates is a man who puts up with endless suffering, in a properly Stoic spirit. He endured poverty, a bad marriage, intractable children, toil, military service, life under tyranny, enmity and finally an indictment, prison and death. Through all this, he never indulged in excessive emotion; he was never, says Seneca, seen either unusually cheerful or unusually melancholy – 'He remained even-tempered in all the unevenness of his fortunes' (*Epistles* 104.27). Socrates' death teaches a Stoic lesson: even pain and misfortune can do us good.

Seneca insists on Socrates as the model for a philosophic life: 'If you desire a model, take Socrates.' But Seneca is also aware of some obvious dangers in the Roman rhetorical reliance on the death of Socrates and other famous deaths – including those of Cato and Theramenes. Perhaps copying other people's behaviour is not really the best way to learn to be good. The result of repeating 'inspirational' stories over and over again may be that it becomes impossible to hear them, just as one cannot look with fresh eyes at the *Mona Lisa*. Perhaps, as Cicero suspected, the example of this famous Greek philosopher was of little use in the political realities of contemporary Rome.

Seneca explicitly addresses this problem. He cites all the usual suspects who are referred to in arguments against the fear of death, including Socrates: 'Socrates conducted a philosophical discussion in prison, and when there were people who promised him escape, he refused and remained, in order to free mankind from fear of the two most terrible things, death and imprisonment' (*Epistles* 24). But then Seneca imagines that the reader may be unimpressed by the cliché: 'You say, all those anecdotes have been told over and over in all the schools; now, since the subject is despising death, you'll be telling about Cato.' Sure enough, Cato's death is next up.

But as Seneca retells the story, Cato's death is not only an example but an illustration of the need for examples. Cato required two things in order to kill himself. One was a sword; the other, a book: Plato's *Phaedo*. Without the example of Socrates ready to hand, Seneca suggests, Cato could not have performed that heroic suicide. 'In desperate circumstances he had provided himself with these two weapons: one, to make him willing to die; the other, to make him able to do so.' Without the death of Socrates, Cato could not have found the courage to die.

THREE WAYS TO IMITATE SOCRATES

The caustic Roman historian Tacitus (AD 55–120) describes a series of three forced suicides under Nero, including that of Seneca himself. Tacitus presents these deaths as three different ways in which a Roman might try to die like Socrates. But he seems to challenge Seneca's claim about the usefulness of the Socratic example. For him, the man who tries hardest to die like Socrates – Seneca himself – is also the man whose death is most tainted by self-consciousness and egotism. Posing as Socrates makes the dying Seneca absurd. Theatre becomes a substitute for true courage.

Nero ordered Seneca to commit suicide in AD 65. Plato insists that Socrates did not commit suicide. But the distinction between self-administered execution and suicide under political duress can be hard to maintain. In Tacitus' narrative (*Annals* book 4), when the philosopher receives the order he turns to his friends and tells them that only one service remains to them, the most beautiful one of all: to bear witness to the image of his life. Thereafter, Tacitus' Seneca seems concerned above all to make the image of his death resemble that of Socrates as closely as possible. Like Socrates, Seneca reproaches his friends when they express grief – though not because the soul is immortal, but because wise men should always show equanimity. He asks, 'Where were those precepts of wisdom, where was the rational attitude against disaster, which they had meditated for so many years?'

He begins to say farewell to his wife, telling her to restrain her grief. But here the Socratic model breaks down, for Seneca's wife, unlike Xanthippe, insists on committing suicide along with Seneca. She is permitted to share in his experience, though she is later rescued from death. This is one way in which the scene is a Romanised version of the death of Socrates: the Romans idealised marriage far more than the Athenians had done.

Seneca and his wife slit their arms with a single cut. But Seneca, being old and feeble as a result of his abstinent way of life, cannot let out enough blood. He slits the veins of his legs and knees also. Being a thoughtful husband, he asks his wife to leave the room, so she will be spared the sight of his sufferings. He remains in full possession of his rhetorical skills and summons secretaries to write down his words. Tacitus remarks drily, 'Since the long discourse he delivered has been published, I spare myself the trouble of writing it down.' The historian need not waste time rewriting the *Phaedo* on behalf of a man who was egotistical enough to dictate his own last words. Tacitus skips over Seneca's final discourses entirely – and leads his readers to believe that they were mere rhetorical posturing.

Seneca's death is an extraordinary combination of almost all possible methods of suicide: wounding and bleeding, poison, suffocation, drowning and finally cremation. Seneca orders a cup of hemlock, because the blood-letting is taking so long – the very same drink, as Tacitus remarks, which the Athenians used to give for public executions. But even hemlock will not work for the Roman philosopher: his limbs are too cold to be affected by the poison. Finally he gets into a hot bath and, as he does so, sprinkles a libation on the nearest slaves, for Jupiter the Liberator. He suffocates in the steam and then his body is burned. In making Seneca die by as many different means as possible, Tacitus seems to cast a satirical eye on the whole notion that philosophy is learning how to die. The philosopher has clearly not learned his lesson very well: he is singularly bad at dying, much worse than most people. It is as if trying to learn about death from Socrates has made Seneca all but incapable of experiencing death for himself. The academic study of the subject has desiccated his body until it has no blood left to spill.

Rubens's painting of the death of Seneca, which was based on a (wrongly identified) ancient sculpture, shows us a hugely muscular, solid-limbed man, standing in a copper basin. His pose echoes the iconography of Jesus' baptism. Seneca's upward gaze seems to look towards an invisible dove. Tacitus tells us that Seneca was too old and shrivelled to let the blood flow from his wrists. Rubens shows us a

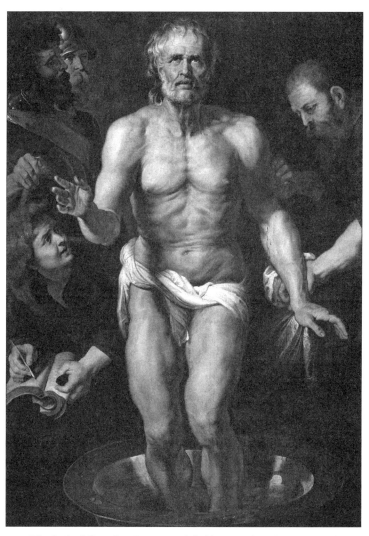

7. The Stoic philosopher Seneca modelled his own forced suicide on that of Socrates. He drank hemlock before slitting his wrists in the bath. This splendid painting by Rubens was based on an ancient sculpture of a fisherman, once thought to be Seneca. To our hero's left, a secretary writes down the great man's final words.

Seneca who is almost too vigorous to die; his legs are strong enough to leap straight from the bath to the next life. Rubens restores some of the dignity that Tacitus tries to remove from the dying Seneca.

Tacitus sets the death of Seneca against those of other people forced to die under Nero. The strongest contrast is with the death of Petronius, author of the raucous satirical comic novel the *Satyricon*. Tacitus presents Petronius as a hedonist and a wastrel who enjoys extravagant pleasures and takes nothing seriously. He is the opposite of a serious-minded philosopher. Tacitus notes explicitly that immediately before he takes the poison, Petronius talks with his friends, but not – like Socrates – about the 'immortality of the soul' (*nihil de immortalitate animae*), but instead he enjoys light songs and frivolous poetry. This is an anti-Socratic death. However, Petronius shows no less courage than Seneca, or indeed Socrates. He makes little of his own demise – in sharp contrast to Seneca's willingness to make himself a spectacle for the admiration of his followers. Petronius sits at table and drowses as the poison takes hold: his death looks like an eternal after-dinner nap.

A final forced suicide is significantly different from those Neronian deaths that preceded it. Thrasea, another Stoic philosopher, is condemned to death by the Senate. When he hears the news, he just happens to be debating 'the nature of the soul and the divorce of spirit and body' with another philosopher. In contrast to Seneca, Thrasea does not have to stage-manage his own death; he is already behaving in the approved manner for a dying philosopher.

However, the nod to the death of Socrates is followed by several details suggesting that Thrasea, the Roman Stoic martyr, is superior to the Athenian Socrates. He is far more solicitous of his family's welfare than Socrates had been. He urges his friends not to risk their lives by associating with a condemned man. Thrasea tells his wife to stay alive and take care of their child – trumping Seneca, who was willing to allow his wife to die by his side. Socrates was made happy by the thought of his own immortality; the dying Thrasea is happy because his friends and family will outlive him. On his request, two friends cut the arteries in each of his arms. His death is bloody and excruciatingly painful – in contrast to the easy end of Socrates.

Thrasea's refusal to limit himself to the Socratic model makes his death far more admirable, in Tacitus' eyes, than that of Seneca. Thrasea is patriotic where Socrates was cosmopolitan. Socrates wanted to pour a libation with the hemlock; Thrasea uses his own blood as a libation to Jupiter the Liberator. Socrates gave thanks for his own safe delivery to Asclepius; Thrasea calls on a god who can aid and liberate the entire city. Socrates submitted to the judgement of his city and died a death without pain. Thrasea, more nobly from a Roman perspective, gives his blood in agony that his city may be free.

THE IRRELEVANCE OF INTELLECTUALS: PLUTARCH AND DIOGENES LAERTIUS

The marginalisation of philosophy, as a speciality occupation or profession, had an enormous impact on the representation of Socrates' life and death in the later Roman Empire. Plutarch, a Greek writer who lived in the first and second centuries AD, remarked that Socrates was 'the first to show that life at all times and in all parts, in all that we suffer and do, always admits philosophy'. But he was also conscious that it may be difficult to integrate our more obviously 'philosophical' activities with the hurly-burly of political and military action.

Plutarch's essay 'On the *Daimonion* of Socrates' uses this topic to mediate on the position of intellectuals in a time of political revolution. It combines historical narrative with philosophical dialogue, on the model of Plato's *Phaedo*. The scene is the city of Thebes one night in December 379 BC. Thebes had been taken over by a Sparta tyranny and many of the most prominent native inhabitants had fled the city. But the exiles are due to return and have plotted a coup to oust the Spartans and take back Thebes for the Thebans.

The house of Simmias – one of the main characters in Plato's *Phaedo* – is the meeting place for the Theban conspirators. While those already inside the city are waiting for the exiles to return, they discuss whether one needs philosophy in order to behave well in politics. Perhaps the bloody takeover of Thebes is out of keeping with philosophical truth. Perhaps philosophers should stay away from killing. Perhaps they should shun all political action. But in that case there is a danger that philosophy will seem irrelevant to the decisions made by politicians in power.

This suspicion is confirmed when the conversation turns to the divine sign of Socrates (the *daimonion*). The characters disagree about what Socrates' sign actually was: one argues that the gods spoke directly to him, while another suggests that he was guided by any random occurrence – such as a sneeze. But all the participants in the conversation agree on one thing: that reason alone cannot be the sole guide for human action. Even Socrates himself used his 'sign', not philosophy, when he wanted to make a decision about anything that mattered. Plutarch's text expresses a common worry of his time: that philosophy may be useless in the real world of politics and war.

Diogenes Laertius, who wrote a set of *Lives and Opinions of the Famous Philosophers* in the third century AD, also reflected the idea that intellectuals are somehow cut off from the realities of politics. He presented Socrates as a suffering sage whose only hope of getting his own back on those who mock and thump him is by neat little witticisms. He often gets beaten up when he goes to the *agora* to discuss his opinions. One day, after he has been pounded and kicked by the populace, a friend expresses surprise that he bears it so willingly. Socrates answers, 'If a donkey kicked you, should I take out a lawsuit against him?' The anti-democratic sentiment is familiar from Plato, but the degree of indignity suffered by Socrates is not.

Diogenes allows Socrates to endure physical as well as verbal humiliation. His memorable anecdotes work to distance the philosopher from the rest of us: Socrates was peculiar and different from everybody else.

Diogenes emphasises Socrates' bad relationship with his nagging wife, or perhaps wives. He tells us that Socrates was a bigamist who was married to Myrto as well as Xanthippe. Like Xenophon, Diogenes emphasises Socrates' ability to deal calmly with a shrewish wife. He reports that one day Xanthippe yelled at her husband and then threw a bowl of slops on his head. Socrates comments, 'Did I not say that Xanthippe's thunder would end in rain?' Xenophon made Xanthippe a nag, but drew the line at chamber pots.

Diogenes introduces a story that became influential in the later tradition: after the death of Socrates, the Athenians deeply regretted what they had done and put up a monument in his memory. The story reinforces the idea that philosophers are never appreciated in their own time. Intellectuals live in an ivory tower, and their ideas are always misunderstood during their life. Philosophy can never be part of the real world. Theory is divorced from practice. These notions are still with us today.

EGOTISM AND THE DRAMA OF SOCRATIC DEATH

For many under the Roman Empire, the dying Socrates seemed too theatrical as well as too theoretical. Lucian, a brilliant comic writer and rhetorician of the second century AD, suggests that imitating Socrates' death is a ridiculously exhibitionistic enterprise.

Lucian reveals, in true tabloid fashion, the dark secrets of celebrities from myth and history. Cerberus, the dog who guards the Underworld, claims that Socrates died bravely only in order to show off to the spectators. His death was not really his own choice. He pretended that he was 'really ready to suffer willingly what he had to undergo anyhow, in order to make the spectators admire his behaviour'.

Lucian tells us that his own time has known just two noble philosophers: Sostratus, also known as Heracles, who was renowned for his extraordinary size and physical strength (about whom Lucian wrote another treatise, now lost); and Demonax, who was, he says, his own teacher. Demonax was, we learn, an eclectic thinker, though 'he probably had most in common with Socrates'. But he was 'a Socrates without the irony', by which Lucian seems to mean that he was more tactful than the Platonic Socrates. He knew how to avoid offending people.

Like his prototype, Demonax was accused of impiety. But Demonax managed to charm even those Athenians who held stones in their hands, ready to hurl at him. He died of his own volition, calmly and cheerfully. He starved himself to death, not forgetting to offer characteristic pieces of advice up to the very end. His death is in many ways comparable to the death of Socrates, down to the philosopher's insistence on not needing a big funeral. But when Demonax is asked how he would like to be buried, he replies, 'Don't bother; the stench will get me buried in the end.' Plato's Socrates insisted that it is only his body, not himself, whom Crito will bury. Demonax identifies himself with his own stinking corpse. In Lucian's eyes, Demonax, unlike Socrates, kept it real.

A text by Lucian about a different contemporary philosopher, *The Death of Pelegrinus*, offers a contrasting image of the worst symptoms of contemporary philosophy. Pelegrinus is, in Lucian's portrait, a fraud through and through. His 'philosophy' is all show, no substance; he is interested in looking like a philosopher rather than being one. One early symptom of his faddish self-aggrandisment is that he falls in with the gullible Christians, who are used to believing all kinds of nonsense and readily accept Pelegrinus as their new cult leader, second in authority only to their founder. An advantage of his brief period as a Christian is that Pelegrinus gets thrown into prison and is able to pretend to be Socrates awaiting execution – but with the added bonus that he survives the ordeal. The culmination of this hypocritical life comes in Pelegrinus' attempt to stage a truly crowd-pulling philosophical death. He leaps on a pyre at the Olympic Games, in the manner of two other models of the philosophical death: Empedocles, the physicist who thought the world was composed of Strife and Love and died by jumping into Mount Etna; and Hercules, beloved by the Stoics, who built his own funeral pyre on the top of Mount Oeta while tormented by the poisoned cloak of Nessus.

The absurdity of Pelegrinus' death lies partly in the attempt to conflate the deaths of Heracles and Empedocles with the death of Socrates. Heracles dies in agony, suffering from fire and poison, which represent, in a common Stoic reading, the torments of the passions. Socrates, by contrast, dies without any pain at all. If death is a spectator sport, it is doubly absurd to try to die like Socrates – in philosophic calm. Lucian sneers at the attempt by a modern philosopher to achieve a death as easy as that of Socrates, but also to get the glory of an agonised death like that of Heracles.

Pelegrinus cannot really live up to either type of philosophical death. He tries to put off the evil hour for as long as possible. What he wants is not to die well, but to be seen to die well. When the crowd starts to urge him to jump at once, he grows rather pale and sickly. When Pelegrinus finally does make his death leap, Lucian is revolted both by the spectacle itself and by its reception. The cynics stand sadly round the pyre, showing a certain amount of grief. Lucian asks them, 'Are you waiting for a painter to come and picture you as the companions of Socrates are portrayed beside him?' The spectators watch this death only in the hope of being watched themselves. Lucian mocks the self-aggrandising egotism, both of those who want to die like Socrates, and of those who want to participate in the scene.

5

PAIN AND REVELATION:
THE DEATH OF SOCRATES AND
THE DEATH OF JESUS

People have been noticing parallels and contrasts between the deaths of Socrates and Jesus since at least the second century AD. The poet Shelley was one of many people through the ages who have named Socrates 'the Jesus Christ of Greece'. Voltaire, more unusually, dubbed Jesus 'the Socrates of Palestine'.

The Italian humanist Marsilio Ficino (1433–99) made one of the most extensive comparisons between the two deaths. He comments that Socrates, like Jesus, turned the other cheek and forgave the enemies who had caused his death. Both Socrates and Jesus were mocked and humiliated. Like Jesus, Socrates submitted meekly to death. Jesus was betrayed for thirty pieces of silver; Socrates offered the price of thirty *minae* in court. Like the Jews after the death of Christ, the Athenians suffered divine retaliation after Socrates' death. Like Jesus, Socrates washed in the evening before his death and exhorted his disciples to piety at dinner-time. The sayings of Socrates were written down not by himself, but by his disciples. Ficino exclaims, 'What am I to say about the fact that, in the same hour [Socrates] refers to the cup, to the

benediction, and in the very hour of his death, to the cock?'
The resemblances seem to go far beyond coincidence. The
dying Socrates, for Ficino, was as like as any human being
could be to the dying Messiah.

But the death of Socrates was different from that of Jesus
in two obvious ways: because Jesus died in agony (not
calmly and painlessly) and because Socrates died without
the benefit of Christian revelation. In the early centuries of
Christianity and in the Renaissance, the comparison of Jesus
with Socrates allowed writers, philosophers and theologians
to think about the relationship of Christian faith to pagan
wisdom, and about whether pain is a necessary element
in an admirable, heroic death. The issue of pain was especially important at the time of the early Christian martyrdoms, while in the Renaissance – as we will see in the second
half of this chapter – knowledge, not pain, became the most
important feature distinguishing the two deaths.

THE TWO CUPS

The writers of the New Testament were often conscious of
the example of Plato's Socrates. Luke's Gospel – the one that
addresses itself most clearly to pagan readers – approxi-
mates Jesus' death on the Cross as closely as possible to the
supposedly painless death by hemlock. Luke puts much
less emphasis than the other Gospel writers on the pain and
humiliation suffered by Jesus at his execution.

After the Last Supper, Jesus goes to the garden of
Gethsemane to pray. In Matthew and Mark, he is 'sorrowful
and troubled': he says to his disciples, 'My soul is very sorrowful, even to death; remain here, and watch with me.' In
all three Synoptic Gospels, he speaks of his coming suffering

and death as a 'cup': 'My father, if it be possible, let this cup pass from me; nevertheless, not as I will, but as thou wilt.' The 'cup' of suffering or of God's anger is a familiar motif from the Psalms and the Prophets, and recurs in Revelation. But a pagan reader might well make the comparison between Jesus' 'cup' and the hemlock cup of Socrates.

The danger, for a Christian author appealing to an audience familiar with the death of Socrates, is that Jesus' desire to have his 'cup' pass from him may seem to compare unfavourably with Socrates' willingness to drink the hemlock. Luke is the only Gospel writer to confront this issue. He solves the problem by an angel: after Jesus' prayer in Gethsemane, Luke tells us, 'there appeared an angel from heaven, strengthening him'. Jesus' internal conflict is fully resolved by the time he goes forward to execution.

Christian attempts to move beyond pagan models often involve subsuming what had once been pagan into Christianity. Paul declares in the first letter to the Corinthians:

> Jews demand signs and Greeks seek wisdom, but we preach Christ crucified, a stumbling block to Jews and folly to Gentiles, but to those who are called, both Jews and Greeks, Christ the power of God and the wisdom of God. For the foolishness of God is wiser than men, and the weakness of God is stronger than men (1 Corinthians 1.22–25).

He may seem to be declaring the absolute novelty of the Christian revelation: through the Incarnation and Crucifixion, God has turned the values of the world on their head. The pain and humiliation of a man on a cross have become the

new wisdom and the new strength. But the passage appropriates the Socratic concept of a foolishness that is wiser than
any supposedly human cleverness, and of a sharp distinction between human and divine wisdom, found in Plato's
Apology. This passage suggests that Jesus trumps Socrates
because he manages to maintain a kind of Socratic irony
right up to the end: his death, like his life, seems foolish and
weak to the many; but to those with eyes to see, it is the
supreme example of wisdom and strength.

A FIGHT TO THE DEATH

Early Christians often turned back to Socrates to find a precedent for Jesus' humble teaching. A striking confirmation
of this comes in the artistic tradition. Socrates was often presented surrounded by six disciples or students. The group of
seven echoed, iconographically, the ancient tradition of the
Seven Sages, the seven wisest men in the world. Christian
artists followed this pose, depicting Jesus with not twelve
but six disciples – as if Jesus were simply a younger version
of Socrates.

During the second and third centuries AD, debates about
the new cult religion often discussed the relationship of Jesus
to the old Greek philosophers, and especially to Socrates.
Socrates was, if anyone could be, the Messiah of paganism.
The death of Socrates, then, became an essential issue in the
controversy about the relative merits of pagan and Christian
morality. Jesus and the Christian martyrs competed with
Socrates for the best death.

The death of Socrates also became a touchstone for those
who hoped to find some way to incorporate elements of the
pagan tradition into Christianity. Perhaps some particu-

larly noble pagans – like Socrates – could set a good moral example, even for a Christian. Some thinkers in late antiquity tried to find a compromise position between paganism and Christianity, suggesting that it might be possible to admire both Jesus and Socrates.

Probably the first Christian to appeal explicitly to the example of Socrates was Justin Martyr (c. AD 100–165; he was roughly a contemporary of Lucian). By birth, Justin was a Greek gentile. He was well educated in Greek philosophy and especially loved Plato. When he was about thirty, he converted to Christianity. Justin ascribes his conversion partly to his Platonism: 'When I was a disciple of Plato,' he writes, 'hearing the accusations made against the Christians and seeing them intrepid in the face of death and of all that men fear, I said to myself that it was impossible that they should be living in evil and in the love of pleasure.' It was because the Christians behaved so much like Socrates in the *Phaedo*, in their courage against death, that Justin realised they must be virtuous people. The dying Socrates led Justin to the dying Christ.

Justin wrote several important treatises defending Christianity to the Greek pagan community. He treats Christianity as the culmination of a tradition begun by the wise men of the Greeks, especially Socrates. 'Those who lived reasonably are Christians, even though they have been thought atheists; as, among the Greeks, Socrates and Heraclitus and men like them.' Justin implies that the main distinctive feature of Jesus' teaching was that he managed to make people believe the message that Socrates and others had been teaching for hundreds of years, without effect. Socrates had already taught his disciples to reject Greek mythology and pagan religion, and exhorted people to get to know the unknown god through reason. Jesus, then, was exactly the same kind of teacher as Socrates; but he was more successful in getting his message across. Justin did not want his readers to abandon the good lessons of Platonism, but to incorporate them into the new Gospel.

Justin's sympathy for the pagan Socrates was fiercely attacked by Tertullian (c. AD 155–230), an influential Church leader who lived in North Africa. Like Justin, and like most Christians of this period, he was a convert from paganism. But whereas Justin stressed the continuity between Greek philosophy and the Christian religion, Tertullian insisted that there must be a radical break between the two.

He argued against the notion that Plato's dying Socrates could be compared either with Jesus or with the Christian martyrs. Two central issues set Christian deaths apart: faith and pain. These two topics recur repeatedly in later discussions of the parallels and differences between Jesus and Socrates.

Tertullian first guns down Socrates' lack of true faith even in the doctrine that he seems to espouse so wholeheartedly in the *Phaedo*: the immortality of the soul. Tertullian suggests that Socrates cannot possibly be taken seriously when he claims to believe that his soul will live for ever, in blessed immortality. How could a pagan possibly have such firm faith? Tertullian insinuates that Socrates' claim to believe in his own immortality was merely a pose, assumed in order to outwit his jailers, and make himself seem to have escaped their prison and their punishment: 'So all the wisdom of Socrates, at that moment, proceeded from the affectation of an assumed composure, rather than the firm conviction of ascertained truth. For by whom has truth ever been discovered without God?' Tertullian refuses to believe in the possibility of pagans attaining access to divine wisdom or truth. The language he uses trades on the famous deceptiveness of Socrates, his *eironeia*. Socrates 'assumed' and 'affected' his confidence: in fact, as a pagan, he could have had no idea of the truth about death. All that calmness was faked for the occasion.

Secondly, Tertullian argues that Christian martyrdoms are always superior to the pagan death of Socrates, because they involve intense pain. Christian martyrdom

> tastes death not out of a cup almost in the way of jollity, but it exhausts it in every kind of bitter cruelty, on gibbets and in holocausts. Meanwhile, in the still gloomier prison of the world among your Cebeses and Phaedos, in every investigation concerning man's soul, it directs its enquiry according to the rules of God.

Tertullian here appropriates the imagery of Plato's *Phaedo* and turns it around. It is the Christians, not the pagan Socrates, who are the real imprisoned philosophers, the ones who always practise how to die, even before their hideously painful deaths. It is they, not Socrates himself, who die in a truly 'Socratic' manner. Tertullian suggests that Socrates, who died so cheerfully and painlessly, knew nothing about death at all, because he failed to suffer.

The Socratic model of open enquiry with people of all different faiths – including Pythagoreans and foreign slaves, 'your Cebeses and Phaedos' – is converted into the Christian struggle to preach the Gospel, even in a world of persecution. Socrates, Tertullian suggests, had it much too easy. It is as if Socrates did not properly die at all, because he seemed to enjoy himself so much.

Pagan opponents of Christianity attacked Jesus' shameful death on the Cross. They mocked Jesus for dying without any interesting last words: unlike Socrates, Jesus produced no final philosophical discourse about the immortality of the soul. One cited various noble pagan deaths, including that of Socrates, and asked, 'What saying equal to these did your god utter in his agony?' Any number of pagans had had a much more impressive death – including Socrates, Seneca and Cato.

But Christians argued that Jesus' death was all the more admirable for its relative silence. According to Origen (c. AD 182–251), who lived in Alexandria and Caesarea, 'The silence of Jesus under scourgings, and amidst all His sufferings, spoke more for His firmness and submission than all that was said by the Greeks when beset by calamity.'

Origen tried to argue on both sides of the fence, treating the death of Jesus as both like and utterly unlike the death of any pagan who came before him. On the one hand, Jesus, like Socrates, died an outcast, condemned by his city and country. Defenders of paganism can therefore not hold this against him. 'Jesus did indeed meet with a most sad death; but the same might be said of Socrates.'

But on the other hand, Jesus' death far outshone that of Socrates or any other pagan. Socrates was called 'wise', but only by a demonic, false pagan oracle: perhaps Apollo favoured him simply because he had bribed him with sacrifices. Jesus, unlike Socrates, died with faith in the true revealed religion. He died in pain, suffering meekly and heroically, and he died in humble silence, not with the chatter so common to Greek philosophers. The theme of Socrates' failure to shut up – or, from a more sympathetic perspective, his ability to keep thinking and talking, even at the moment of death – recurs in discussions of the death of Socrates right up to the twentieth century.

The final words of Socrates – the cock for Asclepius – were an important piece of evidence for Christians trying to argue that paganism was in no way compatible with Christian revelation. Several writers in late antiquity believed that this last allusion to a pagan god undermined all that profound discussion of the immortality of the soul. Origen complains that Socrates and his friends 'pass from those great topics which God has revealed to them, and adopt mean and trifling thoughts, and offer a cock to Asclepius!' Another writer of the period comments that in his final desire to offer a sacrifice to Asclepius, Socrates 'made good his statement' that he knew nothing. Writers of this period often invoked the idea that Socrates was 'the buffoon of Athens'.

By the fourth century AD, it had become much more difficult to assimilate Socrates with Jesus. People began to take sides: one could admire Socrates or Jesus, but not both.

The fourth century was a period of extraordinarily rapid cultural and religious change in the West. Constantine – the first Christian Roman emperor – tried to ensure that Christians would be tolerated throughout his empire. In AD 313 his Edict of Milan outlawed the persecution of Christians. Less than 100 years later, in AD 380, Theodosius adopted Nicene Christianity as the official state religion of the Roman Empire. What had begun as a tiny Jewish-Palestinian cult had suddenly become the world's most powerful ideology. The great eighteenth-century historian Edward Gibbon comments that 'the ruin of Paganism in the age of Theodosius is perhaps the only example of the total extirpation of any ancient and popular superstition, and may therefore deserve to be considered as a singular event in the history of the human mind'.

But paganism did not die without a fight. Throughout
the fourth and fifth centuries, pagans and Christians struggled to convert, convince or suppress each other. In doing
so, both sides turned repeatedly to the connections and contrasts between the death of Socrates and those of Christ and
his followers.

John Chrysostom (c. AD 347–407), a Syrian Christian
who became Bishop of Antioch, explains that the Christian
martyrs were far superior to that most famous of pagan
martyrs. The Christian martyrs would have found it easy to
drink hemlock in their thousands, if only they had thought
it right to do so: 'Had it been lawful when prosecution befell
them to drink hemlock and depart, all had become more
famous than he.' But the Christians were morally superior to
Socrates, because they refused to kill themselves. John reverts
to the possibility that Plato tried to suppress: Socrates' death
may seem like suicide and, as such, an evasion of responsibility.

Somewhat inconsistently, John Chrysostom also argues
that Socrates' death was inferior because it was forced upon
him, not chosen willingly for the greater glory of God.
Socrates drank hemlock when he had been condemned to
death: he 'drank when he was not at liberty to drink or not to
drink; but willing or against his will he must have undergone
it: no effect surely of fortitude but of necessity, and nothing
more.' Moreover, Socrates was old, at an age when he hardly
had any life left to lose by dying: 'When he despised life he
stated himself to be seventy years old; if this can be called
despising.' Xenophon's account of Socrates' reasons to die
becomes fuel for his Christian opponents.

But a few pagan voices still spoke up for the hemlock
against the cross. In his youth, John Chrysostom had been

taught by a pagan rhetorician, Libanius. Libanius retained a lifelong devotion to the old gods and the traditions of antiquity, even when friends, students and colleagues dropped away. Libanius wrote another *Apology* for Socrates. He was not, of course, hoping to save a man who had been dead for over 300 years. He was led to the subject by its contemporary relevance. Libanius' *Apology* can be read as a defence of paganism over the new religion. The emperor Julian ('the Apostate') had recently abandoned Christianity and gone over to pagan neoplatonism. Julian's mentor, Maximus of Ephesus, was a friend of Libanius. The *Apology* may be a veiled argument in favour of Maximus and of a pagan empire, against Christian detractors. The dying Socrates thus becomes an icon for everything that is best and noblest in the pagan tradition.

Libanius also wrote another shorter and stranger piece about Socrates, the *Silence of Socrates*. The premise of this little speech is that Critias has forbidden Socrates to speak at all after his sentence has been passed. It is thus as if the whole conversation reported in the *Phaedo* had been banned. The piece can plausibly be read as a defence of pagan, and specifically Platonic, learning, at a time of Christian–pagan controversy.

Libanius' speaker shows us why we need the *Phaedo*. Plato's dying Socrates represents all the beauty and truth of the pagan past, which is in danger of being lost forever. The speech ends with a plea to Socrates himself: 'to talk even after the hemlock, not to stop even when you die'. The works of the divine Plato have kept Socrates alive.

But the speech also has a melancholy tinge to it. In one of the most heartfelt passages, the speaker reminds his audience that, soon enough, Socrates will be dead, and silent for ever:

'All the haunts of beauty will be taken over by barbarism and silence ... You will indeed have your fill of the absence of Socrates. He will have so many silences.' Libanius mourns the fact that Plato's Socrates has been overshadowed by the pale Galilean.

THE MIDDLE AGES: SOCRATES AS SUFFERING SAGE

During the Middle Ages, the death of Socrates continued to hold an important place in the cultural memory of Europe. But the dying Socrates was a less complex and controversial figure during this period than he had been in antiquity, and would become again.

Many writers and thinkers simply dismissed Socrates. Augustine called him a 'heathen idolator' – although he showed a certain amount of interest in Socratic irony and Socrates' courage in the face of death. In Book Eight of the *City of God* (written in the early fifth century AD), Augustine echoes Cicero's claim that Socrates brought down philosophy from heaven to earth. Augustine's Socrates is a spiritual leader, who hopes to purify the minds of his contemporaries 'from the depressing weight of sinful desires'. He was condemned to death because ignorant men were angry at the revelation of their own folly.

The death of Socrates was most often encountered, in this period, not through Plato's *Phaedo* or *Apology*, but through the Latin writers who alluded to Socrates, especially Seneca and Cicero. This change in sources helps to explain why the Socrates of the Middle Ages often seems so much simpler than the Socrates of earlier or later periods.

Socrates' death became an instance of unjust martyrdom, nobly and philosophically endured. Boethius, for

8. *In this medieval illustration to Augustine's* City of God, *a melancholy and beardless Socrates, clad in a bright purple and green outfit, drinks the hemlock alone in a spindly prison which seems to double as a study: he totters backwards from a desk piled with books. The two kneeling men who point towards him are presumably his accusers, Anytus and Meletus. In the foreground, two men and two women weep for the dying master. Perhaps they are the two disciples, Plato and Xenophon, along with Socrates' two wives, Myrto and Xanthippe.*

example, a Christian philosopher of the sixth century AD, compared his own imprisonment and threatened execution to the sufferings of Socrates in prison. 'Philosophy', who appears to Boethius as a beautiful woman, reminds him of those whom she has aided in the past, including Socrates

9. *Socrates said, when his nagging wife poured a bowl of slops over his head, 'Did I not say that her thunder would end in rain?' In some versions, the bowl contained urine. Socrates' patience with Xanthippe was supposed to illustrate a tag from Horace (Odes 1. 24): 'It is hard, but whatever it is wrong to change becomes easier by patience'. This engraving of the scene is by Otto van Veen (1612); the people in the boat in the background may represent foolish impatience.*

and Plato: 'Socrates won by my aid the victory of an unjust death.'

In the later Middle Ages, Socrates was often seen as a kind of Christian, or at least a monotheist. In the thirteenth century, St Johannes Bonaventura says, 'All true philosophers worshipped one God. Which is also the reason why Socrates, because he forbade men to sacrifice to Apollo, was killed, since he worshipped one God.' In the *Roman de la Rose* (a poem composed in the thirteenth century), we are told that Reason bids us imitate Socrates, who died calmly, bidding his jailers not to swear by more than one God. Socrates' 'impiety', in the eyes of the pagan Athenians, is often taken as a sign that he was 'pious' by the standards of Christianity.

For many writers in this period Socrates became a representative sage – with no more specific characteristics than wisdom and a capacity to put up with bad treatment. In Dante's *Inferno* (composed in the early fourteenth century), Socrates appears as one of Aristotle's underlings, in 'the company of those who know'. Nothing more is said about him, and it is quite possible that Dante himself did not know all that much more.

The story of Xanthippe pouring the contents of a chamber pot over the head of Socrates was popular in the Middle Ages and into the early modern period. Socrates drenched by the slops is very clearly not Plato's Socrates, who is never put in such an undignified position. This Socrates is a fairly unindividuated representative of the life of the mind. The story shows how difficult it is to get on with your thinking in the midst of daily distractions and domestic life.

The vision of Socrates as a comic henpecked husband has resurfaced at various points in western history, to rival the ironic, dying philosopher of Plato. It persisted into the seventeenth century, when an Italian comic operetta, first performed in 1680, evoked *La patienza di Socrate con due moglie* (*The Patience of Socrates with His Two Wives*). The libretto (by Nicolò Minato) was based on the story in Diogenes Laertius that Socrates was a bigamist and had to put up with not one but two shrewish wives. The theme was adapted again by Georg Telemann for his three-act opera on the same topic (*Der Geduldige Sokrates*, 1721).

In more recent times, as we shall see in the last chapter of this book, there seems to have been a return to this vision of Socrates as a generic wise man who struggles to reconcile his work with his home life. The two main reasons for this trend are perhaps the same today as they were in the Middle Ages. First, because few people read Plato, the paradoxes of Plato's Socrates are relatively unknown. In the Middle Ages, the dominant tradition of philosophy was based on Aristotle, not Plato; and few people read Plato in Greek. The same is true today. Secondly, many people became increasingly uncomfortable with many of the values that the dying Socrates seemed to represent – including secular rationality.

SOCRATES' HOLY IGNORANCE

In the fifteenth century, European thinkers were beginning to turn away from the more positive, doctrinal, scholastic tradition of philosophy, influenced by Aristotle, towards a more questioning, more Socratic approach. A key figure in this area was Nicholas of Cusa (1404-64), a German bishop and papal legate. His treatise *On Learned Ignorance* suggested that human senses can never understand God or the universe. Our goal must be to know, like Socrates, that we know nothing.

But the relationship of Socratic ignorance to Christian truth remained deeply controversial in the Renaissance. Erasmus of Rotterdam (1466-1536), one of the most important humanist scholars, saw Socrates as a central figure in his attempt to revive the wisdom of the ancients. Many of his contemporaries were shocked by Erasmus' willingness to admire Socrates. He seems at several moments to put Socrates on a level with Christ himself: 'You will find in Socrates' life what is in harmony with Christ's life.'

For Erasmus, Socrates was an example of how far natural reason and moral sense alone can take a man, even without the light of Christian revelation. He emphasises that the pagans, and perhaps especially Plato's Socrates, anticipated almost all of Christian revelation. As he claims in the *Paracelsus* (*Exhortation to the Diligent Study of Scripture*), which was prefaced to his edition of the New Testament in 1516:

> Socrates (as Plato mentions) taught many reasons why one should not pay back injury with injury. He taught also that since the soul is immortal, one should not mourn those who leave this life, if they have lived well, because they are gone in to a better life. Finally, he taught and urged all men to subdue their physical passions, and to devote their souls to the contemplation of things which are truly immortal, although invisible to mortal sight.

Socrates was an authority for two central tenets of Christianity: that one should turn the other cheek, and that the soul is immortal. The *Phaedo* was a cornerstone for defences of pagan learning, because it showed Socrates arguing for the immortality of the soul, and finally submitting joyfully to death. As the medieval poet Marguerite of Navarre wrote, 'Socrates received the light when he gently accepted the hemlock, in the right belief that the soul is immortal.' Christian readers were, of course, well advised to ignore the fact that the *Phaedo* also seems to argue for reincarnation.

But for Erasmus, Socrates was not merely a representative of ancient wisdom. Other philosophical pagans – like, say, Thales, Aristotle or Plato – would not have served him so well. Socrates seems to anticipate the peculiarly Christian idea that wisdom can invert itself, so that those who seem the most foolish are closest to the truth.

In Erasmus' treatise *The Praise of Folly*, the allegorical figure of Folly launches into an attack on the supposed wisdom of philosophers that culminates in an account of Socrates, wise in philosophy but foolish in everyday life. She asks finally, 'What wisdom made him, once he had been indicted, drink the hemlock? For while he philosophised about clouds and ideas, and measured the feet of a flea and marvelled at the sound of a gnat, he had no idea of the most common ideas of life.' Folly is here, as so often, being foolish. One marker of this is her reliance on the Aristophanic version of Socrates as an egghead with no common sense. In fact – Erasmus seems to hint – it was indeed wisdom that made Socrates drink the hemlock, a wisdom that went beyond the false wisdom of science or reason, to a kind of spiritual insight.

In Erasmus' *Godly Feast*, a theologico-philosophical dialogue in Latin that looks back explicitly to Plato, a group of friends walk through a lovely garden and discuss the beauties of nature. The surrounding scenery provokes a debate about the ways in which God reveals himself. How much of God can one discern even from the natural world, without knowledge of Christ? This leads to an important discussion of the authority of pagan writers: how much could those who lived without revelation have discovered of the truth?

One character, Eusebius ('Pious Man'), declares that even the 'pagans' (*prophani*) should not be called 'profane' if they produced anything good, holy and conducive to goodness in others. When they speak the truth, they have been moved by 'some good spirit'. Cicero and Plutarch make Eusebius feel a better man for reading them.

The friends contrast Socrates' attitude towards death

with that of other noble pagans, such as Cato the Elder. They conclude that Socrates is the closest to Christian faith in his willingness to defer to God's ultimate authority and greater knowledge. This is not Socrates the rationalist, but Socrates the faithful doubter: a man who knows he does not know, but turns to God or the gods as the ones who do know. Another character, Chrysoglottus, remarks, 'This man was so diffident about his own achievements that only his eager willingness to do God's will led him to hope that God in his goodness would feel assured of his having endeavoured to lead a good life.' A third friend, Nephalius, replies, 'When I read such things about men of this kind, I can hardly refrain from saying, "Holy Socrates, pray for us" ["*Sancte Socrate, ora pro nobis*"]'.

This final line is often quoted out of context. It is worth emphasising that Erasmus does not himself, *in propria persona*, declare Socrates a saint; even Nephalius holds back from doing so. But Socrates comes close to sainthood, not through knowledge, but through humility and ignorance. It is because he knows that he knows nothing that Socrates is a man of greater true faith than many a contemporary Christian.

Other humanists, too, presented Socrates as a figure whom Christians could wholeheartedly admire. In this period, more and more scholars were turning to Greek as well as to Latin models. Giannozzo Manetti (1396–1459) wrote a pair of biographies in Latin, a *Life of Socrates* and a *Life of Seneca*. He comments that no Greek can really match the philosophical genius of Seneca; but Socrates is the closest thing. For Manetti, both Seneca and Socrates are valuable as guides to the ethical questions of daily life: 'Their exhortations have awakened men who were asleep or distracted to an incredible love of virtue and detestation of vice.'

Another humanist, Pico della Mirandola (1463–94), treats the dying Socrates as a far more thrilling model. He is interested less in his 'exhortations' than in his joy even in the moment of death: 'Who would not like to be inspired by those Socratic enthusiasms which Plato describes in the *Phaedo*?' The phrase 'Socratic enthusiasms' – *Socratici furores* in the original Latin – suggests that Socrates' death is characterised not by immense calm, but by overwhelming passion: Socratic death is a sublime pleasure that can carry the reader to levels of ecstasy paralleled only by religious – or sexual – enthusiasm.

As we have seen, Marsilio Ficino considered the death of Socrates an exact parallel to the death of Jesus. Socratic humility and Socratic ignorance were for Ficino a precise analogue to the holy simplicity of the saints. He remarks that Socrates, like the early Christian martyrs, seemed simple-minded to fools, but was in fact the wisest of all.

ANGELS AND DEVILS

After the fifteenth century, secular and Christian models again began to diverge. In the sixteenth and seventeenth centuries, most people felt that it was necessary, once again, to make a choice between Socrates and Jesus.

Caravaggio's lost first painting of *The Inspiration of St Matthew* represented the saint as a version of Socrates. Matthew was barefoot and shabbily dressed, and struggled to hold his pen, with a lot of help from a beautiful, androgynous angel. The illiterate saint recalled the Socrates who did not write. The painting used the iconography of Socrates to suggest the limitations of merely human wisdom: even the first Gospel writer was, like Socrates, no more than a holy fool.

10. In this lost painting by Caravaggio, St Matthew looks like Socrates: bare-foot, bald and goggle-eyed, with thick, stone-mason's arms. The saint is, again like Socrates, not accustomed to writing: the the angel has to help him hold his pen. The sinuous, androgynous angel may recall Socrates' sexy young friend, Alcibiades.

But the priests of the Contarelli Chapel, in San Luigi dei Francesi in Rome, who had commissioned the painting, rejected it; this Matthew was too foolish and pagan in his likeness to Socrates, and too little like a Christian saint. Many Reformation thinkers felt that Ficino and Erasmus had gone too far in their admiration for the pagan Socrates. Luther complained, 'Some barely fail to make prophets of Socrates, Xenophon and Plato. But these fine disputations represent supreme ignorance of God and mere blasphemies.' To Luther, even suffering was not enough to please God. The most renowned pagan deaths, even if they had not been as easy as they were, could not please God: the greatest work is nothing without faith in the one true God. 'Even if Cicero or Socrates had sweated blood, that would not make it pleasing to God.'

Milton's *Paradise Regained* (published in 1671) presents Socrates as an inspiration for both Jesus and the Devil. In Book 3, Satan tries to tempt Jesus with worldly glory. In reply, the Saviour gives Satan two examples of those who have managed to achieve glory 'Without ambition, war, or violence'. The first is Job and the second Socrates, 'for truth's sake suffering death unjust', who now lives 'Equal in fame to proudest conquerors'.

But in Book 4, it is Satan who cites Socrates, when he tempts Jesus with pagan philosophy. Socrates, Satan declares, was the one who brought philosophy down from heaven, who was 'pronounced / Wisest of men' by the Oracle, and 'from whose mouth issued forth / Mellifluous streams, that watered all the schools'. Jesus replies that all knowledge offered by pagan learning is 'false, or little else but dreams'. Socrates was the wisest of the ancient philosophers only because he knew that he knew nothing. 'Much of the Soul they talk, but all awry', Jesus declares, suggesting that even Plato's Socratic discussion of the soul's immortality in the *Phaedo* will not stand up to Christian scrutiny.

Satan and Jesus present us with two very different versions of Socrates. For Satan, Socrates is an orator, a public teacher, an inventor of doctrine and the founder of all subsequent philosophical schools. Socrates, in this Satanic view, influenced later philosophy precisely by his words. But Milton's Jesus corrects this Satanic view, suggesting rather that the imitation of Socrates should be much more like the *Imitatio Christi*. Socrates becomes a model for courage in death. He is admirable only for his humble acknowledgement that he knows nothing, and for his submission to unjust execution.

KNOW YOURSELF, KNOW YOUR DEATH

In the sixteenth and seventeenth centuries, Socrates is usually a model for secular doubt, scientific enquiry and, especially, self-knowledge.

A painting by Jusepe de Ribera (*c.* 1591–1652) shows Socrates as a contemporary seventeenth-century gentleman, looking into a mirror. This motif is fairly common in paintings of the period. In other images, Socrates holds up a mirror for a younger man, a boy or a group of younger men. Sometimes this contemplative Socrates comes very close to the figure of Vanitas, and is depicted with skull and book as well as the mirror. Even in Ribera's pared-down interpretation of the theme, Socrates' meditations seem dark and serious, a far cry from the comic Socrates doused in slops. The injunction *'gnothi seauton'* ('Know yourself') seems close

11. In this painting by Jusepe de Ribera, Socrates – dressed as a
contemporary seventeenth-century gentleman – contemplates his own
reflection in a mirror. Socrates was closely associated with the motto, 'Know
Yourself'. Here, his dark reflections also suggest 'Memento Mori'.

to '*Memento mori*'. Socrates sees both his face and his death in the dark mirror he holds.

The three-way association between Socrates, self-knowledge and death became of central importance in the work of Michel de Montaigne (1533–92). Montaigne had a particularly intense and intimate relationship with the figure of Socrates. At times in the *Essays*, Socrates is merely the subject of illustrative anecdotes, like any other character from antiquity. But Montaigne finds that Socrates mirrors himself more closely than any other antecedent.

Socrates, like Montaigne, professed his own ignorance. The ignorance of Socrates was criticised by more positivist scientific thinkers of the period: for instance, Francis Bacon remarks in the *Advancement of Learning* that 'men ought not to fall … into Socrates' his ironical doubting of all things'. Montaigne, on the other hand, admires Socrates precisely for his 'ironical doubting'. In the *Apology for Raymond Sebond*, Montaigne's great profession of faith in ignorance, Socrates becomes a crucial precursor of his own position: 'his best knowledge was the knowledge of his ignorance, and simplicity his best wisdom'.

Socrates, like Montaigne, spent his life trying to understand himself. Montaigne cites Socrates approvingly when he tries to justify his own interest in himself. Socrates earned the name 'wise' because 'he alone had seriously digested the precept of his god: to know himself'.

Montaigne's admiration for the dying Socrates was very great, but not unbounded. The Socrates of the *Crito*, who expressed attachment to his own city over all others, and who refuses to disobey the Laws, was unworthy of a man who claimed to be a citizen of the world. In this respect, if in no other, Montaigne felt himself superior to Socrates himself.

He loved Paris, but considered all men his compatriots: 'I am scarcely infatuated with the sweetness of my native air.' Socrates failed to anticipate fully Montaigne's own cosmopolitan, anthropological broad-mindedness.

But Montaigne was particularly haunted by the nobility of Socrates' last hours. Many of the remarks on Socrates' death were added in Montaigne's final set of revisions: as he approached his own death, Montaigne thought more and more about that of Socrates.

He admired Socrates' lack of concern for his own burial arrangements and was particularly impressed by his constancy in the face of a delayed execution:

> There is nothing, in my opinion, more illustrious in the life of Socrates than having had thirty whole days to ruminate his death sentence, having digested it all that time with a very certain expectation, without emotion, without alteration, and with a tenor of actions and words rather lowered and relaxed than strained and exalted by the weight of such a reflection.

Again, in the essay *On Diversion*, he remarks on Socrates' unusual ability to face death head-on: 'to become acquainted with death with an ordinary countenance, to become familiar with it and play with it'. Socrates and death were on the same kind of terms as Montaigne and his cat: they played together as equals.

In the essay *On Cruelty*, Montaigne argues initially that virtue depends on struggle and the greatest acts of virtue are always painful. Yet Socrates seems not to fit this model. Montaigne is troubled by the problem: 'The soul of Socrates, which is the most perfect that has come to my knowledge, would be, by my reckoning, a soul deserving little commendation: for I cannot conceive, in that person, any power of vicious lust.' Meditation on Socrates prompts him to change his mind and finally adopt a principle completely contrary to that with which he began: the greatest acts of virtue are pleasurable, not painful. Socrates exceeds even Cato in the sweetness and pleasure he found in death. Montaigne exclaims, 'I beg Cato to forgive me: his death was more tragic and more exalted. But *this* death, though I cannot say how, is even more beautiful.' Although he 'cannot say how', the claim itself provides an answer. Virtue, for Socrates even more than for Cato, is not laborious but easy: 'It has passed into [his] nature.' The death of Socrates is admirable precisely because it was not experienced as 'tragic' or 'exalted', but as ordinary, easy, even pleasurable. In the essay *On Physiognomy*, he rejects the story that Socrates' face reflected the innate ugliness of his soul: 'So excellent a soul was never self-made.'

Montaigne argues vehemently against the Platonic notion that virtue should involve a struggle against baser, physical desires. Intellect, and over-intellectualising, are far more likely to lead to evil and suffering than is the simple, unimaginative life of ordinary people. This leads him to suggest at times that Socrates' imperturbability in the hour of his death was not, after all, so unusual. He points to a series of examples of low-born people who approach even torturous deaths with laughter and jokes, toasting their friends and 'yielding in nothing to Socrates'. In *On Cruelty* he implies that Socrates' death was unusual among philosophers, but only because learning makes most scholars blind to their own fundamental ignorance. Socrates died well because he died like one of Montaigne's own peasant neighbours: he was, like them, conscious that he knew nothing about death.

Socrates was thus the founding father of the ideal school of philosophy: the School of Stupidity. Montaigne's Socrates may seem superficially similar to that of Nicholas of Cusa. Both thinkers were interested in Socratic ignorance. But the treatise, *On Learned Ignorance*, is concerned with the metaphysical issue of our inability to comprehend God, while Montaigne's *Essays* are focused on ordinary human experience, in all its complexity. Montaigne's Socrates is surprising precisely because he is not special; he is just a regular man.

Montaigne was particularly interested in the notion that a whole life may be spent in preparation for death. He challenges this philosophical commonplace, claiming that dying is the one great task for which we cannot practise. We undergo death only once, there can be no rehearsal – except through a physical near-death experience. Philosophical injunctions to remember death are absurd. 'If you don't know how to die, don't worry: Nature will tell you what to do on the spot, fully and adequately.' Cicero is wrong to say that 'the whole life of a philosopher is a meditation on death'. Montaigne says 'Death is indeed the end, but not therefore the goal, of life; it is its finish, its extremity, but not therefore its object.' Montaigne does not mention the fact that Cicero borrowed this claim from Socrates himself, in the *Phaedo*.

Montaigne chooses the ironic, questioning defendant of the *Apology* over the dying hero of the *Phaedo*. Socrates is, unlike Cicero or Seneca, a useful philosophic model for those contemplating death, because his attitude towards it is 'nonchalant and mild', 'a sober, sane, plea, but at the same time natural and lowly, inconceivably lofty, truthful, frank, and just beyond all example'.

The true greatness of Socrates' death is that it undermines

the philosophical falsehood that death is a thing apart from the rest of life. In the case of Socrates, the death was no different from the life. Socrates showed how death is always integrated and involved with life. People do not become different, suddenly, on their deathbeds: 'Every death should correspond with its life. We do not become different for dying. I always interpret the death by the life. And if they tell me of a death strong in appearance, attached to a feeble life, I maintain that it is produced by a feeble cause corresponding with the life.' Socrates understood the ordinariness of death as well as its unknowability. He died, as he lived: as himself. Montaigne uses the death of Socrates as an example for ordinary, secular man.

6

THE APOTHEOSIS OF PHILOSOPHY: FROM ENLIGHTENMENT TO REVOLUTION

Benjamin West's first biographer, John Galt, tells a striking story about how the artist came to produce his first history painting, *The Death of Socrates* (1756), at the age of just eighteen. We are told that one client was amazed at the artist's talent and

> he observed to him, that, if he could paint as well, he would not waste his time on portraits, but would devote himself to historical subjects; and he mentioned the Death of Socrates as affording one of the best topics for illustrating the moral effect of the art of painting. The Painter knew nothing of the history of the Philosopher; and, upon confessing his ignorance, Mr Henry went to his library, and, taking down a volume of the English translation of Plutarch, read to him the account given by that writer of this affecting story.

This anecdote is probably complete fiction. Galt presumably means 'Plato' when he says 'Plutarch' – a detail that hardly helps his credibility. In fact, West's striking image of

12. Benjamin West's Death of Socrates *(1756) was his first history painting. The crowded canvas shows Socrates and his disciples confronting a whole army of heavily armed prison guards. West based his composition on an engraving from a popular textbook, Charles Rollin's* Ancient History.

the barbarous guards confronting Socrates and his friends was inspired by an engraving from the frontispiece of Charles Rollin's *Ancient History* (London, 1738–40; engraving by Jacques Philipe le Bas after Hubert Gravelot). The moving description of Socrates' death in Rollin's *History* played a major part in the popularisation of the legend.

But Galt's story marks a turning point in the reception history of the death of Socrates. In the earlier part of the eighteenth century, it was plausible that an intelligent young painter could be only dimly aware of who Socrates was. By the middle decades of the century, the death of Socrates was everywhere. It became an enormously fashionable topic for artists, writers and intellectuals.

Classical deaths in general were popular in this period. Trends in painting and drama had changed, and artists who might, a century earlier, have painted a *Deposition of Christ* or a *Pietà* now searched classical literature for a suitable death. Academic scholarship, archaeology and historical method had produced new discoveries about the ancient world, but also marked a new distance from the lives of the ancients. Ancient deaths were particularly interesting in a period that saw itself as decisively modern: the death of Socrates, Seneca or Cato could hint at the death of antiquity as a whole.

But Socrates was perhaps the most popular dying pagan of them all, at least for the middle decades of the eighteenth century. Until the time of the French Revolution, the death of Socrates was a cultural obsession all over Europe, Britain and America. In England, Joseph Addison considered writing a play about Socrates before settling on Cato – whose patriotic self-disembowelling was often seen as an alternative model of the ideal death. Dramatic representations of the death of Socrates multiplied: in France there were no fewer than three plays called *La Mort de Socrate* in the space of six years, between 1759 and 1764.

One obvious explanation for this flurry of interest in Socrates' death is that the dominant sources had changed. Ficino translated the whole of Plato into Latin, but it was difficult to find vernacular versions of most of the dialogues. By the sixteenth and seventeenth centuries, Xenophon and Diogenes Laertius were becoming much better known. But in the eighteenth century, far more people were reading

Plato's accounts of the last days of Socrates – the *Apology*, the *Crito* and the *Phaedo*. One of Diderot's earliest works was a translation of the *Apology* into French, which Rousseau used for his own study of the *Apology*. The new interest in the death of Socrates was a logical response to this change in source material.

Moreover, European experiences of death had changed radically at this time. Up until the early eighteenth century, most bodies were buried in town churchyards. But urban populations increased enormously around this time, and to deal with the vast numbers of the dead, large burial grounds were built out in the suburbs. Death thus became less visible in daily life. The death of Socrates fitted this newly distanced perspective on mortality in general, since it is a death that seems to deny the fact of mortality.

But neither textual nor social history can fully explain why the use made of Socrates' death in the mid-eighteenth century was so different from that of earlier ages. I would argue that at the time of the Enlightenment, this event was appropriated to serve a specific cultural need: as an image of the social life of the intellectual.

Paintings of the death of Socrates are rare before the eighteenth century, and the exceptions are strikingly different from eighteenth-century versions of the theme. In one painting by an unknown follower of Caravaggio from the early seventeenth century (p. 64), Socrates is saying his last goodbye to his family. The youngest child stretches his arm towards his father, while his mother draws him away. Socrates himself seems to take no notice: all his attention is on higher things. The painting is a rare depiction of the human cost of a life lived for philosophy.

Charles Alfonse Dufresnoy's 1650 *Mort de Socrate* shows

13. In Charles Alfonse Dufresnoy's Mort de Socrate (1650), Socrates and his friends share a large, vaulted space with other prisoners, who are visible in the background lying on the floor. The man in the head-band who stands behind Socrates is presumably the executioner.

a dignified, well-covered-up old gentleman who sips the cup while his friends gesticulate and lament. The scene takes place in what is clearly an open-plan prison: there are other prisoners flopping down in the background, perhaps already dead from earlier hemlock draughts, while some sinister guards in antique helmets lurk by the gate. This painting reminds us that Socrates was by no means the only Athenian to die in prison. One of the friends points to Socrates as he lifts the cup: the suggestion is almost that, without the gesture, we would hardly notice this death among so many.

The Italian painter, writer and satirist, Salvator Rosa

14. François Boucher's grisaille *sketch shows Socrates lying back in a swirl of drapery, clutching his chest as the poison takes hold. We see little of his face, but his strong, sandalled foot is clearly visible, above the empty hemlock cup. Guards watch from the upper level, and disciples crowd round the master. The figures in the foreground may be noting down Socrates' last words – or perhaps sketching the composition.*

(1615–73), painted a *Death of Socrates* which emphasises the master's poverty as well as his cleverness. A skinny, bright-eyed old Socrates smiles knowingly at a few shabby disciples as he prepares to sip his last drink from a rough pewter tumbler.

In the eighteenth-century versions of the scene, by contrast, Socrates always gets his own private room and is always centre stage. By mid-century, the event had become immensely popular among painters, particularly in France; it was the topic for the Royal Academy grand prize in 1762.

In most of these images, Socrates is old, ugly and very

15. *In J. St-Quentin's* Death of Socrates, *which was entered for the 1762 Grand Prix, Socrates has drunk the hemlock, and seems about to topple from his seat. The round cup on the floor echoes the round prison window – recalling Plato's image of death as an escape from prison. The fetters which have been removed from Socrates' legs are also visible on the floor near his feet.*

dead. The central question is the close-knit male social group, which depends – perhaps far too heavily – on this single, wrinkly, floppy old man. Socrates' body is usually heavily-bundled up, and his gaze does not meet the viewer directly. The paintings focus not on the personality of the dying man, but on the effect of his death on his friends.

All the artists who treated the topic were highly conscious of Plato's metaphor of life in the body as imprisonment. The physical prison, a prominent feature of eighteenth-century life and imagination, becomes a prototype for all life on earth. The round, barred prison window offers one means of escape, while the round, empty hemlock cup provides the other. The images echo the traditional iconography for the dead Christ lying in his mother's lap: these are secular *pietàs*. Socrates has taught his disciples about the immortality of the soul, but it is clear that his body will not rise again.

David's painting of 1773 (on p. 13) is very different. Far more than any of his artistic predecessors, David makes Socrates look attractive. He inspires his followers by his shining intelligence and sexiness. The philosopher is shown in the moment of accepting the hemlock cup, when he is still at the height of his powers. The composition is focused on Socrates' torso – naked, muscular and fully lit – and on the twin gestures of his arms. The right reaches for death, while the left points to something beyond death. David's painting is crystal clear, almost cartoon-like in the legibility of its action and its environment. But it is a painting about what happens beyond the frame.

The painting is, of course, a call to revolution. David seems to have imagined his Socrates as a classical forebear for his good friend Robespierre. The invisible world he points to could be death, but it could also be the new France, the future time when heads less sturdy than that of Socrates will rightly roll. David, much more than any of the previous painters, allows room in his painting for spaces beyond the immediately foregrounded composition of the master and his followers: the painting, like its central figure, gestures both backwards (to the wife and family in the distant background, going up the stairs; or to the old world in which values like family might mean anything) and also to the new world of Liberty, Fraternity and Equality, for which we should all be delighted to die. David's painting of Socrates is answered by David's own *Death of Marat* of 1793, where the revolutionary hero is slumped and solitary, murdered in his – extraordinarily vertical – bath.

But the similarities between David's work and the earlier paintings are as important as the differences. All focus on the foreground, in which Socrates is surrounded by only his male friends. None of these painters gives a central place to Xanthippe, as the unknown follower of Caravaggio had done. None of them suggests – as Dufresnoy's seventeenth-century painting had done – that there might have been other prisoners in that Athenian jail as well as Socrates. None of these paintings depicts any earlier moment in the story of Socrates' trial and death. None of these images is explicitly concerned with the confrontation between the individual and the state. Rather, all of them emphasise the intimate male Socratic circle – the closest ancient equivalent to the *philosophes'* salon.

This Enlightenment version of the death of Socrates is quite different from those of earlier ages. We can see the contrast most clearly by looking back to the Socrates of Montaigne, who was a particular hero of the French Enlightenment and whose questioning, secular, tolerant Socrates is the closest precursor. Montaigne saw Socrates as an ordinary hero and as an essentially solitary figure. In the Enlightenment, by contrast, Socrates' death is always seen as the climactic moment of his life – the moment that reveals his true character, or redeems all his faults.

Moreover, in this period the social role of Socrates – as teacher, leader and public intellectual – becomes more important than anything he actually said or did. Enormous emphasis is placed on Socrates' relationship with his friends.

Taking Socrates as the most important ancient philosopher – above either Plato or Aristotle – was a bold, revisionist move, in keeping with the self-perceived radicalism of the Enlightenment. One great advantage of Socrates as a philosophic model was that he wrote nothing, and could therefore be appropriated by later philosophers of all different strands of opinion. It was hard to read Aristotle except through scholasticism, or Plato unmediated by neoplatonism. A return to Socrates seemed to promise a fresh new beginning for philosophy and intellectual life.

Voltaire, Diderot and Rousseau were all seen as versions of Socrates for the modern age. Like Socrates, they risked official disapproval and imprisonment, if not death, for their philosophical beliefs. Charles Palissot's satirical comedy attacking the *philosophes* was scorned by Voltaire as the work of a new Aristophanes.

But in comparison with later uses of the death of Socrates – in, for example, John Stuart Mill's *On Liberty* – the *philosophes* were not primarily interested in using this event to prompt political change. The life of the mind, as practised in the coffee shop, salon or Athenian prison, is represented as an alternative to the active life of politics. The point is clearly illustrated by Dr Johnson, who imagined the following thought experiment: 'Were Socrates and Charles the Twelfth of Sweden both present in any company, and Socrates to say, "Follow me and hear a lecture on philosophy"; and Charles, laying his hand on his sword, to say, "Follow me, and dethrone the Czar"; a man would be ashamed to follow Socrates. Sir, the impression is universal; yet it is strange.' Johnson, like many of his contemporaries, sees the philosophy of Socrates as unquestionably admirable, but also entirely useless.

In this chapter, I show how five very different European writers in this period imagined the death of Socrates:

Diderot, Rousseau, Nicholas Fréret, Voltaire and Moses
Mendelssohn. These writers produced at least five different
versions of Socrates' death. But all of them share the assumptions that the death of Socrates is the central event through
which we can interpret his life and character; and that the
dying Socrates is, or ought to be, a model for the contemporary intellectual in relation to his own social circle, friends
and students. More surprisingly, all are anxious to distance
themselves from this ancient model, even when they hold
up the death of Socrates as an example of philosophic virtue.
Even the most fervent proponents of Enlightenment rationalism and Enlightenment notions of educational and political progress were surprisingly doubtful about whether they
could really be friends with the dying Socrates.

THE QUESTION OF INTEGRITY: DIDEROT AND ROUSSEAU

Denis Diderot (1713–84), the polymath philosopher and
founder of the famous *Encyclopedia*, was obsessed with the
dying Socrates at a period when everybody was thinking
about him. Diderot's Socrates is probably the closest literary
model for the Socrates depicted by David.

Diderot dreamed of writing a drama about the death of
Socrates, although he never actually did so; Voltaire beat
him to it. But it would have been difficult for Diderot to
put Socrates on stage, because he saw him almost as a saint.
Certainly he was that least theatrical of characters, 'a person
without passions', who lived and died for a rational ideal of
virtue.

For Diderot, the dying Socrates was important because he
provided a model of integrity or authenticity. Socrates succeeded in creating a death that was in total accordance with

the principles of his life. Diderot comes close to worshipping his calmness and heroic rationality. Discussing Charles Michel-Ange Challe's (lost) painting *Socrates Condemned by the Athenians to Drink the Hemlock*, Diderot praises the artist's ability to capture the essence of the moment: Socrates' calmness, even in the face of death. '*C'est le plus sublime sang-froid.*'

Diderot himself did not live up to his hero's model. When he was put in prison in Vincennes for impiety in 1749, he failed the Socratic test and chose life over imprisonment or death with dignity, renouncing his own earlier work as 'youthful folly'. This showed considerable chutzpah, since he had written his most controversial work (the *Lettre sur les aveugles)* only just before he was imprisoned.

But the dying Socrates remained the mark to which Diderot continued to look up, the measure of all that humanity might be capable of. In the *Encyclopedia* entry on Socrates, Diderot exclaims, 'Ah, Socrates! I am not much like you; but all the same you make me weep with admiration and joy.' The intimacy of Diderot's engagement with Socrates is evident in his willingness to address him, indeed to *tutoyer* him, even as he points out his own distance from the ideal. Socrates was, for Diderot, an example of a truly authentic and integrated life and death.

Jean-Jacques Rousseau (1712–78), by contrast, thought Socrates' death sat uneasily with his life. Rousseau's Socrates is a man whose integrity is compromised by a willingness to conform to false social ideals.

The trial of Socrates on a charge of impiety seemed to find an obvious parallel in the troubles of Rousseau, whose *Emile* and *The Social Contract* were condemned as impious by the Geneva council in June 1762. The general groundswell of

interest in the death of Socrates in the early 1760s had a lot to
do with what was happening to Rousseau.

But Rousseau himself had extremely mixed feelings
about Socrates. His favoured version of Socrates is an
anti-*philosophe*, a non-philosophical philosopher – just as
Rousseau hoped to be himself. In his *First Discourse (Sur les
Sciences et les Arts)* of 1750, Rousseau celebrates Socrates for
his ignorance and for his rejection of science. He admits that
Socrates is a philosopher, but what makes his philosophy
acceptable is his virtue, as proved by his death.

In the *Profession of Faith of the Savoyard Vicar* in Book 4
of *Emile* (1762), Rousseau seems in many ways to echo the
stance of Socrates in the *Apology*. Like Plato's Socrates, the
Savoyard Vicar is both humble and aggressive: he emphasises his own ignorance, but also reports his discovery that
nobody else is any wiser than himself. Rousseau goes even
further than Plato's Socrates in denying the value of conventional human wisdom: 'The only thing we absolutely do
not know is how to refrain from knowledge.' The Vicar can
begin to learn only when he shuts all his books and turns
instead to the book of nature.

But then Vicar launches a fierce attack on Socrates, asking
how anybody could dare to compare his easy death – *facile
mort* – with the truly horrible, and truly admirable, suffering of the divine Jesus: 'If this easy death had not honoured
his life, we would be unsure whether Socrates, with all his
esprit, was anything other than a sophist.' Rousseau seems
to hesitate even as he condemns Socrates. On the one hand,
his death *is* admirable; on the other hand, Socrates was, in
life, nothing but a sophist. His death was the only admirable
moment of his life – and even that moment was not so great,
after all.

The problem with Socrates' death is that it was too easy: Socrates was too theoretical, too little rooted in the body. He did nothing but talk about what other people had actually done. The philosophical calm of the dying Socrates, which had been for Diderot a major reason to admire him, was for Rousseau a mark of his inadequacy. Socrates had become associated with rationalist contemporary philosophers – including Rousseau's one-time hero Voltaire. Socrates, despite his claims to know nothing, remained tainted by Voltaire's pretence that he had mastered the whole world by reason.

The most extensive discussion of the death of Socrates by Rousseau comes in a strange, unfinished work that was not published in his lifetime, the *Fiction or Allegorical Fragment on Revelation*. It describes how a terrible false temple, representing Fanaticism, is challenged by three people in turn. The first challenger is the first philosopher on earth – a brave but feeble figure, who can see the truth but is instantly slaughtered by the priests of intolerance.

The second is not named, but he is clearly identified as Socrates: 'an old man with a fairly ugly face, but attractive manners and an intimate, profound style of conversation which soon made one forget his physiognomy'. He tries to explain to the people why they should turn from false idols, urging them, 'Worship the one who wants universal happiness, if you want to be happy yourselves.' Rousseau then offers a brief but highly sympathetic summary of the death of Socrates as described in Plato's *Phaedo*. Socrates comments that he has to die in order to prove that he is more than a sophist: 'I would be suspected of having lived as nothing but a sophist, if I feared to die as Philosopher.'

But this noble death is marred by the old man's last

words, which were 'a distinct homage' to Fanaticism itself. Rousseau suggests that Socrates' death represents a lack of integrity, since it fails to match the great deeds of the character's life.

The third figure to combat the great evil is, predictably enough, Jesus, who seizes the false idol and stands up in its place, and speaks in such a simple, convincing way that everyone listens and believes. Jesus is ultimately a more admirable model than Socrates: his teaching is more effective, and his life and death are more of a piece.

For Rousseau, Socrates is admirable as a representative of philosophical ignorance; and yet he is still too confident in his own mental powers, too reliant on his mind. Jesus beats Socrates at his own game. Similarly, Socrates is admirable for his willingness to face death, to defy priestly superstition and to stand up for the truth. But again, Rousseau suspects he may be still in league with the powers he seems to oppose; and hence, again, Jesus is a more trustworthy representative of the virtues for which Socrates is celebrated. The sources of Rousseau's admiration for Socrates' death are also the sources of his suspicion.

THE BATTLE AGAINST FANATICISM

The Enlightenment critique of the dying Socrates became part of the Enlightenment's own mythology. Nicolas Fréret (1688–1749) was a talented scholar who devoted much of his energy to challenging false myths. He was confined to the Bastille for his claim that the Franks, and hence the modern French nation, were not descended from the ancient Trojans, but were in fact a league of south German barbarian tribes, with no particular classical association or claim to free blue blood.

In 1736 he gave a lecture at the Académie Royale that aimed to debunk the idea of Socrates as a martyr to truth, unjustly condemned by sophists, intolerant politicians or priests. He presents his own work as a challenge to preconceived ideas: 'The idea of the wisdom and worth of Socrates that we acquire in the first years of our education gives us an illusion which our more adult reflections have difficulty in dissipating.' Fréret argues that the real grounds for the trial were political: Socrates was charged with impiety, but he was really hated as the teacher of Alcibiades and Critias. This reading has recurred many times over the years since Fréret; the most famous recent example of the genre was I. F. Stone's *Trial of Socrates*, published in 1988 (discussed in the following chapter).

Fréret based his conclusion on a careful analysis of the ancient sources. Like later scholars who adopt this reading, he presented it as truth to challenge generations of myth. The lecture is a classic example of Enlightenment rationalism, although turned in this instance against an Enlightenment myth. Fréret was troubled by two aspects of Socrates as depicted in Plato's *Apology*: his reliance on the *daimon* and his defiant attitude towards the jurors and towards the Athenian government in general. He was aware of what modern scholars call the *Apology–Crito* problem, and was deeply disappointed that the Socrates of the *Apology* seems to betray the principle so eloquently expressed by the Laws in the *Crito,* that the citizen must always submit to the rules of his own society. Socrates' reliance on his *daimon* seemed a betrayal of Socrates' rationalist principles. Even worse, it set a precedent that might do untold political harm: 'By means of the *daimon*, Socrates opened the door to fanaticism.'

Paradoxically, then, Fréret presents Socrates himself as the representative of fanatical religious belief, *fanatisme*. He died not because he was a philosophical free-thinker, but because he favoured superstition and hated democracy. For Fréret, as for Voltaire, Socrates' death undermines his identity as a wise philosopher. Fréret thus produces an inverted version of the idea that the death of Socrates was a philosophical 'apotheosis'. Truth and reason triumphed not through the defiant challenges of one brave gadfly, but through the judicial system that put to death a man who threatened the well-being of the state.

Even Voltaire (1694–1778), the Enlightenment intellectual who made most extensive use of the death of Socrates as a political myth, had surprisingly deep reservations about whether he could really admire the man. Voltaire celebrated Socrates as one who spoke truth to power, while corrupt priests, popular ignorance and an oppressive government were blamed for his death. 'The death of this martyr was in effect the apotheosis of philosophy', Voltaire declared.

But he had relatively little sympathy with Socrates himself. Voltaire's account of the death of Socrates is conflicted because he wanted to see the death of Socrates as a precursor to the deaths of innocent victims of intolerance in his own day, such as Jean Calas, a Huguenot who had recently been tortured and executed for the murder of his son, which he almost certainly did not commit. But Voltaire refused to beat the Athenians with the stick he aims at his own contemporaries. He insisted on a difference between his own age and that of classical Athens, even when he drew the parallel. Socrates was 'the only person the Greeks ever killed for his opinions'. The Athenians put only *one* philosopher to death, and an irritating one at that – and then they felt bad about it afterwards. The pagans thus, as often in Voltaire, put Catholic France to shame.

He notes that no fewer than 220 jurors voted *against* the death penalty. Some 220 enlightened philosophers in a single city? As Voltaire remarks, 'That is quite a lot.' Moreover, as we learn from Diogenes Laertius, the Athenians were soon ashamed of having killed Socrates and erected a temple in his memory. Voltaire concludes, 'Never has philosophy been so well avenged, nor so brilliantly honoured.'

Voltaire associated his own activities with those of Socrates, but only up to a point. In his play *La Mort de Socrate*, the names of the priests who bring down Socrates recall Voltaire's own personal enemies. Socrates is, like Voltaire himself, a deist, who lectures his prosecutors about his faith in a single God. This famous trial for impiety provided an obvious pretext for attacks on contemporary intolerance and the corruption of clergy.

But Voltaire remained reluctant to idolise Socrates, who had far too little common sense to be his ideal philosopher. Even in the play, he pays surprisingly little attention to Socrates' actual death. He invents a lot of extra stage business that has nothing to do with the trial. Socrates has a young female ward with a troubled love life; it eventually gets sorted out. It is as if Voltaire cannot imagine that his audience will care enough about Socrates to sustain their interest in him for a whole evening.

In private, Voltaire viewed Socrates as a show-off, calling him in a letter to Frederick the Great 'this snub-nosed sage', the 'Athenian chatterbox'. He deliberately challenges the notion that Socrates preserved his moral integrity by his willingness to die. For Voltaire, the truly intelligent philosopher was one who could stay alive. He claimed triumphantly,

'I am cleverer than Socrates' ('*Je suis plus sage que Socrate*'). After all, Voltaire was smart enough to have challenged religious authority and survived. In the *Treatise on Tolerance*, he remarks that Socrates' willingness to make enemies of powerful people 'was hardly worthy of a man whom an oracle had declared to be the wisest on earth'. In other words Socrates, for all his wisdom, was a fool.

MOSES MENDELSSOHN: FAITH, REASON AND THE JEWISH SOCRATES

In Germany, debates about the dying Socrates were ostensibly centred less on the role of *philosophes* in society than on the relationship of faith to reason. But here too the death of Socrates raised important questions about the social position of the modern intellectual.

Moses Mendelssohn (1729–86), a celebrated Jewish writer, thinker and theologian, was dubbed 'the Socrates of Berlin'. His rewriting of Plato's *Phaedo* (*Phaidon*, 1767) was a sensation in its own time. Mendelssohn uses the same basic structure, situation and characters as Plato had done. But he radically alters the Platonic arguments for the immortality of the soul. He presents an image of the dying philosopher who, even more vehemently than the Platonic original, denies human mortality and asserts that reason, virtue and human dignity can rise above all worldly spheres. Mendelssohn's new 'proof' of the soul's immortality depends primarily on belief in a benevolent Providence that allows no evil thing to happen to us. We are all protected by a good God: not only the philosopher, but all humanity is under his eye.

Mendelssohn's Socrates is a humanitarian, a benefactor to mankind: one who 'gave up, in the most loving fashion, health, power, comfort, reputation, peace, and in the end, life itself for the well-being of his fellow humans'. Socrates died to prove to us that we need not die. He died to save us all from the sins we might commit, were we unsure of the ultimate welfare of our souls. Mendelssohn's dying Socrates is a secular, ecumenical kind of new Messiah. He sacrifices himself for our redemption.

The *Phaidon* became the locus for debates about the scope and limits of natural reason, unilluminated by Judaeo-Christian faith. It prompted the notorious 'Lavater Affair' of 1769, in which Johann Kaspar Lavater challenged Mendelssohn to convert to Christianity. Lavater presented conversion to Christianity as the Socratic path: Mendelssohn, he said, should 'do as Socrates would have done', had he read modern defences of Christianity. He would have converted. Lavater implied that Socrates was not, after all, an ecumenical hero equally available to both Jews and Christians. Socrates – and perhaps the whole heritage of classical antiquity – belonged only to Christians.

But Mendelssohn refused to convert. He replied with a defence of both religious and philosophical toleration. He distinguished revealed from natural religion, arguing that only the latter was an appropriate topic for philosophy – and natural religion was common to Jews and Christians alike.

The Lavater Affair was an important moment in the modern cultural reception of antiquity. Mendelssohn had, through his rewriting of the death of Socrates, shown a way to reconcile the heritage of Greek philosophy with both Judaism and Christianity. But Lavater insisted that the Christians, not the Jews, were the cultural heirs of the Greeks – and in particular of the dying Socrates. In his later writings, Mendelssohn addressed a purely Jewish readership and abandoned the attempt to create an ecumenical theology.

Mendelssohn's *Phaidon* had been an attempt to reclaim the death of Socrates – as well as Socrates' views of death – for all the people of Europe, Jewish and Christian alike. It failed, and with its failure, marked by the Lavater Affair, came the awareness that the death of Socrates could not be used to create a new kind of companionship between all intellectuals, whatever their race or religious beliefs.

David's painting marked a moment of change, from a time when the dying Socrates was seen primarily in relationship to his own social circle – as an intellectual leader, teacher and friend – to a time when he was seen primarily as a solitary individual who stood up against the will of the masses and who was destroyed by them. We are, in this respect at least, the heirs not of the French Enlightenment, but of the French Revolution.

The Marquis of Condorcet (1743–94) remarked in 1793 that the death of Socrates was 'an important event in the history of humanity: it was the first crime which marked this war between philosophy and superstition, a war which still continues among us, as does the war of philosophy against the oppressors of humanity'. By the time Condorcet wrote these words, the association between the death of Socrates and crimes against individual human freedom had become well established as a core myth of the Enlightenment. But Condorcet's aphorism was, of course, a radical simplification of Voltaire's view about the death of Socrates. Voltaire was interested in the squabbles between one philosopher and another, and specifically in his own superiority over Socrates. By the 1790s the battle lines had hardened and there was no longer room to admit that 'philosophy' could mean more than one thing.

A year later, in 1794, Condorcet was himself arrested and condemned by the radical party in the French republican government, led by Robespierre. His death is mysterious, but he probably drank poison in prison – like his hero before him. Condorcet's own death was also an important event in the history of humanity. It marked, as Edmund Wilson has noted, the end of the French 'Enlightenment'. After the killings of 1794, the dying Socrates lost much of his cultural popularity. The possibility of calm, philosophical death no longer seemed realistic. Artists and writers turned back to the more brutal, and far more directly political, death of Cato the Younger. Cato's hands-on death, by self-disembowelment (see Guérin, page 123), corrects the false politeness of that poor, fey, wizened old man sipping his polite little hemlock drink. The painting seems also to invert the earlier model of the master who can teach his disciples how to die by his friendship and his example. Cato is not setting an example. He is not a teacher surrounded by devoted followers, but a rebel trying to escape. In Guérin's painting, he leans away from the other figures as he searches for his entrails with his own fingers. The painting rejects not only the calmness, but also the possibility of a shared life of the mind that had been implied by mid-eighteenth-century depictions of Socrates' death.

7

TALK, TRAGEDY, TOTALITARIANISM: THE PROBLEM OF SOCRATES IN MODERN TIMES

Thomas Carlyle (1795–1881) – the great historian of the French Revolution and one of the most influential writers of the Victorian age – was unimpressed by the death of Socrates. When asked whether he admired the conversation of his last hours, he commented damningly, 'Well, in such a case, I should have made no discourse; should have wished to be left alone, to profound reflections.' Carlyle, who recommended the 'worship of silence', condemned Socrates for talking too much – a complaint that would recur throughout the nineteenth and twentieth centuries.

In modern times, Socrates' death has generally been seen in two main ways: as the conflict of the individual with the state and as the downfall of rational, talkative man. Through meditating on the death of Socrates, modern writers and thinkers wrestled with their own doubts about civic disobedience, the power or limits of human reason and modernity itself. Socrates' death was seen as an iconic moment in the formation of modernity. Many of the most influential philosophers of the nineteenth century – including Hegel, Kierkegaard and Nietzsche – looked back to this moment as

16. Antonio Canova made a series of reliefs of scenes from the life of Socrates, including Socrates' rescue of Alcibiades, his dismissal of his family from the prison and the moment when Crito closes the master's eyes; the set has been called 'a secular stations of the Cross'. In this relief from 1794, Socrates, holding his hand to heaven, defends himself before the Athenian jury; his three accusers stand to his right.

the beginning of modern ethical and political thought, and sometimes as the beginning of modernity itself.

Socrates' talkativeness identified him as a modern person: like us, he talked too much. Because his main expertise lay not with the sword, but with the tongue, he was a hero for our times.

But Socrates' chatter came under new suspicion in the nineteenth century, because he was no longer valued as a representative of intellectual friendship. Socrates now seemed to be talking, ineffectually, to himself. The Enlightenment emphasis on Socrates' death as an image of shared mental life disappeared at the time of the French Revolution. Thereafter, Socrates was presented not in dialogue with his friends, but in conflict – set against his judges or his city, or struggling (and failing) to control his most unruly students.

The calm, philosophical death of an old man, surrounded

by his devoted followers, was out of keeping with Romantic cultural ideals. Félix Auvray's version of the theme, probably painted around 1800, shows the dying Socrates as a clean-shaven young man, expiring in a lonely garret, in the manner of Chatterton or Keats.

When Socrates is shown with his pupils, he is no longer the successful patriarch. J. B. Regnault's painting *Socrates Tears Alcibiades from the Embrace of Sensual Pleasure* (exhibited 1791) shows Alcibiades lurching drunkenly in the arms of Pleasure, while Socrates grabs his other arm. The topic was a popular one in nineteenth-century art, while Socrates' sociable, sublime death fell from favour among visual artists. In Regnault's painting the scowling philosopher holds up his left arm to heaven, in a mirror image of the pose of David's dying Socrates, while with his right, he grabs at Alcibiades, trying to lead the sybarite away from the brothel to higher things.

The image is a meditation on the French Revolution: the hedonistic aristocrat is dragged from his palace by a rough, poorly dressed revolutionary. But it seems likely that the mission of this old red cap will fail. Socrates cannot teach Alcibiades self-control unless he wants to learn. The conflict can be resolved only by violence and death.

Antonio Canova's relief of Socrates facing his judges (1794) is ostensibly very different: the figures are relatively static, and the white marble contrasts with Regnault's colourful canvas. But in both these images from the 1790s Socrates is shown not with his friends and followers, but with his opponents. He faces the hostile jury alone. Moreover, Canova's relief does not suggest any kind of connection or conversation. Socrates does not meet the eyes of either jury or viewer; instead, he looks upwards, perhaps seeking his own divine guidance.

Despite the vast number of images of the dying Socrates in the eighteenth century, there had been (to my knowledge) no earlier depiction of Socrates on trial. Canova's focus of the solitary Socrates, facing the judgment of his fellow-Athenians, foreshadows the major concerns of modern readings. From this moment onwards, Socrates was always on trial. The Socratic point of view – reason, science, irony or 'subjective' morality – always opposes some other value (such as pleasure or traditional morality). His death was tragic not because it was unjust, but because two different and equally valid models of justice came into conflict.

Modern philosophical accounts of the death of Socrates begin with G. W. F. Hegel's series of *Lectures on the History of Philosophy*, given during the years 1805 to 1830. Hegel argues that Athens was right to condemn Socrates and Socrates was also right to resist Athens: these two sides inevitably, and tragically, clashed. For Hegel, Socrates represents the beginning of modern ethical philosophy and modern theories of the self, in that he introduced a new style of ethics (*Moralität*) that depends on an individual's subjective judgement. This new style necessarily conflicted with traditional morality based on social conventions (*Sittlichkeit*).

Hegel presents the death of Socrates as a turning point in world history, because it marks a significant shift in human attitudes towards ethics. After Socrates, it was no longer possible simply to act by the wisdom handed down from one generation to another, such as the idea that sons should honour their fathers. The Athenian jury destroyed Socrates; but Socrates even more thoroughly destroyed the Athenian culture in which he had been born, because he introduced the notion that everyone must decide what to do for themselves.

Hegel saw Socratic individualism as neither entirely good nor entirely bad, but as an inevitable development in the process of history. His treatment of Socrates is bound up both with his theory of history and his theory of tragedy. Socrates is, like Antigone, a paradigmatic tragic figure. Hegel challenges the conventional view that this death is tragic because Socrates died unjustly. Rather, he says, 'Innocent suffering would only be sad and not tragic.' The death of Socrates is genuinely tragic because the Athenian decision to kill him was as valid, in moral terms, as his own resistance to Athenian conventions: 'Two opposed rights come into collision, and one destroys the other.' This is, for Hegel, the essence of tragedy.

Søren Kierkegaard (1813–55) was always haunted by the figure of the dying Socrates. His first book was a dissertation on Socrates that took him over ten years to complete: *The Concept of Irony with Constant Reference to Socrates* (1841). This work partly echoed Hegel's ideas, but Kierkegaard resisted his claim that Athens was justified in killing Socrates. Kierkegaard's meditation on the trial and death of Socrates allowed him to come up with a new account of ethics. He argued that Hegel was wrong to invoke collective morality. For Kierkegaard, all morality was subjective. He also condemned Hegel for neglecting Socrates' divine mission. Inspired by Socrates' *daimonion*, Kierkegaard argued that morality is inseparable from spirituality.

Kierkegaard remained heavily influenced by Hegel's vision of the death of Socrates as a tragedy. But he wanted to concentrate on the dying Socrates as tragic hero, not on the Athenian jury. He noted in *Fear and Trembling* that Socrates was 'an intellectual tragic hero': such a hero 'always dies before he dies'. Socrates is an emblem of conscious death, a hero who is fully, albeit paradoxically, aware of his own encounter with the unknown.

The German classicist and philosopher Friedrich Nietzsche (1844–1900) was also obsessed with the idea that Socrates' death was fully conscious and fully rational: an intellectual encounter with an irrational force. Nietzsche had a love-hate relationship with Socrates, whom he sometimes idolised, sometimes villainised. His changing attitudes towards Socrates were prompted by his mixed feelings about the value of reason itself.

Whereas Hegel saw the death of Socrates as a tragic event, for Nietzsche Socratic philosophy was the death knell for tragedy and the beginning of cultural decadence. He declared in *The Birth of Tragedy* (1872) that the philosophy of Socrates signalled 'the death of tragedy': 'Consider the consequences of the Socratic maxims "Virtue is knowledge; man sins only from ignorance; he who is virtuous is happy." In these three basic forms of optimism lies the death of tragedy.' Socrates was too much of a rationalist to allow for tragedy. His death, in particular, suggested that reason could conquer all the dark side of life: 'The *dying Socrates* as man raised above the fear of death by reason is the escutcheon which above the entrance gate of science reminds everyone of its mission: to make existence appear as intelligible and hence as justified.' This was, for Nietzsche, the great lie.

Nietzsche's essential philosophical disagreement with Socrates centred on the ideas that reason is the strongest motivation in human life, and that life is ultimately comprehensible. Nietzsche insists that people are not purely, or even primarily, rational: even Socrates was much less rational than he and his followers would have liked to think. Nietzsche mocks the last words as absurd: what kind of philosopher dies babbling about a rooster? The famous *daimonion* of Socrates was, according to Nietzsche, probably just an ear infection. But Nietzsche's views of Socrates were constantly changing. He acknowledges that 'Socrates, to confess it frankly, is so close to me that I almost always fight against him'. He admired and wanted to emulate the Socrates who was ironic, funny and unpredictable. If it came to a contest between Jesus and Socrates, Nietzsche thinks Socrates would win hands down. He remarks in *Human, All Too Human* (1878), 'Socrates excels the founder of Christianity in his cheery earnestness and prankish wisdom. Besides, he was smarter.'

By the time he was writing *The Gay Science* (1882), Nietzsche again turned savagely against Socrates, treating him as the precursor to a decadent and corrupt civilisation. Nietzsche even suggests that Socrates was perhaps not really Greek at all; his famous snub nose sounds suspicious from the point of view of genetic purity. In *Twilight of the Idols* (1888) he tells us, 'Socrates belonged by extraction to the lowest of the people: Socrates was rabble. We know, we can even still see, how ugly he was ... Was Socrates actually really a Greek?' The ancient problem of Socrates' physiognomy becomes more hazardous and sinister in a period of eugenic experimentation and racial segregation. If not Greek, what was Socrates? African? Semitic? Nietzsche does not say, but his hints are dark.

Perhaps, Nietzsche seems to imply, the Athenians should not have limited themselves to exterminating just one Socrates. Nietzsche suggests not only that clever-clever non-Aryan intellectuals ought to be killed, but also that their own ultimate desire is for death: 'Socrates wanted to die – it was not Athens but he himself who administered the cup of poison; he forced Athens into it.' He tricked the Athenians into bringing shame on themselves by awarding him as a punishment the death that he had wanted all along.

The German-Jewish writer Walter Benjamin (1892–1940) is a good candidate for the role of twentieth-century Socrates. A serious moral thinker whose written work is fragmentary, he killed himself while trying to escape from Occupied France. In his doctoral thesis and only finished work, *The Origins of German Tragic Drama*, Benjamin revisits and revises Nietzsche's distinction between the tragic hero and the dying Socrates.

Benjamin argues that the most important characteristic of the tragic hero is his silence. However much he may speak on stage, 'tragic man' is essentially silent and inarticulate about his relationship to the gods and his own death. Tragedy is viewed as a struggle or *agon* between a single, isolated figure and the ancient gods. It is a struggle that the hero is bound to lose, dying as a sacrificial victim for the onward progress of his community: tragic death is a form of atonement. The hero has to die. He shrinks before death 'as a power familiar, personal and inherent in him'. The hero's sublime silence marks both his limited awareness of his own situation and his defiance. There is a vast gulf between the ideals of the hero and those that hold sway in his society and his world. The tragic hero's thoughts are, necessarily, unspeakable in his language. Benjamin observes, echoing an earlier German critic, that 'in tragedy pagan man realizes that he is better than his gods, but this realization strikes him dumb'.

Socrates, by contrast, dies talking. For this reason, the death of Socrates is not tragic; it is 'a parody of tragedy'. Socrates, unlike the tragic hero, understands his situation perfectly. He is fully conscious of his relationship towards death, and the gods, and his own society: 'In one stroke, the death of the hero has been transformed into that of a martyr.' The *Phaedo* reveals how far Socrates stands from the tragic hero. Socrates dies talking about immortality. Death itself is for him entirely alien, or unreal: beyond it, 'he expects to return to himself'. The possibility of total annihilation and loss of consciousness, which is always present for the tragic hero, is impossible for the *Phaedo* Socrates. Instead of sacrificial death, Socrates dies to set 'the example of the pedagogue'. The moral of his death is all on the surface, articulated by the dying man himself. It seems, in Benjamin's account, as if Plato's dialogues are bad art compared to Greek tragedy. Plato's Socrates seems to make the fatal, philistine moral error of telling us what to think.

TOTALITARIANISM

One of the most important issues in modern responses to the death of Socrates has been whether Socrates can be distinguished from his pupil and creator, Plato. George Grote's monumental history of Greece (finished in 1856) made a sharp and influential distinction between Socrates – the open-minded teacher of the *Apology* – and Plato. This distinction allowed many thinkers of the twentieth century to condemn Plato's politics as proto-fascist or worse, while admiring or worshipping Socrates for his free-spirited individualism.

The Swedish playwright August Strindberg's play about the death of Socrates, *Hellas* or *Socrates* (1903), implies a parallel between Athens and contemporary Europe. Both are decadent imperialist societies, overrun with awful women and immoral playwrights, which will be destroyed by war and corruption, and in the process the best minds of their generation will also be destroyed.

The temptation to draw parallels between Athens and Europe became even stronger after the Second World War, which seemed to many to resemble the Peloponnesian War. If so, the death of Socrates began to look like a terrible fore-shadowing of the effects of fascism, Marxism or totalitarian-ism – in effect, a one-man Holocaust.

Perhaps the most compelling twentieth-century evoca-tion of Socrates' death written in the aftermath of the Second World War is Mary Renault's novel *The Last of the Wine* (1956). Renault evokes the whole history of Athens, from the time of the Great Plague (430 BC) until immediately before the trial. The book is told from the perspective of a fictional young man called Alexias, who stands on the edge of Socrates' circle and suffers through the turbulent final years of the Peloponnesian War and its aftermath.

With admirable restraint, Renault avoids describing the actual death of Socrates; Plato had done that already. Instead, his death is foreshadowed in the death of the narrator's young uncle, also called Alexias, at the very beginning of the story. When his boyfriend is dying of plague, Alexias goes to him and takes hemlock with him, 'so that they should make the journey together'. With the hemlock dregs, he writes the boyfriend's name, Philon ('Dear one'), 'as one does after supper with the last of the wine'.

Renault does not associate Socrates with any single strand of political opinion. For her, what is lost after his death is precisely a capacity for human love, loyalty and intellectual exploration, free from the restraints of politics. Socrates, like Alexias, will take the hemlock by his own choosing, for the sake of the dying things he loves: beauty, truth and the city of Athens. The world is less magical without him.

Most twentieth-century retellings that link the Peloponnesian and world wars do so in a less restrained way. Karl Popper argued in a book written during the Second World War (*The Open Society and Its Enemies*, 1945) that Plato was at the root of western totalitarianism – including both Marxism and fascism – while Socrates fought and died for the opposite of totalitarianism: 'the faith in man, in equalitarian justice, and in human reason': 'He showed that a man could die, not only for fate and fame and other grand things of this kind, but also for the freedom of critical thought, and for a self-respect which has nothing to do with self-importance or sentimentality.' Like many thinkers after the war, Popper believed that the world needed a return to Socrates, away from the terrible dangers of Platonism.

The American playwright Maxwell Anderson wrote a play about the death of Socrates in 1951, *Barefoot in Athens*, which provides a celebration of Socrates' death as a heroic symbol for modern democratic society. Anderson's version of the story sets it firmly in the context of the Cold War between America and the Soviet Union. Socrates' Athens is, like America, a democracy whose freedoms are under threat of a takeover by a communist power: Sparta. Anderson assumes that freedom of speech, to which Socrates devotes his life, is possible only under a democracy.

The dramatic climax of Anderson's play is the final moment in prison, when Pausanias, the King of Sparta, offers Socrates the opportunity to escape with his family to a Spartan palace. Socrates refuses, because he would be unable there to speak his own mind freely to people of every class and position. There is, he claims, no other city in the

Greek world where he can do this, because 'Athens is the only democracy'. Historically, all this is nonsense. But the point of the play is contemporary American ideology, not historical accuracy. Anderson presents the trial of Socrates as a symbol of democratic glory as well as democratic shame: only in a democratic system could such a trial take place.

The play shifts attention away from Socrates' relationship with his friends to his relationship with his wife and family. It tells the story of a final reconciliation between an old married couple. Socrates tells Xanthippe, 'Athens has been the great love of my life, and after Athens, you.' She is, understandably, jealous: she wants her husband to love her enough to put food on the table. She also reminds Socrates that his love for his country is, necessarily, unrequited: 'No matter how much you love Athens it doesn't love you.' But the play presents love – and especially unrequited or not-quite-requited love – as the most beautiful state of being, which again is possible only in a democratic society. Socrates dies for love of Athens, while Xanthippe remains in Athens in order to continue her love for Socrates. The lights dim as Socrates and Xanthippe sit cuddled up together, praying in darkness for 'beauty in the inward soul'. Socrates has now become the hero of a new kind of enlightenment. He is a man who dies for love of personal freedom, who does not know much about earning a buck, but knows for sure that love is all you need.

The last work of the great Italian film director Roberto Rossellini was a stiff but dignified television film of Socrates' last days (*Socrate*, 1970), which celebrates Socrates as an anti-totalitarian, a man who is always willing to question received prejudices. Rossellini's Socrates is a defender of the liberties of the modern city, which Rossellini had seen compromised in fascist Italy.

But for others, Socrates himself was on the side of the fascists. The journalist I. F. Stone wrote a popular and readable book, *The Trial of Socrates* (1988), in which he returned to the old argument that the real charge against Socrates was hatred of democracy. Stone suggests that Socrates may even have engineered his own death in order to bring Athenian democracy into disrepute.

Stone's book was criticised by many reviewers and scholars, who noticed that it provides a view of history highly coloured by Stone's own radical politics. But the book was also extremely influential. It inspired a television play by the British playwright Peter Barnes (*The Trial of Socrates*, 1992). Barnes's Socrates is, like Stone's, an anti-democrat who resists any form of political participation. He deserves to die for his hatred of democracy. The greatest injustice is that it is he, not more deserving men, whose death will bring endless fame.

In the eighteenth century, as we have seen, figures like Voltaire and Moses Mendelssohn proposed a new vision of Socrates as a great teacher, friend, and philanthropist, a man whose life, death and example can improve life on earth for all mankind. Modern readers have often felt sceptical of this vision.

A comment from one of the greatest twentieth century admirers and scholars of Socrates, Gregory Vlastos, takes us back to the old comparison between Socrates and Jesus, and articulates why many modern readers feel that Socrates was ultimately less admirable, and even less likable. 'Jesus wept for Jerusalem. Socrates warns Athens, scolds it, exhorts it, condemns it. But he has no tears for it.' We come back to the age-old criticism of Socrates for not suffering enough pain, in comparison to Jesus' agony on the Cross. But the main concern has altered, from physical to emotional pain. Vlastos, like many twentieth century readers, is particularly upset by the fact that Socrates showed no grief for his companions or family – and therefore, showed no love. Socrates is now seen as a loner, not the centre of a community. Twentieth century readers assume that the life of the mind must be separate from the passion and tears of the heart.

METAPHYSICS AND COMMON SENSE

Socrates has often been admired for his willingness to 'speak truth to power', and die in the telling. But it is unclear what truth, specifically, he told. The Romantic French poet Alphonse de Lamartine's influential and ecstatic *La Mort de Socrate* (published with the first collecction of *Méditations Poétiques*, 1820), presented Socrates as a mystical figure, who had glimpses of eternal life beyond our ken. Lamartine's Socrates gazes out over the sea, and rejoices to see the sail which brings his death. The contemplation of nature inspires in him a hysterically exclamatory happiness at God's benevolence and at his own pure eternal soul. Death liberates him from the chains of life on earth, into new birth: 'Death is not death, my friends, but only change!'

But another possibility was to see Socrates as an anti-metaphysician, an ordinary man whose greatest heroism lay in the revelation of his own commonplace ugliness. The idea of dying may be brave, but wanting to live, and admitting it, is even braver. The concept of Socrates as a man of the people whose wisdom and courage are both of a simple, common-sensical kind, has been popular in twentieth-century responses to the myth.

A sharp little story called 'Socrates Wounded' by the

great German dramatist Bertolt Brecht (1898–1956), written during his exile from Germany in the war years, focuses on Socrates in the Battle of Delium. Brecht's Socrates is a fat little cobbler who is rightly renowned for both cleverness and bravery – but bravery 'of a special kind'. When the battle begins, Socrates is clever enough to try to run away, rather than be trampled by Persian infantry. But other people are convinced, in the scrum of the battle, that he has really acted like a hero. Socrates is the Falstaff of Athens. Once he gets home, he is faced with a dilemma. Should he admit that he does not really deserve the laurel for bravery? Finally he tells Alcibiades and Xanthippe the truth. Xanthippe bursts out laughing, while Alcibiades says that he wishes he had brought his wreath to give to Socrates. 'You can take my word for it, I think you're brave enough. I don't know anybody who in this situation would have told the story you've just told.' Brecht suggests that the courage to tell the truth, when not compelled to do so and at the risk of embarrassment and shame, is more deeply admirable than the courage to run at an enemy in battle; the latter seems phoney and foolhardy.

Opponents of metaphysics may, like Brecht, discover or invent a non-metaphysical Socrates. Alternatively, common sense may lead one to reject the whole story of Socrates' death. A very funny piece by Woody Allen (from his collection *Side Effects*, New York, Random House, 1981) evokes what would have happened at the time of Socrates' death, if Allen put himself 'in this great philosopher's sandals'. Allen's Socrates spouts some of the usual stuff about the immortality of the soul and the 'principles of truth and free enquiry'. But he is, of course, far too neurotic and cowardly to want to die, or even to suffer any inconvenience. His friend Agathon protests, 'But this is your chance to die for truth!'. Allen-as-Socrates replies, 'Don't misunderstand me. I'm all for truth. On the other hand I have a lunch date in Sparta next week and I'd hate to miss it.' Agathon is shocked: 'Is our wisest philosopher a coward?' he asks. The Woody Allen Socrates answers, 'I'm not a coward and I'm not a hero. I'm somewhere in the middle'. Allen's dialogue returns to the old problems of whether Socrates was ordinary or extraordinary, and whether he was really able to 'bring down philosophy from heaven to earth'. It suggests that a Socratic death could never happen, in the real modern Manhattan world of eggs and smoked salmon bagels. Philosophy is just an academic subject, not a mode of life and death – in contrast to what Seneca, Montaigne, or Voltaire might have hoped. Agathon protests, 'But you have proved many times that the soul is immortal!' Allen's Socrates replies, 'And it is! On paper. See, that's the thing about philosphy – it's not all that functional once you get out of class.'

Another solution for those suspicious of abstractions and metaphysics is to concentrate on other characters in Socrates' story, setting rational male philosophy against feminine intuition. *Xanthippe* by the Viennese writer Fritz Mauthner (1884; translated as *Mrs Socrates* by Jacob Hartmann, 1926), is a surprisingly successful novelistic account of the effect of Socrates' life and death on his wife. Mauthner's Xanthippe is an honest, intelligent but uneducated lame peasant woman who suspects, quite rightly, that her husband's philosophy will get him into trouble. Socrates cannot restrain himself from delivering a lecture in which he acknowledges his doubts about the mythological gods of the city, and his fate is sealed. Socrates himself does not seem particularly upset about dying; his last words, according to Mauthner, are, 'Recovery at last! If the gods exist, I should like to thank them for my recovery!'

But for Xanthippe, things do not look so rosy. Left a single parent with a young child (Lamprocles), she settles as a country village farmer and makes a life for herself and her son. But she refuses to allow her boy to learn to read or to daydream. She has retained her husband's philosophical works, but eventually burns them after Plato and Xenophon try to buy them from her. Pure metaphysics, 'pure sunlight', is fatal, she believes. Socrates chose perfection of the work, not perfection of the life. His calm, philosophical death condemns Xanthippe and her child to a life of poverty and struggle. Whereas Socrates died for his own belief in reason, she dies trying to rescue her fellow peasants from an accidental fire in a granary. Xanthippe's death is the more admirable of the two.

The German artist Franz Caucig (1762–1828) painted a *Death of Socrates* which echoes the themes of Mauthner's novel. In this painting, Socrates lies on a wooden, straw-filled prison pallet, his eyes half-closed. A jug and cup stand on the bedside table; apparently he has already taken his dose. The male disciples and the executioner are shadowy figures in the background; the scene is focused on domestic tragedy. Xanthippe bends over her husband's prone body and clasps one of his hands; with the other, this stubborn old philosopher is still gesturing upwards, still trying to make some metaphysical point. Xanthippe wears a blue, Madonna-like robe, and a sturdy, tearful toddler boy is clinging to her neck. The child, whose face is at almost the exact centre of the canvas, is the real focus of our attention; his orphaning is the most important effect of the father's wilful death.

A similar story, but in a comic mode, is told by Roger

Scruton's *Xanthippic Dialogues* (1998), which offers a witty critique of Plato's version of Socrates. The women who were (in Plato's account) excluded from the Socratic circle, and from Plato's Academy, are now able to offer devastating rebuttals of these male philosophers. Scruton reminds us that Plato's Socratic dialogues are not the whole truth, either about Socrates or about the world.

THE PROBLEM OF MODERN SOCRATES

The dying Socrates proved particularly problematic for philosophers and theorists in the last decades of the twentieth century, because Socrates has so often been seen as a hero of reason – and reason itself has become a dubious value. In some cases, the death of Socrates has to be reimagined not as a demonstration of the power of reason, but as a final revelation of the impossibility of total rationality and total control over mysteries such as death. One striking modern painting of the death of Socrates, by the German artist Johannes Grützke, corrects David's controlled, triumphant death. It shows a man who looks crazed and convulsed, dying less with calm control than in the frenzy of a mad dog. The painting illustrates the impossibility of approaching death reasonably.

Postmodernist or poststructuralist critiques of traditional western notions of reason and logic may end up condemning the calm, classical image of the dying Socrates as the source of all our rationalist, 'logocentric' ills. The French theorist Jacques Derrida's famous essay *Plato's Pharmacy* (1972) studies the multiple meanings of the Greek word *pharmakon*: drug, cure, poison, talisman, medicine, magic. Plato uses *pharmakon* as an image of writing. Derrida uses a close reading of the ambiguities of this word to conduct a wholesale critique of 'western metaphysics', beginning with Plato.

Plato sets up distinctions between inner truth and external means of conveying truth, such as language. But these distinctions turn out to be confused and unviable, according to Derrida. The supposedly secondary terms are used to explain the primary terms, in a whole series of key oppositions: absence informs presence, play work, essence supplement, outer inner, language truth, representation reality, written spoken, son father.

Derrida's reading implies a new interpretation of the death of Socrates. As he notes, *pharmakon* is also the only word used by Plato for the hemlock that Socrates drank. Platonic metaphysics, for Derrida, is all motivated by a combination of mourning and guilt for the death of Socrates. Socrates, Derrida claims, functioned both as Plato's father and as his brother. Echoing Freud's account of the origins of religion in an original family murder (*Totem and Taboo, Moses and Monotheism*), he notes that Plato 'repeated the father's death', writing or rewriting his death sentence even as he tries to undo it.

This relationship to the death of Socrates explains all the contradictions in Plato – including the paradox that Plato, who condemned writing and cast the poets out of his Republic, should have written so much. He writes to unwrite or overwrite the indictment of Socrates. The cost of Platonic metaphysics, the cost of rationality, is death, Derrida seems to suggest. At other moments he implies that we turn to Platonic metaphysics because, like children, we fear to die and can exorcise our fear only by the 'antidote' of dialectics. Derrida calls for a new kind of enlightenment, through an alternative metaphysics. This new mode of thought will be possible only if we can move beyond Plato's mode of imagining the death of our father or brother – Socrates. It is unsurprising, then, that so much of Derrida's own writing is about death, including evocations of his own dead philosopher friends. He tried, throughout his life, to find alternatives to the Platonic death of Socrates.

While Derrida insisted that Plato's Socrates must be held accountable for much of what is wrong with western metaphysics, another French theorist, Michel Foucault, tried to reclaim a less rational or 'logocentric' side of the dying philosopher. In his last lectures before he died, given in the Collège de France in 1984, Foucault suggested that all western thought went wrong through a misreading of Plato's *Apology*. Socrates is associated in this text, Foucault argued, with two central phrases: 'know yourself' and 'the care of the self'. Foucault prefers the idea of self-care over the all-too-cognitive, all-too-rational concept of self-knowledge. He argues that Plato's *Apology*, too, evokes a Socrates who seeks knowledge only in the service of the care of the self, not the other way around. According to Foucault, we should – like Socrates – try to look after ourselves. Knowing ourselves is of secondary importance.

Foucault's own early death perhaps prevented him from developing an account of the relationship between death and care in the *Apology*. But he hints that Socrates' choice of death is the culmination of his care for himself, as well as his culminating act of self-recognition. Socrates died in order to preserve his true self. Foucault's reading is in many ways a return to Stoic accounts of Socrates' death: like Seneca, Foucault thinks Socrates chose death because it allowed him to be, remain or become himself. It was the hemlock that made Socrates great.

SOCRATES AND EUTHANASIA: THE HEMLOCK SOCIETY

For many readers throughout the tradition, the essential meaning of Socrates' death lies in the fact that he died by his own choice.

The Hemlock Society was the oldest and one of the most successful 'right-to-die' or 'assisted suicide' organisations in America. It was founded in 1980 as a simple 'Mom and Pop' enterprise by one Derek Humphry, an outspoken advocate of euthanasia. Humphry's first wife, Jean, suffered from painful and terminal bone cancer and in 1975 she killed herself with his help. His book about her death, *Jean's Way* (1979), was a bestseller. The Hemlock Society provided literature to explain the best ways to concoct homemade suicide potions and set up a network of 'Caring Friends' to ensure 'maximum personal support' in the last hours, as well as advocating legal reform to allow physician-assisted suicide for the terminally ill. The organisation's slogan was 'Good Life, Good Death' and it used the hemlock plant as an emblem.

To readers of Plato, the name might seem less than apt. There is, after all, an important difference between deliberate suicide for personal reasons and submitting to state execution by poison after a legal court has passed a death sentence. Plato insists that Socrates' death was not suicide: his hero resists killing himself on his own terms in prison and instead waits patiently for the state's punishment to be carried out. Xenophon's Socrates is perhaps more readily assimilated into the model of assisted suicide for the terminally ill, since, you will remember, he claims to choose death in order to avoid the inevitable decline into senility associated with old age. In justifying the name, the Hemlock Society emphasised 'the principle of personal choice central to Socrates' action'. He chose death rather than exile, an

17. An American pro-euthanasia organisation, the Hemlock Society, used the poison which killed Socrates as a symbol for 'Good life, good death'. More recent incarnations of this society have dropped all allusion to the death of Socrates.

option that was unacceptable to him, 'much like terminally ill people today' (most of whom, one might quibble, do not have the option of moving to Thessaly).

But the name proved increasingly controversial, both within the organisation and outside it. Many members of the society felt that association with Socrates was impeding their hopes of legislative reform: it carried, some said, too much 'baggage' and was too 'elitist'. The organisation has since gone through various mergers with other euthanasia groups. After a brief phase under the name 'End of Life Choices', it now calls itself 'Compassion and Choices', and traces its roots back only as far as the beginning of the twentieth century, when the modern 'choice-in-dying' movement began in America. Compassion and Choices promises 'state-of-the-art care at the end of life'. Humphry himself mourned the eventual decision to change the name and condemned the ignorance that prompted it: 'Socrates' death in 329 BC [*sic*] was a noble and self-chosen one,' he argued, and one that had instant name recognition.

It is not clear whether the abandonment of the Socratic model will help the society achieve its legislative goals. Hostility and anxiety about legalising the 'ultimate civil right' remain strong in both the US and the UK. It is unlikely that people will worry less about the morality of suicide and the possibilities of abuse now that the name of Socrates is no longer attached to the movement.

But the change of name signifies more than simply a decline in classical education in US and UK schools. It suggests that our society has, even in the course of the last twenty years, moved further and further away from the idea that death is part of life, and may itself be an act of heroism. The newest name emphasises 'compassion' and 'comfort' even over that crucial buzz-word 'choices'. The dying person is conceived as weak, ill and in need of nurture, not a triumphant fighter in the final moral struggle of life.

RELEVANCE AND IRRELEVANCE: HOW THE DEATH OF SOCRATES CAN CHANGE YOUR LIFE

It is striking that, for much of the twentieth century, most major writers, philosophers and artists have paid relatively little attention to Socrates. Few of those who have cared about the death of Socrates in the twentieth century have had the intellectual and cultural stature of Erasmus, Voltaire or even Foucault. The dying Socrates seems to have fallen away from his central place in western culture.

One reason for this change is that Socrates seems to many people to be tainted by his association with the dead-white-male western tradition. The death of Socrates is no longer often cited in calls for tolerance and civil liberty, as in the days of Voltaire, Condorcet, John Stuart Mill or even Martin Luther King.

Socrates is an unlikely icon for an age of gender equality. An exception will help illustrate the rule. Elsie Russell is the only woman known to me to have painted a 'Death of Socrates'. Russell's Socrates is a tired old man sitting in a dark, under-lit prison. The painting is suggestive less of calm than of stagnancy: a dead white patriarch has had his day. But there are sympathy and softness in the depiction of Socrates' and Crito's sagging breasts. Russell manages to domesticate and feminise the scene. It almost seems like a group of quiet old ladies preparing to drink a nice hot cup of tea. Socrates earns his place in the tableau only at the cost of losing his heroic stature.

More generally, modern culture has often doubted the value or relevance of antiquity. Socrates, as the most famous of all the ancient Greeks, has fallen out of favour along with the decline of classical learning. Again, the exceptions are revealing. For a few avant-garde artists and composers in the twentieth century, Socrates' antiquity and irrelevance have been precisely the reason for his attraction. A so-called dramatic symphony (for four female voices and a small orchestra) about the death of Socrates, composed by Erik Satie (*Socrate*, 1916), evoked the death of Socrates by setting to music three passages from Plato, culminating in the death scene from the *Phaedo*. Satie viewed Socrates as a representative of the 'purity' of antiquity. He prepared to write this piece by eating only white foods: he hoped to produce 'white emotions' in the listener, including wonder and tranquillity. The music itself achieves a beautifully clean minimalism. The dying Socrates was an attractive subject because it was almost meaningless. Antiquity in general, and Socrates in particular, have beome pure white nothing. John Cage adapted Satie's *Socrate* to make it even more minimalist, in his *Cheap Imitation* (finished in 1969): he eliminated the human voices and set the entire work for piano.

In the works of both Satie and Cage, the individuality of Socrates – that goggle-eyed old ironist – no longer matters at all. His attraction, for both composers, lies partly in the fact that he died peacefully. But even more important is the fact that he lived and died a very long time ago – and can therefore represent an almost abstract human experience. The point is clear in a striking painting by the Belgian artist Jan Cox that was inspired by Satie's work, *De Dood van Socrates* (1979). The solitary figure represented here is barely recognisable as a man. Pain triumphs over reason, and even over humanity.

If we move from high to low culture, Socrates is used to mean anything or everything. He can take on an enormous number of banal meanings, since his actual character is almost entirely undefined. Those searching to add a little extra cultural capital to a self-help manual by invoking the ancient world can always appeal to Socrates as an authority for any old truism. William Bodri's *Socrates and the Enlightenment Path* (2001) treats Socrates as a figure who unites western and eastern wisdom, and can guide us in the West towards Buddhist or Confucian enlightenment. Mark Forstater's *The Living Wisdom of Socrates* (2004) offers an account of how Socrates, through 'personal struggle', achieved 'a life infused with spirit'. The spiritual side of Socrates is also emphasised in Dan Millman's semi-autobiographical novels *Way of the Peaceful Warrior* (1980), *Sacred Journey of the Peaceful Warrior* and *The Journeys of Socrates*, in which a teacher named 'Socrates' appears as a New Age guru.

In Alain de Botton's enjoyable book *The Consolations of*

18. The Belgian artist Jan Cox painted this disturbing, semi-abstract Death of Socrates *in 1979, a year before he killed himself. To the right of Socrates is a bushy-tailed cockerel – an allusion to Socrates' last words.*

Philosophy (2000), the death of Socrates is a reminder that we should not worry too much about popularity. What other people think of us matters only if they are right: truth is always more important than opinion. The lesson is a good and useful one. But, as de Botton himself recognises, its application is doubtful. Perhaps the death of Socrates teaches modern democratic governments and juries to look without prejudice at social minorities and socially unpopular opinions. But perhaps it only teaches de Botton himself not to worry so much about whether strange policemen will like and approve of him. De Botton's chapter on the death of Socrates begins by juxtaposing two drinks: the hemlock in David's painting and the Nesquik chocolate milk enjoyed by de Botton himself after viewing *The Death of Socrates*. Moral seriousness and heroism can hardly be maintained for more than a few words in a world where adults consume mass-produced children's drinks.

All these books try to reclaim Socrates from academic philosophy and put him back in the marketplace. But the quest risks denying some of the most well-attested facts about Socrates: that he was clever, provocative and liked asking questions. As in the Middle Ages, Socrates is often turned into a representative sage or wise man. Plato's ironic, questioning Socrates is abandoned in favour of Xenophon's bland advocate of traditional morality. These versions of Socrates reveal how little tolerance our culture has for genuine moral or political dissent.

There have been a few attempts to bring Socrates the gadfly into the modern world. But these versions of Socrates often seem severely restricted in the issues they are willing to address. One example is Christopher Phillips's inspiring but oddly limited *Socrates' Café: A Fresh Taste of Philosophy* (2002). In coffee shops all over America, Phillips raised big questions about life, such as 'What is love?' and 'What is work?', and talked them through with whoever happened to be in the café.

But Phillips's version of the Socratic gadfly is always terribly careful to avoid offending people. He combines Socratic questioning with the charming geniality of the Oprah Winfrey show. If only he could have asked the workers and managers of the Starbucks chains he patronised, 'What is global consumer capitalism?' This is a Socrates without ideology, and in fact Socrates without the death: it is a Socrates whom nobody would ever want, or bother, to kill.

The thriller writer Walter Mosley – one of Bill Clinton's

favourite writers – has come much closer to creating a modern Socrates whose moral choices really do matter. Socrates Fortlow, who appears in *Always Outnumbered, Always Outgunned* and *Walkin' the Dog*, is a contemporary black man. Out of prison after serving a life sentence for murder, Socrates walks the dirty streets of downtown LA, trying to find a way to be good and redeem himself for his crimes. He is a murderer-cum-philosopher, living on extra time, who needs to examine his life again every day – and, if possible, avoid killing any more black people.

In the Socrates Fortlow books, Mosley claims for the black community this icon of white western culture. But in doing so, he shows why it is not possible for a modern Socrates to be a citizen of America in the way that the old Socrates was a citizen of Athens and of the world. Socrates Fortlow feels loyalty only to his own people. The worst of his crimes, in his own eyes, is the fact that the people he killed were black. Mosley's Socrates lives in a world which is so deeply divided by race and class that his quest for human wisdom can be relevant only to himself.

ALTERNATIVE HISTORIES

It is hard not to wonder what the cultural and intellectual history of the West would have looked like if Socrates had died in his bed. Would the world record on human rights and toleration have turned out better, worse or much the same? Would our notions of reason, truth, heroism and the soul be radically different without the image of this death? Or has our culture changed so much, since the time of ancient Athens or even since the eighteenth century, that Socrates' death no longer matters to us?

Thomas Disch's dystopian futurist novel, 334 (1974), describes a young college student in the early twenty-first century struggling to make sense of a reproduction of David's painting, *The Death of Socrates*. The task seems, at first, impossible: 'He stared at the picture of Socrates in the bad light. With one hand he was holding a big cup, with the other he was giving somebody the finger. He didn't seem to be dying at all.' The inability of this boy to understand the gestures in the painting reflects the poverty of the world he lives in, which is dominated by desire and aggression ('the finger'). But Socrates turns out to be relevant even in this bleak future, as a reminder of what is missing. The authorities, in Disch's world, pretend to be able to know everything about everybody. They provide tests and assemble statistics, to decide which citizens may have children and which may not. What the future still needs is Socrates' awareness of his own ignorance. Even though he does not understand David's work, the student finds himself crying over it: 'A tear fell into Socrates' cup and was absorbed by the cheap paper'.

Two more recent science fiction novels suggest a more hopeful vision of how Socrates can still save the world. The continuing dominance of this ancient philosopher over modern imaginations is shown very clearly by these works, which depict what would happen if the original death were reversed, and Socrates were brought back to life in the present or the future.

In God's Name (2001), written under the pseudonym Robert Verly, begins with God, who has realised that nobody on earth really understands Him/Her/It. The solution, of course, is to bring back Socrates from Limbo. He appears, in a rather Xenophontic guise (where Xenophon meets Benjamin Franklin), and explains that all religions are wrong, the

American Founding Fathers were right about almost everything and we should all be less judgemental of one another.
He is glad to learn some new scientific facts about black
holes and happy to have been of use, although he recognises
that 'beneficial changes came more from inevitable trends of
history than from his efforts'. Eventually his soul – or rather,
his plasma – will be recycled all over again.

A slightly less crazed experiment with reversing the
events of 399 BC is Paul Levinson's *The Plot to Save Socrates*
(2006). This novel describes what happens when a New York
graduate student of the 2040s sees part of a new Platonic
dialogue, set just after the *Crito* and ready-translated into
implausible nineteenth-century English in the manner of
Benjamin Jowett. The student herself wishes Socrates had
stayed alive to fight for a better world. In the new text, he
is offered another chance to escape from prison and death.
A clone can take the hemlock in Socrates' stead, while he
himself will be whisked away in a time machine. Through
the rest of the novel, the student travels through time, back
to Socrates' prison cell as well as to Alexandria and nineteenth-century London, in search of the truth. Perhaps, she
realises, Socrates never really died at all.

The major premise of the book is fundamentally silly,
since obviously the ethical problem of whether Socrates
should have escaped from prison remains the same whether
he uses a time machine, cloning or a chariot. But the book
raises important and interesting questions. How has the
death of Socrates already changed our world? And does
this event belong only to Plato or can it be appropriated and
reappropriated by all of us?

Plato's creation of Socrates' character, and of the scene of
his death, can be seen as a kind of identity theft. The myth of

222 THE DEATH OF SOCRATES

the death of Socrates has been stolen so many times that it is, by now, unclear to whom it really belongs.

This idea is strikingly expressed in a piece by the Swiss dramatist Friedrich Dürrenmatt (1921–90; most famous for his play *The Visit,* 1956). Dürrenmatt's Socrates is a jolly, fat, popular old man, a heavy drinker, whose sole failing is a tendency to steal knick-knacks from his hosts' houses when everybody but himself is lying about drunk. He donates the spoils to an 'antiques' shop run by his wife, Xanthippe. Plato, an 'introverted intellectual' who has 'resolved to change a world he held in contempt', persuades Socrates to allow him to perform a much more serious kind of theft or borrowing: Plato 'steals' Socrates' conversations, to create his own written dialogues. He passes off that dangerously antidemocratic text, the *Republic,* as Socrates' own opinions, and Socrates is put on trial. Socrates, a relaxed, lackadaisical man who has no sense either of strategy or of words as private property, is unable to learn his own defence speech; he is condemned to death.

But, in a surprising twist, Aristophanes offers to die in Socrates' stead. After all, Aristophanes remarks, it would be a pity to waste such a dramatic script as Plato's *Phaedo,* which he has already composed. Socrates would be sure to fluff the lines. Aristophanes suggests that there are two quite different ways of dying with integrity. For himself, as a dramatist, it makes sense to die in character, in the last great performance of his life. For Socrates, on the other hand, there is still time to die as Socrates, not as Plato's version of himself. Socrates is shipped off to Syracuse, where Plato hopes that he will be able to convince Dion the tyrant to become a philosopher. 'Unfortunately, Dion had vowed that anyone who drank him under the table had to die. Socrates drank Dion under the table. Now Socrates had to drink the hemlock after all.' But Socrates flouts Dion's expectations of a big spectacle by dying without saying a single word.

The piece ends with a great speech by Socrates' wife, Xanthippe, in which she gives words to Socrates' silent death. She declares that Socrates was the only man who knew what all women know: how to be himself, rather than simply play at being himself. In the final twist of the story, Xanthippe reveals that she has bought the enslaved Plato, using the profits from the shop which Socrates stocked with his thefts. Plato, the only character in the story who claims absolute knowledge of himself and believes in his inalienable right to his own words and opinions, becomes an object for Xanthippe's new shop.

Dürrenmatt's Plato, who thinks he can change the world, can be possessed by others. But Aristophanes, Socrates and Xanthippe, who make no such claims, remain free to be themselves, without play-acting, ownership or robbery. Xanthippe tells us that her husband's death by hemlock was simply 'the natural consequence of being such a good drinker'. 'Socrates died as Socrates', she declares. Xanthippe, who has been so often excluded from the story of her husband's death, finally gets the last word.

FURTHER READING

GENERAL

Translations from Greek and Latin are, except where stated, mine. There is a huge bibliography on Socrates. The following suggestions are certainly not exhaustive, and do not reflect everything I read while writing this book.

There are two good collections of texts and quotations about Socrates in English: *The Socratic Enigma*, edited by H. Spiegelberg (Indianapolis, Bobbs-Merrill, 1964), and *Socrates: A Source Book*, edited by J. Ferguson (Buckingham, Open University Press, 1970). Unfortunately both are out of print, but they can be tracked down in second-hand shops or libraries.

An excellent collection of essays about Socrates and the Socratic tradition, *A Blackwell Companion to Socrates*, edited by Sara Ahbel-Rappe and Rachana Kamtekar (Blackwell 2006) appeared just as I was finishing this book.

A useful overview of the reception of Socrates throughout the western tradition is James Hulse's *Socrates: Reputations of a Gadfly* (New York, Lang, 1995). Also helpful is Mario Montuori's *Socrates: Physiology of a Myth* (first published in Italian, 1974; very poor English translation, published Amsterdam, J. C. Gieben, 1981).

INTRODUCTION

The epigraph from this chapter comes from a letter by T. B. Macaulay, written from Calcutta to his friend Ellis, dated 29 May 1835. Macaulay responds favourably to Plato, but not to Socrates, and writes, 'I am now deep in Plato, and intend to go right through all his works. His genius is above praise. Even where he is most absurd, – as, for example, in the *Cratylus*, – he shows an acuteness, and an expanse of intellect, which is quite a phenomenon by itself. The character of Socrates does not rise upon me. The more I read about him, the less I wonder that they poisoned him. If he had treated me as he is said to have treated Protagoras, Hippias, and Gorgias, I could never have forgiven him.'

Nicander's *Alexipharmaca* is available in English translation in *Nicander: The Poems and Poetical Fragments*, edited with translation and notes by A. S. F. Gow and A. F. Scholfield (New York, Arno Press, 1979). On the painful symptoms of water hemlock poisoning, see C. Gill, 'The Death of Socrates', *Classical Quarterly*, 23, 1973, pp. 225–8. Gill's account is corrected by Enid Bloch, 'Hemlock Poisoning and the Death of Socrates', in Thomas Brickhouse and Nicholas Smith's *The Trial and Execution of Socrates: Sources and Controversies* (Oxford, Oxford University Press, 2002). On uses of hemlock versus other methods of state killing, see *Capital Punishment in Ancient Athens*, Irving Barkan (Chicago, Chicago University Press, 1936).

1 SOCRATES' PHILOSOPHY

In general, the most ancient important sources used here are: Plato's *Euthyphro*, *Apology*, *Crito* and *Phaedo*, all available in *The Last Days of Socrates*, translated and edited by Hugh

Tredennick and Harold Tarrant (London, Penguin Books, 2003); Plato's *Gorgias*, translated by Chris Emlyn-Jones and Walter Hamilton (London, Penguin Books, 2004); and Plato's *Protagoras and Meno*, translated by Adam Beresford, with an introduction by Lesley Brown (London, Penguin Books, 2006). The contrast between water, which can be transferred from one cup to another on a piece of wool, and wisdom, which cannot be so easily transferred, comes from Plato's *Symposium*, translated by Christopher Gill (London, Penguin Books, 2003). The *Symposium* is also the most important source for Socrates' appearance and his relationship with Alcibiades, discussed in Chapter 2. Aristophanes' *Clouds* is available in many translations, including *Lysistrata/ The Archarnians/The Clouds*, translated by Alan Sommerstein (London, Penguin Books, 1974).

On Aristophanes' *Clouds*, see the introduction to the edition by K. Dover, which is mostly accessible to those who have no knowledge of Greek.

On Socrates' philosophy, see Thomas Brickhouse and Nicholas Smith's *The Philosophy of Socrates* (Boulder, Co., Westview Press, 2000) and Gregory Vlastos, *Socrates: Ironist and Moral Philosopher* (Ithaca, NY, Cornell University Press, 1991). Vlastos' view of Socratic irony is challenged by many other Platonists, including Alexander Nehemas (*Art of Living: Socratic Reflections from Plato to Foucault* (Berkeley, University of California Press, 1988)) and Iakovos Vasiliou ('Conditional Irony in the Socratic Dialogues', *Classical Quarterly*, 49(2), 1988, pp. 456–72).

Robert Nozick discusses Socratic ignorance in *Socratic Puzzles* (Cambridge MA, Harvard University Press, 1997). Also see *Socratic Questions: New Essays on the philosophy of Socrates and its significance* edited by Barry S. Gower and

Michael Stokes (Routledge, London, 1992); *Essays on the Philosophy of Socrates* edited by Hugh H. Benson, Oxford University Press, 1992; and *Remembering Socrates: Philosophical essays* edited by Lindsay Judson and Vassilis Karasmanis (Clarendon, Oxford, 2006), which includes two essays on reception.

Mario Vegetti's essay, 'The Greeks and their gods', is in *The Greeks* edited by Jean-Pierre Vernant, translated by Charles Lambert and Teresa Lavender Fagan (Chicago, Chicago University Press, 1995, pp. 254–84).

Leo Strauss's *The City and the Man* (Chicago, Chicago University Press, 1964) discusses Plato's *Republic*.

A lively recent account of Socratic philosophical method is Debra Nails's *Agora, Academy, and the Conduct of Philosophy* (Kluwer, Dordrecht and Boston, 1995). Charles Kahn's *Plato and the Socratic Dialogue* (Cambridge, Cambridge University Press, 1996) provides an energetic and controversial introduction. These books offer an introductory glimpse into the Socratic problem.

On the Athenian religious context for the trial, see Robert Garland, *Introducing New Gods: The Politics of Athenian Religion* (Ithaca, NY, Cornell University Press, 1992), and especially the magisterial overview in Robert Parker's *Athenian Religion: A History* (Oxford, Clarendon, 1996). On Socrates' own religious views, a good starting point for the scholarly debate are the articles collected in Brickhouse and Smith's *The Trial and Execution of Socrates* (see especially the articles by M. F. Burnyeat and Mark L. McPherran).

The money equivalences given in this chapter are based on *Antiphon and Andocides* translated by Michael Gargarin and Douglas M. MacDowell (University of Texas Press, Austin, 1998, pp. xxv–xxvi).

2 POLITICS AND SOCIETY

Our main source for the Peloponnesian War is Thucydides (*The History of the Peloponnesian War*, translated by Rex Warner, Penguin, London, 1954).

A very useful book on all the characters who appear in Plato's dialogues is Debra Nails's *The People of Plato* (Indianopolis, Hackett, 2002).

For more on the historical Socrates, a good place to start is Brickhouse and Smith's *The Trial and Execution of Socrates*. This includes extracts from the ancient sources and a selection of modern scholarly essays. It has a useful introduction by the editors that surveys the state of current opinion.

A good non-specialist introduction to the historical issues is given by James A. Colaiaco, *Socrates against Athens: Philosophy on trial* (Routledge, New York and London, 2001).

Douglas MacDowell's edition of Andocides' *On the Mysteries* (Oxford, Clarendon, 1989) contains a useful appendix on the events of 415 BC, which is comprehensible without Greek.

For more detailed discussion of the political context of the trial, see Mogens Herman Hansen, 'The Trial of Socrates from the Athenian Point of View', *Historisk-Filosofiske Meddelelser*, 71, 1994.

Andrea Nightingale offers an interesting account of the development of philosophy as a discipline in the fifth and fourth centuries BC, including discussion of why it matters that Socrates, unlike the other sophists, did not take money: see *Genres in Dialogue* (Cambridge, Cambridge University Press, 1995). The Lysias passage discussed in this chapter is included in *Lysias*, translated by S. C. Todd (Austin, University of Texas Press, 2000).

On visual representations of Socrates and other philosophers of antiquity, see John Henderson, 'Seeing through Socrates: Portrait of the Philosopher in Sculpture Culture', *Art History*, 19, 1996, pp. 327–52; and Paul Zanker, *The Mask of Socrates: The Image of the Intellectual in Antiquity*, translated by Alan Shapiro (Berkeley, University of California Press, 1995). On associations between Socrates and satyrs, see Daniel McLean, 'Refiguring Socrates: Comedy and Corporeality in the Socratic Tradition', unpublished PhD dissertation, University of Pennsylvania, 2002.

The translation of Aristophanes cited comes from Jeffrey Henderson's Loeb edition (*Frogs, Assemblywomen, Wealth: Aristophanes* Vol. 4, Boston, Mass., Harvard University Press, 2002).

3 PLATO AND OTHERS

The Penguin translations of Plato and Xenophon are excellent. See Xenophon's *Conversations of Socrates*, translated and edited by Hugh Tredinnick and Robin Waterfield (Harmondsworth, Penguin Books, 1990), and Plato's *The Last Days of Socrates*, translated and edited by Hugh Tredennick and Harold Tarrant, (London, Penguin Books, 2003).

Other Latin and Greek fragmentary sources, untranslated, may be found in the indispensable scholarly collection, edited by Gabriele Giannantoni, *Socratis et Socraticorum Reliquiae*, 4 vols. (Naples, Edizioni dell' Ateneo, 1990).

On Xenophon's *Memorabilia*, see A.-H. Chroust, *Socrates: Man and Myth: The Two Socratic Apologies of Xenophon* (London, Routledge, 1957). The methodology used in this book is dubious, but Chroust provides an essential starting point for those hoping to reconstruct Polycrates' *Prosecution of Socrates* from Xenophon's *Defence*. Vivienne J. Gray's 'The Framing of Socrates: The Literary Interpretation of Xenophon's *Memorabilia*' (*Hermes*, 1998, pp. 1–202) offers a worthy defence of Xenophon's merits.

There are, of course, an enormous and ever-growing number of excellent books and publications about Plato. The following list is extremely selective; it will lead you to more.

The introduction to Michael Stokes's edition of Plato's *Apology* (Warminster, Aris and Phillips, 1987) is accessible to the Greekless and provides a stimulating account of why Plato is little or no use as a source for the historical Socrates. For a different approach, see C. D. C. Reeve, *Socrates in the Apology: An essay on Plato's Apology of Socrates*, Indianapolis IN, Hackett Publishing, 1989.

Recent 'literary' or 'dramatic' readings of Plato's dialogues include James A. Arieti, *Interpreting Plato: The dialogues as drama* (Rowman and Littlefield, Savage, MD, 1991; and Ruby Blondell, *The Play of Character in Plato's Dialogues* (Cambridge, Cambridge University Press, 2002).

A helpful attempt to grapple with the different voices of Plato's *Crito* is Roslyn Weiss, *Socrates Dissatisfied: An Analysis of Plato's 'Crito'* (Oxford, Oxford University Press, 1998); even more useful is Verity Harte's article 'Conflicting Values in Plato's *Crito*', *Archiv für Geschichte der Philosophie*, 81 (2), 1999, pp. 117–47, which distinguishes the voices of Crito, Socrates and the Laws. A sympathetic and stimulating account of Socrates' interlocutors, including both Crito and Euthyphro, is John Beversluis's *Cross-examining Socrates* (Cambridge, Cambridge University Press, 2000). More classic articles on the *Apology*, *Crito* and *Euthyphro*, and further bibliography, can be found in Brickhouse and Smith, *The Trial of Socrates*.

On the last words, see Glenn Most, 'A Cock for Asclepius', *Classical Quarterly*, 43, 1993, pp. 96–111. Most gives a clear account of various possibilities and points to further bibliography. His own interpretation is that the words refer to Plato's illness. See also George Dumézil, *The Riddle of Nostradamus: A Critical Dialogue* (Baltimore, Johns Hopkins University Press, 1999), for a further attack on the 'life-is-sickness' interpretation.

4 'A GREEK CHATTERBOX'

A translation of Diogenes Laertius' *Life of Socrates* is included in Ferguson (ed.), *Socrates: A Source Book*. Diogenes' *Life of Socrates* is also included in *The Unknown Socrates*, edited and translated by Bernhard Huss et al. (Wauconda, Bolchazy-Charducci, 2002). This is a helpful collection of four late antique sources, with parallel English translations: as well as Diogenes, it includes Libanius' *Apology*, Maximus of Tyre's *Whether Socrates Did the Right Thing* and Apuleius' *On the God of Socrates*.

Regretfully, I have passed over the fascinating topic of Socrates' influence on Hellenistic philosophy. On the influence of Socrates on the development of Greek philosophical schools, especially Cynicism, much has been written, but relatively little is in English. The classic study is Klaus Döring, *Exemplum Sokrates: Studien zur Sokratesnachwirkung in der kynisch-stoischen Popularphilosophie der frühen Kaiserzeit und im frühen Christentum* (Wiesbaden, Franz Steiner, 1979). See also M. Gigante Giannantoni et al. (eds), *La Tradizione Socratica: Seminario di studi* (Naples, Bibliopolis, 1995). A useful introductory article in English is A. A. Long's 'Socrates in Hellenistic Philosophy', *Classical Quarterly*, 38, 1988, pp.

150–71. A good collection of scholarly essays in English is *The Socratic Movement*, edited by P. V. Waerdt (Ithaca, NY, Cornell University Press, 1984).

Mark Morford surveys Roman ambivalent attitudes to philosophy in *The Roman Philosophers: From the Time of Cato the Censor to the Death of Marcus Aurelius* (London, Routledge, 2002); Morford discusses Cato's rejection of the Athenian embassy.

Little has been written about Cicero's relationship to Socrates. There is an article by Raymond DiLorenzo, 'The Critique of Socrates in Cicero's *De Oratore*, *Philosophy and Rhetoric*, 11, 1978, pp. 247–61.

The death scenes of Seneca, Petronius and Thasea in Tacitus are discussed by Catherine Connors, 'Famous Last Words', in *Reflections of Nero: Culture, History and Representation*, edited by Jás Elsner and Jamie Masters (London, Duckworth, 1994, pp. 225–36).

5 PAIN AND REVELATION

In general, see G. Hanfmann, 'Socrates and Christ', *Harvard Studies in Classical Philology*, 60, 1951, pp. 205–33.

Links between the Gospel of Luke and the death of Socrates are discussed in Peter J. Scaer, *The Lukan Passion and the Praiseworthy Death* (Sheffield, Phoenix Press, 2005).

On Libanius, see William Calder, 'On Libanius' *Silence of Socrates*', *Greek, Roman and Byzantine Studies*, 1, 1960, pp. 185–201).

The *Apologies* of Justin Martyr are available in a recent English translation: *The First and Second Apologies*, translated by L. W. Barnard (New York, Paulist Press, 1997).

On Erasmus and other humanists, see R. Marcel, '"Saint"'

Socrate, patron de l'humanisme', *Revue Internationale de Philosophie*, 5, 1951, pp. 135–43.

On Montaigne's responses to Socrates see the final chapter of David Quint's *Montaigne and the Quality of Mercy* (Princeton, NJ, Princeton University Press, 1988); also Joshua Scodel, 'The Affirmation of Paradox: A Reading of Montaigne's *De la phisionomie*', in *Yale French Studies*, 64 (*Montaigne: Essays in Reading*), 1984, pp. 209–37; and Nehemas, *Art of Living*, pp. 101–27.

6 THE APOTHEOSIS OF PHILOSOPHY

For those who can read French, Raymond Trousson's excellent and lively book discusses the relationship of three eighteenth-century French writers to Socrates: *Socrate devant Voltaire, Diderot et Rousseau* (Paris, Minard, 1967).

For those who can read German, a very thorough account of the relevant sources is given by B. Böhm, *Sokrates im Achtzehnten Jahrhundert* (Leipzig, Neumünster, 1929).

Mario Montuori's two (overlapping) edited collections of essays are both useful for this period: *De Socrate iuste damnato: The Rise of the Socratic Problem in the Eighteenth Century* (Amsterdam, J. C. Gieben, 1981; note that the essays in this volume are not translated from their original languages); and *The Socratic Problem: The History, the Solutions. From the 18th Century to the Present Time* (Amsterdam, J. C. Gieben, 1992). The 1981 volume reproduces the Fréret essay discussed in this chapter.

An excellent social history of death in eighteenth-century France is John McManners' *Death and the Enlightenment* (Oxford, Clarendon, 1981).

Michael Fried's *Absorption and Theatricality: Painting*

and Beholder in the Age of Diderot (Berkeley, University of California Press, 1980) is a stimulating introduction both to Diderot and to French painting of this period.

Philippe Ariès' major work on death is translated into English by Helen Weaver as *The Hour of Our Death* (Oxford, Oxford University Press, 1991).

Voltaire's *Treatise on Tolerance* is available in English, with introduction and commentary, in the *Cambridge Texts in the History of Philosophy* series, edited by Simon Harvey, 2000. The *Philosophical Dictionary* is available in Penguin Classics, translated by Theodore Besterman, 1984.

The best translation of Rousseau's *Emile* is by Allan Bloom (New York, Basic Books, 1979).

As far as I know, no complete English translation of Moses Mendelssohn's *Phaidon* is currently available. Parts of it are included in *Moses Mendelssohn: Selections from His Writings*, edited and translated by Eva Jospe (New York, Viking, 1975).

7 TRUTH, TALK, TOTALITARIANISM

A fine overview of much of the material covered in this chapter is Paul Harrison's *The Disenchantment of Reason: The Problem of Socrates in Modernity* (Albany, NY, State University of New York, 1994). This book discusses Hegel, Kierkegaard, Nietzsche and also – briefly – Derrida and Foucault. See also Sarah Kofman, *Socrates: Fictions of a Philosopher* (Ithaca, NY, Cornell University Press), which also focuses on Hegel, Kierkegaard and Nietzsche.

Hegel, Kierkegaard, Nietzsche and Benjamin are all readily available in English translation:

- G. W. F. Hegel, *Lectures on the History of Philosophy: Greek*

Philosophy to Plato, translated by E. S. Haldane (Lincoln and London, Nebraska University Press, 1995).
- Søren Kierkegaard, *The Concept of Irony with Continual Reference to Socrates*, translated by Howard V. and Edna H. Hong (Princeton, NJ, Princeton University Press, 1989).
- Friedrich Nietzsche, *The Birth of Tragedy and Other Writings*, edited and translated by Raymond Geuss and Ronald Speirs (Cambridge, Cambridge University Press, 1999); *The Gay Science*, edited by Bernard Williams (Cambridge, Cambridge University Press, 2001); *Human All Too Human*, edited by R. J. Hollingdale (Cambridge, Cambridge University Press, 1996); *Twilight of the Idols and the Anti-Christ*, translated by R. J. Hollingdale (1990).
- Walter Benjamin, *The Origins of German Tragic Drama*, translated by John Osborne (London, Verso, 1998).

Much has been written about Nietzsche's responses to Socrates. There is a useful chapter in Nehemas, *Art of Living*, pp. 128–56. The best single work on the subject is Werner J. Dannhauser's *Nietzsche's View of Socrates* (Ithaca, NY, Cornell University Press, 1974).

Derrida's essay 'Plato's Pharmacy' is available in Jacques Derrida, *Dissemination*, translated, with helpful introduction and notes, by Barbara Johnson (Chicago, Chicago University Press, 1981).

Michel Foucault's *Hermeneutics of the Subject: Lectures at the Collège de France, 1981–82* was edited by Frédéric Gros and translated into English by Graham Burchell (New York, Picador, 2006).

Foucault's views of Socrates are discussed by Nehemas, *Art of Living*. Melissa Lane's *Plato's Progeny: How Plato and Socrates Still Captivate the Modern Mind* (London, Duckworth,

2001) gives an excellent account of responses to Socrates by twentieth-century historians and philosophers.

Modern dramatic representations of Socrates are discussed by R. Todd, 'Socrates Dramatized', *Antike und Abendland*, 27, 1981, pp. 116–29.

Other books mentioned in this chapter include I. F. Stone, *The Trial of Socrates* (Boston, Ma, Little, Brown, 1988); Alain de Botton, *The Consolations of Philosophy* (New York, Vintage International, 2001); Christopher Phillips, *Socrates Café: A Fresh Taste of Philosophy*, (New York, Norton, 2002); Mark Forstater, *The Living Wisdom of Socrates* (Hodder Mobius, 2004); Walter Mosley, *Always Outnumbered, Always Outgunned* (New York, Washington Square Press/Simon and Schuster, 1998); Roger Scruton, *Xanthippic Dialogues* (St Augustine's Press, South Bend, IN,1998); Thomas Disch, *334: A novel* (Vintage 1st edition, 1999; the first section of the book is called 'The Death of Socrates'). Dürrenmatt's *Death of Socrates* is available in English translation in *Dimension2*, a journal of contemporary German-language literature, Vol. 3(3), 1996. Another interesting recent account of the continuing relevance of Socrates is Jonathan Lear's *Therapeutic Action: An earnest plea for irony* (New York, Other Press, 2004).

There are several available recordings of Erik Satie's *Socrate* and John Cage's *Cheap Trick*. Both pieces are included on a CD from the Wergo music label (1993), performed by Herbert Henck, Hilke Helling and Deborah Richards.

LIST OF ILLUSTRATIONS

ACKNOWLEDGEMENTS

I am grateful to the American Association of Learned Societies, the American Academy in Rome, and the Cambridge Center for Research in the Arts and Social Sciences for helping me complete this project.

My interest in Socrates began at Oxford High School, where I was lucky enough to study Greek with three wonderful teachers: Eda Forbes, Caroline Mayr-Harting and Deborah Bennett.

I would like to thank a number of people who have given help, corrections, suggestions or support of various kinds while I was writing this book. These include Craig Arnold, John Bodel, Christopher Borg, Jenny Davidson, Lowell Edmunds, Joseph Farrell, Carmela Franklin, Sam Hood, James Ker, Robin Kirman, Melissa Lane, Rebecca Lindenberg, Stefannie Markovits, Bridget Murnaghan, David Quint, Ralph Rosen, Marco Roth, Joseph Schwartz, Clara Waissbein, Andrew Wilson, Bee Wilson and Ann Vasaly. The list should be longer; apologies to all those whom I have failed to mention.

I would also like to thank my colleagues and students in the Department of Classical Studies at the University of Pennsylvania, and the audiences at talks I have given on Socrates at Penn, New York University, Princeton University,

Richard Stockton College and the American Academy in Rome.

Particular thanks to Mary Beard, for her patient and inspiring work as editor of the book; to Peter Carson, Penny Daniel and Nicola Taplin at Profile Books; to Cecilia Mackay for her help with the pictures; and to the external readers for Harvard University Press, who have all helped to improve this book.

I am especially grateful to my mother, Katherine Duncan-Jones, who read a rough draft at an early stage and made very helpful comments.

INDEX

PROFILES IN HISTORY

The *Profiles in History* series will explore iconic events and relationships in history. Each book will start from the historical moment: what happened? But each will focus too on the fascinating and often surprising afterlife of the story concerned.

Profiles in History is under the general editorship of Mary Beard.

Already available:

David Horspool: *King Alfred: Burnt Cakes and Other Legends*

James Sharpe: *Remember, Remember: A Cultural History of Guy Fawkes Day*

Ian Patterson: *Guernica and Total War*

Claire Pettitt: *Dr. Livingstone, I Presume? Missionaries, Journalists, Explorers, and Empire*

Greg Woolf: *Et Tu, Brute? A Short History of Political Murder*

Forthcoming:

Christopher Prendergast: *The Fourteenth of July*